TERTIARY LEVEL BIOLOGY

Environmental Microbiology

W. D. GRANT, B.Sc., Ph.D.
Lecturer in Microbiology
University of Leicester

and

P. E. LONG, B.Sc., Ph.D.
Lecturer in Botany
University of Leicester

Blackie

Glasgow and London

Blackie & Son Limited
Bishopbriggs
Glasgow G64 2NZ

Furnival House
14–18 High Holborn
London WC1V 6BX

British Library Cataloguing in Publication Data
Grant, W. D.
  Environmental microbiology. — (Tertiary level biology)
  1. Ecology
  I. Title   II. Long, P. E.   III. Series
  574.5   QH541

ISBN 0–216–91153–2
ISBN 0–216–91152–4 Pbk

Filmset by Advanced Filmsetters (Glasgow) Ltd

Printed in Great Britain by
Thomson Litho Ltd, East Kilbride, Scotland

Preface

The nature and scope of the text

The environment in which we live has to a large extent been determined by the activities of innumerable organisms interacting with each other and with their immediate surroundings. From the point of view of the microbiologist, it is obvious that microbial activity has a great part to play in the continuing maintenance of conditions suitable for other forms of life on this planet. There has therefore always been an awareness of the need for a good understanding of how microorganisms react in the environment, and this has been heightened from time to time as detrimental microbial activities become evident under certain conditions. The need for a good understanding has recently assumed a new importance as the era of microbial manipulation dawns—microbiology has always been a practical discipline, and the possibilities of beneficial modification on a global scale may be within our grasp.

The growing interest in environmental microbiology can be gauged from the increase in relevant undergraduate teaching. However, one of the most serious problems confronting the student is the dearth of appropriate texts. In part this is a reflection of the plethora of potential subject matter. The study of the relationships of microorganisms with each other and with their environments—"microbial ecology"—constitutes a subject area which is far from precisely circumscribed, and each researcher or teacher has his own personal notion of which topics are appropriate. It follows that the scope of any book purporting to fall within this general area will be the subject of dispute. In the end, what is included is the subjective choice of the author.

Texts do, however, often evolve from teaching experience with particular groups of students. In our opinion, "microbial ecology" is best taught at senior undergraduate level following a basic training in microbiology, and we have assumed that the readers of this book will have some knowledge of the major microbial groups and will be familiar with the special features of prokaryote structure and function. However, we believe that the text is intelligible to those biologists with only a rudimentary knowledge of microbiology.

What kinds of environment are appropriate for consideration in a text of this kind? It is possible to argue indefinitely about what constitutes a "natural habitat"; for example, animals represent important and significant microbial habitats, and the relationship between man and microbial populations is important enough to be considered as a separate and distinct topic. However, the microbial population inhabiting animals may matter less in the long term maintenance of the biosphere than do the activities of certain groups of microorganisms such as sulphur oxidizers in soils and waters (7.1). We therefore consider the animal to be outside the scope of this book, except for a discussion of certain interrelationships in the rumen which have parallels elsewhere (4.8, 9.4).

It is clear that soil and water represent by far the most significant microbial habitats, in terms both of microbial biomass and microbial activity. It is beyond dispute that these habitats constitute "natural environments", and that microbial activity within these habitats is essential to the maintenance of the environment. A substantial section of the text is therefore concerned with the nature of microbial activity within soil and water. Further sections deal with the effects of microbial activity within these main habitats in both the short term and the long term, and how microorganisms in these habitats react under certain exceptional circumstances imposed by the "pollutant" activities of man.

Although existing texts cover some aspects of these topics, no single text at present covers all the aspects in detail. We have here attempted to fill the gap. Another important function of a book directed at senior undergraduates is to point the reader towards relevant literature. The breadth of the subject matter covered in this text is such that certain topics are inevitably not considered in great detail, but the reader should be able to find appropriate references leading to the detailed information in the literature. Particular care has been taken in the selection of recent key articles and books, and in compiling reference lists which are both concise and comprehensive.

We are indebted to Dr Johannes Imhoff, Professor Don Kelly, Dr Frank Odds and Professor Hans Trüper for invaluable discussions on sections of the text. Ian Riddell, Angela Chorley and Julia Polonski helped greatly with the illustrations. We are particularly grateful to Grace Redfern for patiently deciphering and typing the whole manuscript.

W.D.G./P.E.L.

Contents

INTRODUCTION

THE SIGNIFICANCE OF MICROORGANISMS IN THE ENVIRONMENT

The role of microorganisms in providing inorganic compounds at a valence state appropriate for assimilation into higher plants is well understood, and the largely microbially-mediated nitrogen and sulphur cycles (6.1, 7.1) are often quoted and discussed. Less attention is given to the contribution of microorganisms to the continuing decomposition and mineralization of carbon compounds, other than a cursory acknowledgement of their contribution to decay.

In fact, in most ecosystems, the largest part of the organic production is not consumed and utilized by herbivores or carnivores, but becomes part of a pool of dead organic material (detritus). For the continued balance of the biosphere it is necessary that such a pool should remain in a steady state. Herbivore consumption decreases in importance with increasing size of the primary producers (see table), partly because higher organisms do not decompose a number of higher-plant polymers (5.4, 5.5), but partly also because macrophytes have an inappropriate carbon : nitrogen ratio. Animals at all trophic levels (with the exception of ruminants) require a diet with a $C:N$ ratio of less than $17:1$, and the woody tissues of macrophytes have much higher $C:N$ ratios ($\sim 200:1$) than does phytoplankton ($\sim 20:1$). This is reflected in the relative extents of utilization by herbivores (table). Microbial decomposition of such recalcitrant materials is also less restricted by the type of nitrogen available and is thus essential to a balanced carbon cycle. An additional advantage accrues from microbial activity, in that microorganisms ($C:N \sim 6:1-12:1$) themselves become part of the detrital material, increasing the nutrient value for herbivores. The mammalian rumen (4.8) is a special example of this kind of effect.

Microorganisms are also vital to the anoxic decomposition of organic

1

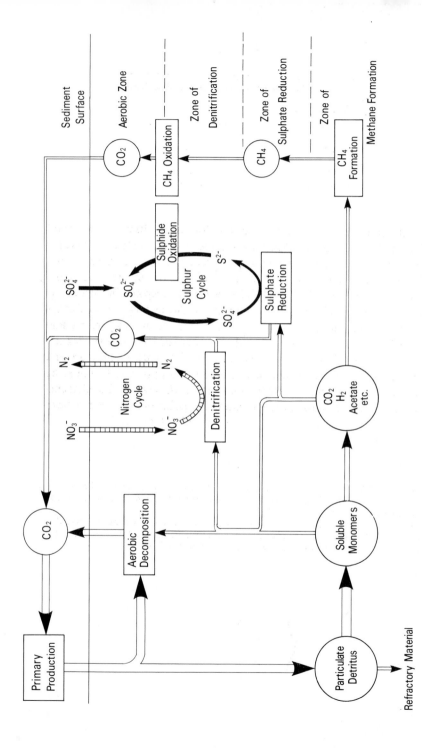

Pathways of carbon during anaerobic decomposition in an aquatic sediment, and their relationship with the sulphur and nitrogen cycles (modified from Fenchel and Jørgensen, 1978).

Table Fraction of primary production consumed by herbivores (abbreviated from Fenchel and Blackburn, 1979)

Plant community	% production consumed
Phytoplankton	60–90
Grasslands	12–45
Kelp beds	10
Deciduous forests	1.5–5

material. Sulphate respiration accounts for some 50% of the total oxidation of organic material in some marine environments (7.1), and the utilization of CO_2 as an electron acceptor by methanogenic bacteria has a profound effect on the overall oxidation of organic material in many anoxic environments (4.8, 9.4). Reduced electron acceptors in turn act as energy sources elsewhere in the environment. Accordingly, microbially-mediated transformations of various kinds enmesh in complicated and sometimes less than obvious ways in the maintenance of the environment. As an example, the intricate interrelationships of the carbon, nitrogen and sulphur cycle in an anoxic sediment are depicted opposite. It would be possible to draw up similar interrelationships for these and other elements in any environment, illustrating the important point that the planet owes its continued equability as an environment to microbial activity.

REFERENCES

Fenchel, T. and Blackburn, T. H. (1979) *Bacteria and Mineral Cycling*, Academic Press.

Fenchel, T. and Jørgensen, B. B. (1978). Detritus food chains of aquatic ecosystems: the role of bacteria. *Adv. Microbial Ecol.* **2**, 1–58.

Paul, E. A. and Voroney, R. P. (1980). Nutrient and energy flows through soil microbial biomass, in *Contemporary Microbial Ecology*, editors, D. C. Ellwood, J. N. Hedger, M. J. Latham, J. M. Lynch and J. H. Slater, Academic Press, 215–238.

PART 1—HABITATS

CHAPTER ONE

THE SOIL

1.1 Physical aspects of soil structure—the microhabitat concept

A fully developed soil is an intricate mixture of inorganic and organic components, a complex product of parent material, topography, climate, time and biological activity. In an average fertile loam (a good agricultural soil), mineral matter from weathered rock usually accounts for some 50% by volume, and organic matter from plants, animals and microorganisms for 10–15%. Air and water occupy most of the remaining volume in a complicated system of pores and channels where the amount of air and pore space is a function of the water content of the soil. In general, living organisms occupy considerably less than 1% of the total volume. Other types of soil may have much higher proportions of organic material (up to 30% v/v in peaty soils) or much lower proportions (as little as 1% v/v in tundra soils). It is convenient to consider the inorganic and organic components separately, although any soil is truly a composite entity, its properties depending on the exchange and interaction between organic and inorganic fractions.

Soil develops when rock is changed by a series of processes collectively known as *weathering*. The parent rock is broken down into small fragments by temperature changes, the action of water, extremes of acidity or alkalinity, and other chemical effects produced by biological activity. While the parent rock is disintegrating under a combination of these effects, it exchanges material with its immediate environment, and the final product consists of a surface layer of soil physically and chemically distinct from the underlying material. The most abundant elements in the mineral component of soil are Si, Al, Fe and O, the mineral component being mainly composed of silicates, exemplified by the simplest form silica (SiO_2)—the abundant mineral quartz for instance, is almost exclusively composed of SiO_2. The aluminosilicates constitute another large class of silicates where tetravalent Si is partially substituted by trivalent Al. Consequently these minerals often have a net negative charge.

The atoms of many silicate minerals are arranged in negatively-charged pyramids, or silica tetrahedra, held together by other atoms, especially Ca(II) and Mg(II). There are various distinct weathering processes; an important one is hydrolytic attack, in which Mg(II) and Ca(II) are replaced by H^+, producing an unstable structure (7.5). Microorganisms quickly colonize freshly quarried stone surfaces, and a number of common soil fungi, bacteria and blue-green algae have been shown to contribute towards the weathering of rocks by mediating such effects. In addition, microbially-mediated weathering appears in part to be due to the production of organic acids, such as 2-ketogluconic acid, which remove divalent cations from silicates by chelation, producing an effect analogous to hydrolytic attack. Lichens are often colonizers of bare rock surfaces, and many lichens produce a variety of unusual phenolics and terpenes that have considerable chelation properties, and which over many years may decompose even the exceptionally stable mineral quartz—as exemplified by the etching of glass under lichen growth on old church windows.

The composition of the mineral fraction of a soil markedly influences the properties of the soil. Particularly significant is the relative proportion of primary minerals (those remaining unaltered from the original parent rock) and secondary minerals (those modified by the weathering process). One of the most important consequences of weathering is the production of *clays*. Clays are secondary minerals, and consist of minute aluminosilicate particles which constitute the smallest size class of the particles found in the soil mineral fraction (table 1.1). Of the four main types of clay found in soil, three (illite, montmorillonite and kaolinite) have a distinct crystalline structure, whereas the fourth type, amorphous clay,

Table 1.1 Classification of the sizes of soil particles

	Texture class	International scale (mm)	American scale (mm)
Primary Minerals	Gravel	>2.0	>2.0
	Coarse sand	2.0 → 0.2	2.0 → 0.25
	Fine sand	0.2 → 0.02	0.25 → 0.05
	Silt	0.02 → 0.002	0.05 → 0.002
Secondary Mineral	Clay	less than 0.002	less than 0.002

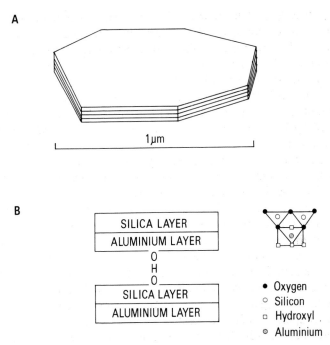

Figure 1.1 A. A clay micelle. Clay micelles are large, flat, leaf-like surfaces with silicon and aluminium atoms arranged alternately with oxygen atoms in a sandwich-like structure.
B. Diagrammatic representation of kaolinite showing a layer of silicon atoms joined to a layer of aluminium atoms (1:1 clay). This structure is then joined to the next leaf by a hydrogen–oxygen bond. The arrangement of atoms in one of the bilayers is shown on the right (redrawn from Courtney and Trudgill, 1976). Montmorillonite and illite have a layer of aluminium sandwiched between the two silica layers in each leaf (2:1 clays).

lacks any well defined structure. The crystalline types have a micellar structure composed of several layers or leaves of aluminosilicate material which expand or contract, depending on the degree of hydration bonding between the individual layers (figure 1.1). The overall electrical charge on clay particles is negative, due to replacement of Si(IV) by Al(III), and so cations are attracted to the particle surfaces, forming a layer of positive charge. Because sorbed cations include many plant nutrients, soils with high concentrations of clays are fertile, whereas soils having high concentrations of primary minerals with negligible ion exchange capacity are less fertile.

Soil classification systems often reflect the agricultural potential of a soil or its textural properties. Texture is an important classification feature

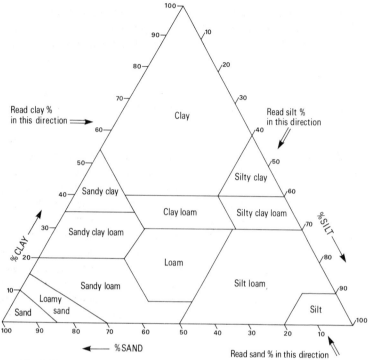

Figure 1.2   Soil texture graph.

related to particle size, and relative proportions of different size classes of particles derived by sedimentation or sieving procedures may be plotted on a triangular texture graph (figure 1.2). It can be seen that a sandy soil for instance is a coarse-textured soil with good drainage properties but is likely to be low in nutrients, due to the absence of significant amounts of clay. In contrast, a clay soil may be poorly drained, because of the preponderance of very small particles, but is high in plant nutrients. Loam soils (mixtures of sand, silt and clay) are clearly the most desirable agricultural soils, with intermediate drainage and nutrient properties.

Groups of mineral particles usually contribute to well-defined composite structures, sometimes called soil aggregates or *peds*. The type of structure found, which is governed by the texture of the soil, can be described by various terms—platy, blocky, spheroidal—and the tilth of a particular soil reflects the structure of the aggregates. Soil aggregates contain organic as well as inorganic material, and the major components determining aggregate stabilities are clays, certain organic materials including humic substances (1.2), and exopolysaccharides produced by microorganisms. The importance of exopolysaccharides produced by common soil bacteria such as *Bacillus* spp. has been demonstrated by showing that soils subject to periodate treatment (which destroys polysaccharides) often lose their aggregate structure. Fungal hyphae and other filamentous structures may also contribute towards binding mineral particles together. It is also thought that humic substances may act together with clays as a cement in binding groups of smaller particles. An idealized representation of a soil aggregate is depicted in figure 1.3. Microorganisms are present in larger pores, but there are also pores too small to permit the access of microorganisms, and which contain humic material and domains or packs of clay micelles or platelets. Such a model has considerable microbiological implications. Since there is no microbial access to the smaller pores, the organic material in them will be protected, and this may account in part for the longevity of humic substances in soil (1.2). Further consideration of the structure of the soil aggregate depicted in figure 1.3 leads to the conclusion that microbial life must exist in many discrete microhabitats that may undergo quite independent environmental fluctuations. In the absence of appropriate techniques with which to

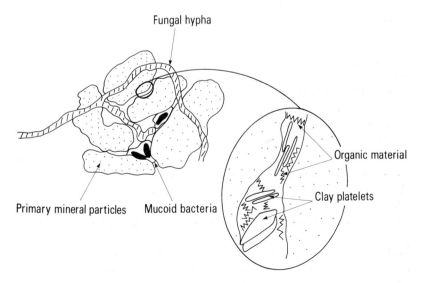

Figure 1.3 Diagrammatic representation of a soil aggregate.

approach the study of individual microhabitats, it is clear that assessments of the activity of soil microorganisms represent, at best, the net result of a large number of presumably rapid and independent fluctuations in microhabitat conditions, and so must provide an over-simplified and generalized view of microbial behaviour.

Natural soil-forming processes do not produce a uniform homogeneous soil throughout the depth of the soil layer. If a vertical section of uncultivated soil is examined, it is usually possible to see several distinct layers or *horizons* which collectively form the soil profile. These horizons are a consequence of weathering, leaching, and the mobilization and accumulation of clays, chelates and humic material at different depths. The general term *eluviation* is often used for the washing out or removal of materials, and the term *illuviation* for the washing in and immobilization of materials in a horizon.

Horizons are usually differentiated on the basis of colour, texture, mineral content and organic content. There are many subdivisions depending on the differentiation scheme used, but the three major horizons recognized are the A, B and C horizons (figure 1.4). The uppermost, or A horizon, is where humic material accumulates derived from plant and animal litter (if a permanent litter layer exists it is sometimes referred to as the A_0 horizon), and the layer is characterized as a zone of maximum eluviation; it is usually subdivided into an upper humus-rich layer, and a lower layer which is an area of maximum leaching of silicates, Fe and Al. Below this, the B horizon is a zone of maximum illuviation, where

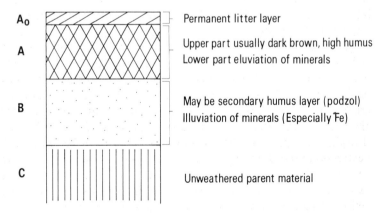

Figure 1.4   Diagrammatic representation of a soil profile.

accumulation of silicates, Fe and Al occurs. The underlying C horizon is a zone little affected by biological processes, where unweathered parent rock occurs.

The thickness and characteristics of each major horizon depend mainly on the topography of the site, plant cover, pH and rainfall. Under deciduous trees, soil profiles known as *alfisols* ("brown earths") develop with a permanent litter layer, and a relatively unleached humus-rich A horizon. Under coniferous cover, acid profiles known as *spodosols* develop, also with permanent litter layers. Acid soil profiles are often known as *podzols*—the process of podzolization is basically one of acid leaching. Podzols are unusual in that the B horizon is very extensively illuviated, containing much Fe, and the upper part of this horizon contains a humus layer separate and distinct from the humus layer in the upper part of the A horizon, a consequence of the mobilization of organometal complexes and microbial activity at a particular depth in the profile. Many different types of soil profile exist, ranging from highly organic soils like bog soils (histisols) to desert types (aridisols), and the extensively leached types under tropical rain forests (oxisols or latosols). Under waterlogged conditions all soil profiles may undergo a process known as *gleying*, where anoxic conditions develop, Fe(III) is reduced to Fe(II) (7.3) and SO_4^{2-} reduction occurs (7.1), resulting in a bluish colouration or mottling due to FeS generation.

1.2 Chemical aspects of soil structure

When organic residues are deposited in soils, a proportion escapes oxidation to CO_2 and H_2O, and this fraction is slowly transformed to a brown, insoluble residue. The classical approach to determining the structure of this material has been to apply particular extraction techniques designed to recover various classes of compound, and often these compounds are characterized as distinct and separate chemical entities. There is good reason to suppose, however, that the mature organic material in soils can be regarded as one giant molecule, and it can therefore be misleading to consider certain fractions in isolation. Nevertheless, it is usual to discuss separately those components which can be removed by mild extraction procedures, the intractable, insoluble residue which is left after these mild procedures being treated separately, and referred to as *humus* or *humic substances*. It is likely that, in part, the relatively easy extraction of certain classes of substance is a reflection of incomplete humification.

The soil organic fraction contains small amounts of many different classes of organic compound which are in the process of transformation, but it is the stable forms which concern the soil scientist, since these are the substances which are important in ion exchange and soil aggregate structure (1.1). Soils also have considerable enzyme activity which is retained after sterilization by irradiation. Many different kinds of enzyme have been detected, although the protein content of soils is negligible. Enzyme activity is associated with the clay fraction of soils, and is presumed to be derived largely from microbial cells. There is some correlation between enzyme activity and soil fertility, both in the range of enzyme activities and the levels detected. There have indeed been attempts to monitor enzyme activity as a measure of soil condition, following long-term administration of herbicides, but in common with most other procedures used to monitor soil performance over a long period, the results obtained have been inconclusive.

Soil organic phosphorus

The stable organic fraction of soils often contains more than 90 % of the total soil phosphorus. A certain proportion of the soil P is in the form of phosphate esters in the humic fraction, but frequently a large fraction (20–80 %) can be readily extracted, and is found to be present as phosphate esters of inositol isomers such as myoinositol (figure 1.5A). Most of the phosphorylated isomers of inositol, from monophosphates to hexaphosphates, have been detected in soils. The only inositol phosphate which is present in significant amounts in higher plants is myoinositol hexaphosphate (phytic acid), and it is assumed that the other forms found in soils are a consequence of microbial activity. Organic P seems to be largely unavailable to plants, and plants often show P deficiency in areas where the soil organic P content is high (7.4). Precisely why organic P should be so stable is not clear, since many common soil microorganisms possess phytases and acid phosphatases which might be expected to release inorganic P. Presumably the highly charged inositol phosphates are extensively bound to clays, rendering them less susceptible to microbial attack.

Soil polysaccharides

Soil polysaccharides are often characterized as separate and distinct entities. There is some justification in treating microbial exopoly-saccharides separately—these are extremely resistant to degradation or

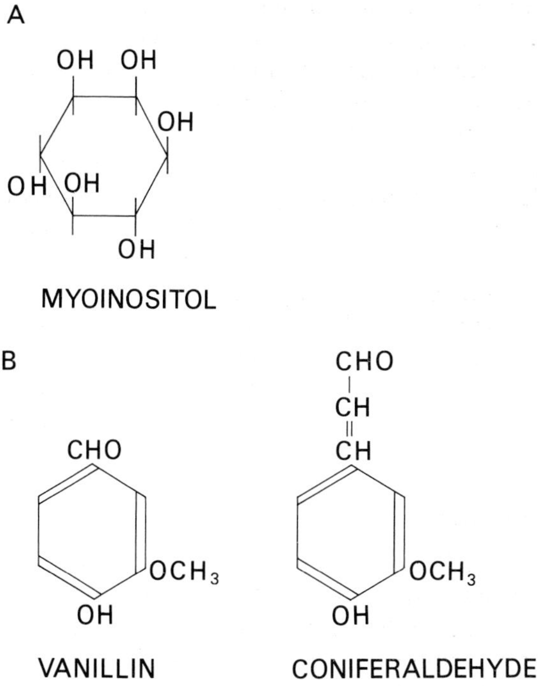

A

MYOINOSITOL

B

CHO

VANILLIN

CHO
|
CH
||
CH

OCH₃

OH

CONIFERALDEHYDE

Figure 1.5 A. Myoinositol. Phytic acid has a phosphate group esterified to each of the hydroxyl groups.
B. Humus hydrolysis products.

modification, and their importance in the structure of the soil aggregate has already been discussed (1.1). Microbial exopolysaccharides may make up 0.1% of the organic material in soils. The rest of the carbohydrate material in soils makes up $5-20\%$ of the total organic matter, and $10-20\%$ of this carbohydrate is fairly easily extracted, consisting in the main of modified higher plant polysaccharides such as cellulose, pectins and hemicelluloses. The rest of the carbohydrate material is difficult to remove and characterize, and presumably represents significantly altered plant (and some microbial) polysaccharides that are firmly complexed within the molecular structure of humus.

Humus

The major portion of organic material in soils, however, is made up of the insoluble brown residue known as humus. Three fractions of humus are recognized. *Fulvic acid* (MW 2000–9000) is soluble in acid and alkali; *humic acid* (MW 5000–100 000) is soluble in alkali and insoluble in acid; *humin* is the insoluble residue remaining after acid and alkali treatment. These three fractions probably represent different size classes of the same polymer, since they yield identical results when subjected to end group analysis and nuclear magnetic resonance spectroscopy (NMR). Humus is far from homogeneous in composition, varying from soil type to soil type, and from site to site within any one soil type. There has been much speculation as to its origin, but one is inexorably drawn to the conclusion that much of the material derives from lignin (see figure 5.3), one of the most important structural polymers of higher plants. There is a compelling similarity between the hydrolysis products of lignin and those of humus, and generally the distribution of the residues derived from humus is consistent with the structure of the lignin in the prevailing plant cover. Many phenolic residues based on the phenylpropane unit of lignin have been isolated following the hydrolysis of humic substances (figure 1.5B), but additional aromatic and phenolic compounds not found in lignin have also been identified, and it is likely that other plant compounds such as flavonoids are the source of certain of the unique humic hydrolysis products.

There is now a considerable body of evidence to suggest that microbial synthesis is also in part responsible for the formation of humus. Many soil microorganisms produce brown polymers which resemble humus in end group analysis and NMR patterns. Bacteria and actinomycetes such as *Azotobacter* spp., *Streptomyces* spp., and fungi such as *Aspergillus* spp., *Epicoccum* spp. and *Stachybotrys* spp., produce a variety of dark, resistant polymers when grown in pure culture. Furthermore, clay minerals often markedly enhance the chemical polymerization of phenolic compounds produced in microbial cultures. Co-polymers of microbially-produced phenols and humus hydrolysis products can also be readily produced in microbial cultures. This suggests that humus is almost certainly produced as a collaborative venture between those microorganisms that hydrolyse and modify lignins, and those that produce phenolic polymers. The resultant product is presumably chemically reactive at least in the early stages, and forms complexes with a variety of soil organic and inorganic compounds to produce the final stable macromolecule.

The basis of the remarkable persistence of humus in soils has been the subject of considerable discussion—estimates of the mean residence time of various humic substances range from 5–2000 years depending on soil type. In part the persistence may be a reflection of microhabitat topography (1.1). However, the undoubted recalcitrance of lignin, one of the starting materials, must also play a part. In view of the size and complexity of the molecule, it is not difficult to imagine that many enzymic steps would be necessary before suitable growth and energy substrates are obtained. Microbial modification of the developing polymer may also block potential ring cleavage sites (see 5.5, 8.6). Humus-degrading micro-organisms, which usually also degrade lignin, frequently require an additional carbon and energy source (and source of reducing power) before humus decomposition can take place. Also, since the properties of enzymes often change markedly following sorption to a surface, it may be that sorbed soil enzymes are important in modifications that determine persistence.

1.3 The methodology

In view of the heterogeneity of the soil environment and the consequential existence of different microhabitats which may be close together (1.1), the application of most of the currently available microbiological techniques to soil analysis yields data which represent an average or summation of microbial activities within many microhabitats. Such data is however not without value, and a variety of techniques has been applied to soils with a view to relating soil condition and performance to microbial activity. A list of such techniques is shown in table 1.2, which is by no means a comprehensive survey of the methodology employed, but designed to illustrate the aims often pursued, and the methodology which has developed accordingly. In essence, at one extreme, soil can be disrupted and its component parts and microorganisms extracted, monitored and enumerated, or at the other extreme, it can be treated as a tissue, whose physiological performance can be assessed by a variety of non-disruptive procedures.

Procedures designed to isolate microorganisms usually depend on enrichment or selection of a particular group, since direct micro-manipulation techniques are extremely time-consuming. *Enrichment* or *selective* procedures clearly do not give any indication of the original numbers present, but nevertheless, are useful in detecting rare micro-organisms. The techniques used range from simple batch culture enrich-ments, or soil perfusion columns, where a variety of parameters can be altered to select for particular microorganisms, to the insertion of specific "baits" into soils. Spread plate cultures, which are used in viable-counting procedures, are also selective cultures in a sense, since the composition of the media is of great importance in determining what will grow.

Table 1.2 Methodology applied to soils

	Aims	Procedures
1. Isolation		
	(a) Direct	Micromanipulation
		Sieving and dilution
		Pour or spread plates of nutrient media
	(b) Indirect	Enrichment procedures
2. Enumeration		
	(a) Direct	Counts of microorganisms by microscopy
	(b) Indirect	Viable counting procedures
		Substrate utilization
3. Biomass		
	(a) Total	Calculations based on counts by microscopy
		ATP
		$CHCl_3$ fumigation
	(b) Specific groups	Calculations based on counts by microscopy
		Assay of group specific substances
4. Distribution		
	(a) Direct	Microscopy of soil preparations
		Scanning electron microscopy of soil preparations
	(b) Indirect	Buried slides, capillaries, nylon mesh, etc.
5. Growth and activity		Changes in number or biomass
		Soil replica plates
		Colonization of buried slides, capillaries, etc.
		Measurement of O_2 uptake
		Measurement of CO_2 evolution
		Measurement of substrate utilization
		Measurement of product appearance
		Measurement of temperature increase by microcalorimetry

The most widely-used *direct enumeration* procedures are based on the Jones and Mollison technique, where a known amount of soil is suspended in agar, and a standard volume allowed to set on a slide. Suitable staining procedures can be used to distinguish the microbial flora from detritus. Epifluorescence microscopy, where a fluorescent dye is excited by incident illumination from the top, has proved particularly useful, since there is no requirement for the illumination to pass through a thick, relatively opaque specimen.

Enumeration procedures based on culturing particular groups are also widely used, but of course depend completely on careful selection of the media used. Although the well-known spread plate procedures give little indication of the *total* microbial population, they are useful in that they allow the isolation and identification of the organisms concerned. Such procedures overemphasize the importance of fungi that sporulate heavily in soils, and consequently representatives of the genera *Aspergillus*, *Cladosporium* and *Penicillium* are often the only fungi enumerated by these procedures, although it is unlikely that these are the major fungal types in all soils. *Most Probable Number* (MPN) procedures (also known as extinction dilution procedures) are based on the concept that the level of dilution of the original sample needed to obtain a negative result in a particular physiological test, or in a particular growth medium, is related to the size of the population in the original sample. The Presumptive Coliform Test (8.2) is an MPN test, and the technique is useful for the rapid estimation of particular physiological groups, rather than the entire microflora. Substrate utilization studies can also be of use in indirectly enumerating certain groups, and independent estimations of numbers of nitrifiers in soils have been made in this way (6.3).

Biomass estimates can be achieved by directly counting and measuring the size of microorganisms in soils, and applying appropriate mass conversion factors for each of the major groups. However, such procedures are extremely laborious and subject to considerable operator error, although this procedure still remains one of the best ways of determining individual biomasses for different morphological groups of micro-organisms.

In recent years, the *ATP assay*, a rapid and convenient procedure, has been increasingly used as a sensitive way of measuring total biomass. The rationale behind this procedure is that cells contain a relatively constant proportion of ATP relative to biomass under most conditions. There is some evidence which suggests that ATP levels may fluctuate considerably depending on the state of the cell; ATP assays are nevertheless widely used, although the extraction of ATP from soils presents problems not encountered in the aquatic environment (2.3). The sensitive assay of ATP relies on the light-emitting properties of the enzyme system responsible for bioluminescence in the firefly. The enzyme luciferase oxidizes its aldehyde substrate luciferin in the presence of O_2 and ATP, emitting light in the process. The amount of light is proportional to the amount of ATP present, provided all other components are in excess, and the light emitted can be measured in a sensitive photometer. It is possible to detect 10^{-14} g ATP using this procedure, and in theory, this should enable detection of ten bacterial cells, although in practice this level of sensitivity cannot often be achieved in a difficult environment like soil.

The so-called *chloroform fumigation procedure* is also used extensively to determine total biomass in soils. In this technique, a small amount of untreated soil is added to a chloroform-sterilized sample, and the evolution of CO_2 followed over a 10-day period. The evolution of CO_2 is considered to result when "dead" microbial carbon is oxidized by the reintroduced soil microorganisms, and it is assumed that about 40 % of the original microbial carbon is released as a CO_2 "flush" in this way.

Specific biomass estimates (bacteria, fungi, etc.) can be achieved by direct counting and measuring procedures, but it is also possible to assay for *group-specific substances* like muramic acid (bacteria) or chitin (fungi). Chemical procedures may not be entirely satisfactory, since, for example, chitin is also found in insect exoskeletons, and muramic acid contents differ from genus to genus.

The distribution of microorganisms in soil can be determined by preparing soil samples in a variety of ways and examining these by light microscopy or electron microscopy. These procedures do not usually enable identifications to be made, although it is sometimes possible to label specific microorganisms with fluorescent immunoglobulins, which can then be visualized. Buried slides and capillaries also give some indication of the arrangement and distribution of microorganisms. The examination of flat-sided capillaries buried in soils (pedoscopes) and sediments (pelo-scopes) has proved of particular use in the detection of appendaged bacteria involved in ore deposition (7.7). However, all of these techniques cause significant soil disruption, or the introduction of unnatural surfaces, and as yet there is no technique which can be applied to undisturbed soils.

Growth and activity estimates are often based on changes in microbial numbers or biomass over a period. The rate of colonization of slides or capillaries can also be used to monitor soil activity, and the *replica plate procedure* has been used extensively in the laboratory. In this procedure, known microorganisms are placed at particular points on the surface of plates of soil, and their growth and spread monitored by periodically replicating from the plate (using a multipoint replicator) on to plates of appropriate nutrient media. The effect of clays on microbial growth and activity has been studied using this procedure (1.5). Activity measurements often involve treating soil as a tissue, and monitoring various parameters like O_2 uptake or CO_2 evolution. The rates of appearance and dis-appearance of various substrates and products have also been widely used as indicators of soil condition, following the long-term applications of pesticides.

Assessing how useful all of these procedures are, and indeed if different kinds of measurement are reasonably consistent with one another, is a long-term and labour-intensive process which has seldom been undertaken. However, there is some evidence to suppose that "physiological" measurements such as O_2 uptake and CO_2 evolution are consistent with biomass estimates, viable counts of microorganisms, and substrate utilization. The application of principal components analysis and factor analysis has simplified the processing of the plethora of data that any soil study generates, and some progress has been made towards predicting which data are most useful in rapidly relating changes in microbial populations and activities to soil performance in general. There have also been some preliminary attempts to mathematically model soil systems, incorporating appropriate terms for biomass, substrate disappearance, O_2 consumption and so on. It is to be expected that in the future such techniques may be useful for predicting patterns of decomposition at various times during the year, or during particular treatments.

1.4 Soil structure and water

The water regime of a particular soil is largely a function of capillarity effects that are in turn dependent on soil texture and concomitant particle size. Simple measurements of water content on a volume or weight basis do not indicate how much is actually *available* to plants and microorganisms. This is clearly shown by the observation that different types of soil dried down to the "wilt point" for higher plants may have quite different water contents expressed on a volume or weight basis. For this reason it has recently become fashionable to describe the water relations of microorganisms in thermodynamic terms, rather than relating microbial growth or activity to water content *per se*. Under conditions where a microorganism has to expend an additional amount of energy to obtain water as a consequence of the presence of solutes, the system is conveniently treated in terms of *water activity* (a_w). Simply, a_w is a measure of the amount of free water in a system, which is effectively decreased when a solute is dissolved in water, because some of the water becomes bound to the solute.

Numerically, $a_w = P/P_0$ where P and P_0 are the vapour pressures of solution and pure solvent respectively. For an ideal pure solvent, $a_w = 1$; in all other cases $a_w < 1$. For a microorganism suspended in a particular medium, a_w provides a measure of the degree to which it is stressed in terms of its water relations. The term a_w is extensively used as a descriptive parameter in the food industry, and can be readily applied to any homogeneous environment, including saline lakes and other such environments under extreme water stress (3.2). Water can not only be bound by solutes, but interfaces such as are provided by particles suspended in aqueous solution, and water/gas interfaces, also bind water molecules, effectively decreasing their availability. Either of these effects lowers a_w, and this is reflected in a lowering of the vapour pressure of the system relative to that of pure solvent.

There is no reason to suppose that microorganisms react differently depending on how a particular a_w is achieved, and a_w could equally well be used as a useful descriptive parameter applied to the water regime of soils, but largely for historical reasons, a different parameter, *water potential* (ψ) is normally used. This directly measures the amount of work that must be done by an organism to obtain water, and is related directly to a_w as follows:

$$\psi = RT \ln a_w$$

where R is the gas constant and T the absolute temperature. Alternatively, in potential terminology:

$$\psi = \psi_p - \psi_s - \psi_m$$

where ψ_p represents the hydrostatic potential (which is negligible in most terrestrial environments), ψ_s the potential of water as reduced by the presence of solutes (negligible in all but exceptionally dry or saline soils), and ψ_m the potential of water as reduced by interaction at interfaces (matric potential). Interface effects produce the main water stress experienced by microorganisms in soils under most conditions, and ψ_m rather than ψ is most commonly measured in practice. ψ_m is a reflection of surface tension forces acting at menisci of water columns in capillary pores. If a soil pore has an effective radius r (cm), the suction necessary to absorb water can be expressed as $\psi_m (\mathrm{N\,cm^{-2}}) = 2\gamma r^{-1}$ where γ is the surface tension of water ($\mathrm{N\,cm^{-1}}$). Much of the literature expresses ψ_m (and ψ) in the non-SI unit "bars" with a negative sign (1 bar = $10\,\mathrm{N\,cm^{-2}}$ = 0.987 atm = $1022\,\mathrm{cm\,H_2O}$.) ψ_m is also sometimes expressed in logarithmic pF form, where $pF_x = 10^x\,\mathrm{cm\,H_2O}$. There are several methods for determining ψ_m, usually manometric procedures which measure the amount of suction required to bring a soil to a particular water content. Measurements of ψ usually rely on directly or indirectly measuring vapour pressures and deriving ψ from a_w.

Since it is relatively simple to subject an organism to osmotic stress (ψ_s) in a homogeneous medium, most information relating microbial growth and activity to water stress has been obtained in this way (3.2). The growth

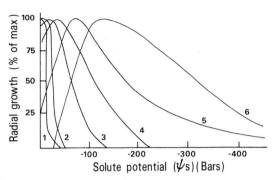

Figure 1.6 The effect of solute potential on the radial growth rate of representative fungi. 1, *Clavulina amethystma*; 2, *Phytophthora cinnamoni*; 3, *Fusarium* spp.; 4, *Aspergillus, Penicillium* spp.; 5, *Aspergillus amstelodami*; 6, *Xeromyces bisporus* (redrawn from Griffin and Luard, 1979).

responses of certain representative fungi to a range of values of ψ_S are shown in figure 1.6, and some limiting a_w values are shown in table 3.2. ψ_m curves are generally broadly similar in shape, but the limiting values for ψ_S are normally lower than the corresponding ψ_m values, probably as a consequence of different rates of nutrient diffusion in the two systems rather than an effect on ψ_m *per se*. The particularly xerotolerant types such as *Xeromyces bisporus* (table 3.2) are not found in soils, the most ubiquitous xerotolerant soil fungi being members of the genus *Penicillium* and *Aspergillus*, which are as common in soils with high rainfalls as in desert soils. It is clear that certain fungi are active in soils at ψ_m values of -200 bars ($a_w \sim 0.87$) and many are active at ψ_m values of -100 bars ($a_w \sim 0.92$), whereas higher plants are unable to generate sufficient suction to overcome ψ_m values of -15 bars ($a_w \sim 0.99$—the "wilt point"). Soil bacteria are generally limited to ψ_S values above -100 bars, although a few *Bacillus* and *Micrococcus* spp. can grow at ψ_S values of -200 bars. In soils, ψ_m affects bacteria in an important indirect way, since they require a surface film of water equivalent to the diameter of a cell for movement. It can be calculated that at ψ_m values below -1.5 bars ($a_w \sim 0.999$), soil pores large enough to permit the passage of a bacterial cell of radius 1 μm will drain, and therefore it can be predicted that bacterial activities would be markedly reduced at such ψ_m values due to localized depletion of nutrients. Observations of sequential bacterial activities such as sulphur oxidation and nitrification bear out this supposition, and it is clear that bacterial metabolism in soils effectively ceases at ψ_m values below -5 bars

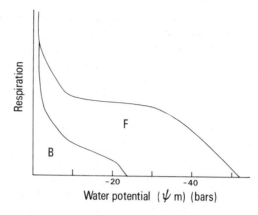

Figure 1.7 The relationship between respiration of soil microorganisms and soil water, potential (ψ_m). B and F represent the contributions of bacteria and fungi respectively (redrawn from Griffin and Luard, 1979).

as a consequence of reduced mobility, despite the ability of most common soil bacteria to grow in osmotically stressed media at much lower ψ_s values. Fungi (and presumably actinomycetes) are able to bridge air gaps by virtue of their hyphal mode of growth, and although inhibited to some extent by nutrient availability, are thus able to utilize nutrient sites elsewhere. Fungal activity in soils is therefore directly affected by ψ_m, rather than indirectly via mobility, and fungi make the major contribution to soil respiration under all but the wettest conditions (figure 1.7).

1.5 Soil structure and sorptive effects

Although microorganisms are considered to be aquatic and therefore physiologically restricted by the availability of the aquatic phase, soil microorganisms exist in soil in a sorbed state, colonizing a relatively small fraction ($<1\%$) of the available surface area of a soil, and therefore are not suspended in water layers for any significant period of time. It would be expected that the degree of sorption between soil microorganisms and soil particles would be broadly related to the surface charge of a soil particle. Accordingly, the clay fraction (and to some extent the organic fraction), is usually considered to be the most important soil fraction with regard to sorptive interactions. Sand and silt-sized particles, because of their relatively low surface area/mass ratio and negligible ion exchange capacity, probably do not maintain permanent microbial surface populations, and this is reflected in E.M. scanning studies of soil particles which indicate a low surface colonization of such particles (< 0.02 %) compared with clay and organic fractions (up to 15 %). The fact that microorganisms are sorbed in soil has considerable practical implications for enumeration techniques (1.3), and even the most vigorous treatments designed to disrupt soil aggregates generally fail to release more than 10 % of added marker bacteria.

Mechanisms of short-term sorption are complex and are thought to include the formation of cation bridges between negatively-charged bacterial surfaces and negatively-charged clay micelles. However, other mechanisms of sorption are probably also important, since sorption occurs in soils under conditions when relatively small amounts of cations are present, or when the pH is such that bacterial cells are not negatively charged. Such mechanisms probably include van der Waal's forces and changes brought about in the free energy of surfaces by prior sorption of organic macromolecules. Permanent adhesion involves the synthesis of attachment appendages such as holdfasts or fimbriae (pili), or the synthesis of exopolysaccharide cement—many soil bacteria when first isolated are fimbriate or mucoid.

Most solid surfaces when immersed in water assume a net negative charge, and consequently even relatively inert soil minerals like quartz can participate in sorption interactions to some extent . Any negatively charged surface can attract cations and organic macromolecules, and microorganisms may then be attracted along a concentration gradient of potential nutrients. The importance of the concentration of nutrients at interfaces is illustrated in figure 1.8, where a dramatic variation is seen in the numbers of bacteria that can be supported in low concentrations of nutrients in the presence and absence of glass beads.

Inorganic nutrients are probably obtained by microorganisms by an ion-exchange mechanism, whereby H^+ produced during metabolism is exchanged for various cations, so that a highly charged surface such as a clay surface fulfils two functions, that of nutrient supply and pH buffer. The buffering capacity of various soils is thought to be an important factor in the distribution and spread of certain fungal diseases, notably those produced by *Fusarium oxysporum* var. *cubense* (banana wilt) and *Histoplasma capsulatum* (human histoplasmosis). Both diseases, which are largely confined to tropical and sub-tropical regions of the Americas, are spread through soil. Soil containing significant amounts of clays have been found to be virtually free of the pathogens, whereas soils lacking clays, often in the same locale, are described as "high risk". This has been

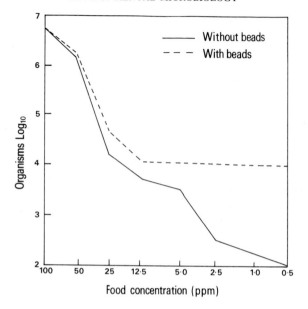

Figure 1.8 The effect of glass beads on the survival of *Escherichia coli* under low nutrient conditions (after 72 h incubation) (redrawn from Henkelekian, J. and Heller, A. (1940), *J. Bacteriol.* **40**, 547–560).

attributed to the pH buffering capacity of clay-containing soils, which promotes bacterial activity and consequent antagonism towards fungi, whereas in low clay soils, lower pH and consequent inhibition of bacteria results in extensive fungal spread.

It might seem at first sight that sorptive effects are likely to be universally of benefit to the microbial population of soils, but the literature is full of conflicting results showing sorption-mediated stimulation or inhibition of almost any parameter it would be possible to measure, including S oxidation, nitrification, soil respiration, microbial growth etc., and it would be fair to say that no simple coherent rationale exists to explain the contradictions in the plethora of data. Occasionally it is possible to relate a particular phenomenon to nutrient enhancement, or buffering capacity, but in general terms the only thing that all investigators are agreed upon is that interfaces are of fundamental importance in the behaviour of a particular soil and the concomitant microbial growth and activity therein.

1.6 Other consequences of the microhabitat existence

A further assumption to be derived from the microhabitat concept is that a localized environmental change may markedly alter the microbiological balance of one habitat without necessarily affecting adjacent habitats. Redox and pH are parameters that are particularly susceptible to change, dependent largely on the clay content and water regime of a particular microhabitat. Bulk pH measurements of soil give no indication of pH variations within soil aggregates, or variations over short distances within the charged surface layer of clay particles (1.1). Soil sectioning procedures used in conjunction with colorimetric pH measurements often reveal pH differences of more than 2 units over short distances in soil, and calculations of pH within charged surface layers indicate the possibility of considerable pH difference over very short distances from the surface of clay micelles. Similarly, microhabitats separated by only short distances may have quite different redox potentials as a consequence of the water regime of a particular soil—at ψ_m values of about -0.1 bars, pores of diameter $10\,\mu m$ and smaller are filled with water and could conceivably become anoxic due to microbial activity and poor oxygen transfer rates, since the diffusion coefficient of O_2 in water is about 10 000 times smaller than in air, whereas larger pores would contain an air space and presumably be oxic.

The succession of microorganisms and chemical effects that would be predicted following pH or redox changes within microhabitats is not thought to be significantly different from those observed following such changes on the macroscale (3.3, 3.4). Denitrification (6.4), SO_4^{2-} reduction (7.1), methanogenesis (9.4), and the related release of PO_4^{3-}, Fe(II) and Mn(II) (8.3), are readily observed in waterlogged soils, but can sometimes also be detected in trace amounts in relatively well-drained soils. Very acid or alkaline soils have characteristic populations of fungi and bacteria respectively, similar to those found in comparable "extreme" environments (3.3), but it is significant that examples of microorganisms considered to occupy extreme environments can be isolated from quite unexceptional soils, supporting the view that microhabitats undergo extreme conditions periodically, including extremes of temperature produced by day/night fluctuations.

The soil atmosphere

The soil atmosphere occupies the water-free pores between particles or aggregates. Its volume thus directly relates to the matric potential in a particular soil. Exchanges between the soil atmosphere and the overlying air are slow, and are vulnerable to any occlusion of the soil pores. Consequently, the composition of the soil atmosphere departs from that of normal air, with O_2 depleted, and CO_2 enhanced by the respiration of soil organisms and plant roots. High CO_2 concentrations inhibit the growth of many microorganisms, but partial pressures of CO_2 in the soil atmosphere are generally low, between 0.002 atm and 0.02 atm, occasionally reaching 0.1 atm. Some fungi can grow faster at these concentrations than in normal air (0.0003 atm CO_2), and it is possible that these fungi can obtain a significant amount of their biomass carbon from anaplerotic CO_2 fixation, which might be an important asset in soil where the supply of assimilable organic carbon is often localized and fluctuating. CO_2 at soil concentrations promotes perithecial formation in *Chaetomium globosum* and conidiation in *Fusarium* spp. but inhibits chlamydospore formation in the latter, and fruiting body formation in basidiomycetes such as the cultivated mushroom, *Agaricus brunnescens*. In the case of the mushroom, the effect may have a survival value as it restricts fruiting to near the soil surface, thus minimizing the carbon and energy required to raise the spore-bearing surfaces above the soil and into the air where spore dispersal occurs.

The soil atmosphere also contains other biologically active gases including NH_3 and various volatile metabolites including ethylene (C_2H_4). C_2H_4 is well known as a plant growth regulator; at high concentrations (> 5 ppm), it can also inhibit root development and root nodulation (4.6). C_2H_4 is produced by soil bacteria and fungi as well as by higher plants. There is no evidence, however, to suggest that microorganisms are adversely affected by C_2H_4 at the concentrations normally experienced in soils, and indeed, certain soil bacteria (*Mycobacterium* spp.) may use C_2H_4 as a source of carbon and energy.

1.7 The distribution and composition of the soil microflora

The literature contains numerous counts of various classes of microorganisms related to soil types, seasonal variation within soils, depths in soil profiles, and so on. The students of such data will notice disturbing variations in results (often 1–2 orders of magnitude) between counts made on samples of soil taken from sites only a few cm apart, or even between replicate counts on the same sample. These differences to some extent reflect the inadequacies of the enumeration procedures (1.3), but also probably reflect real differences imposed by the heterogeneity of the soil environment. Whatever the reason for these variations in results, statistical analyses should never be far from the mind of anyone trying to relate environmental influences to changes in the soil microflora.

Occasionally, attempts have been made to relate enumeration data to the physical and chemical characteristics of particular sites, and such work has confirmed what was to some extent intuitively obvious, namely that the number of microorganisms is related to moisture content, pH, organic content, and temperature. Thus, neutral fertile soils in relatively warm high rainfall areas tend to have the highest numbers of microorganisms, and on the basis of total microbial numbers, chernozems (wet grassland) > brown earths > podzols > tundras > latosols. The particularly significant correlation between organic content and microbial numbers is illustrated by the increased numbers of microorganisms in the rhizosphere (4.4), and the association of microorganisms with the humus layer(s) in soil profiles. Thus in all soils the largest number of microorganisms is found in the upper layer corresponding to the humus-rich A horizon, and in podzols a second peak of microbial numbers is seen in the upper humus-rich layer of the B horizon (table 1.3). Unexpectedly, anaerobic bacteria are found in greatest numbers in the upper layers, supporting the idea of anoxic microenvironments at any depth, dependent on the water regime.

Seasonal variations in microbial numbers are often difficult to estimate for the reasons already mentioned, and may also have to be assessed against a background of almost equally large, possibly real, daily or weekly fluctuations. However, a peak of microbial numbers is often observed in summer months, presumably as a reflection of increased temperature and litter input. Soils which are frozen in winter often show a peak of microbial

Table 1.3 Numbers of various kinds of microorganisms as determined by viable count ($\times 10^{-3}$ g dry soil^{-1})

Horizon	Aerobic bacteria	Actinomycetes	Anaerobic bacteria	Fungi	Algae
(1) Brown earth					
A (upper)	9500	1800	2000	400	25
A (lower)	2000	150	400	50	5
B (upper)	10	0	0	6	0
B (lower)	1	0	0	3	0
(2) Podzol					
A (upper)	5200	600	1000	580	100
A (lower)	1800	50	10	230	20
B (upper)	2900	180	100	400	0
B (lower)	80	40	10	10	0

Table 1.4 Biomass estimates for a wood soil (abbreviated from Lynch, 1979)

Group	Dry matter biomass (kg ha^{-1})
Bacteria	36.9
Actinomycetes	0.2
Fungi	454.0
Protozoa	1.0
Earthworms	12.0
Other biota	23.0
Annual litter production	7640.0

number immediately after the spring thaw, and this is thought to reflect the increased availability of nutrients following physical disruption of the soil structure. Ploughing of land produces the same effect. Comparisons of total counts of bacteria (by microscopic procedures) and viable counts (by plate spreading procedures) reveal that total counts are usually 2–3 orders of magnitude higher than the corresponding viable counts, and there is some evidence that the divergence is even greater at depth in the soil profile. This is to some extent also a reflection of the inadequacies of the enumeration procedures, but may also reflect the moribund state of a considerable fraction of the soil population as a consequence of nutrient deprivation (2.6).

Viable-counting procedures give an erroneous impression of the relative importance of the various groups of microorganisms, and in particular imply that bacteria constitute the most significant group of microorganisms in soils (table 1.3). Fungi are under-estimated, since viable-counting procedures effectively enumerate fungal spores only. On the other hand, estimates of biomass made by various procedures (1.3) indicate that fungal biomass generally exceeds that of bacterial biomass by anything from 2 : 1 to 20 : 1. The predominance of fungal biomass in a particular soil is illustrated in table 1.4, which also serves to indicate the significance of the microbial flora compared with the rest of the soil biota. Differential respiration studies using specific inhibitors of various microbial groups further illustrate the importance of fungi, since fungal respiration rates usually exceed bacterial respiration rates several-fold, even in non-acid soils (see figure 1.7).

The plethora of information about microbial numbers is matched by the vast amount of information on the types of microorganisms found in soils.

Soil is a giant repository for microorganisms, and nearly all types end up in soil at some time or another, leading to somewhat sterile arguments about the constitution of the indigenous and the transitory population. As far as bacteria are concerned, identification depends on the capacity to culture the organism, and what is isolated depends on the procedures used. There are periodic reports of the isolation of unknown bacteria that comprise significant fractions of the bacterial population of certain soils, so it is possible that a substantial fraction of the bacterial population of soils remains to be isolated and identified. However, there appears to be a general consensus that the majority of the aerobic, organotrophic bacterial population of most soils is composed of Gram-positive types. It is unwise to generalize about the percentages of various groups, but it is not uncommon to find that up to 70% of all bacterial isolates from soil are Gram-positive so-called coryneform bacteria of the poorly defined genus *Arthrobacter*, with *Bacillus* and *Micrococcus* spp. making up most of the rest of the Gram-positive aerobic population. The Gram-negative population is usually largely composed of *Pseudomonas* and *Flavobacterium* spp. and strict anaerobes seem to be mainly members of the Gram-positive genus *Clostridium*. Other relatively common genera that are considered to be indigenous include *Acinetobacter, Agrobacterium, Alcaligenes, Brevibacterium, Cellulomonas, Corynebacterium* and *Nocardia*. The major actinomycete genus is probably *Streptomyces*, and the characteristic "wet earth" smell associated with soils is produced by these prokaryotes. Soils under stress (extremes of water activity, temperature, pH, etc.) generally have more *Bacillus* spp. The preponderance of these particular Gram-positive types in almost all soils examined may reflect their resistance to the kinds of environmental fluctuation associated with microhabitats. Bacteria such as nitrifiers, S oxidizers, N_2 fixers and SO_4^{2-}-reducing bacteria, despite their enormous importance in the environment, apparently account for only a small fraction of the total bacterial population (seldom exceeding 10^2–10^3 g^{-1} dry weight) except under exceptional circumstances related to availability of specific substrates.

Representatives of all the major groups of algae, fungi and protozoa can also be found in soil, and in the case of algae and protozoa, the types do not differ significantly from those found in the aquatic environment. Algae are particularly important in preventing surface erosion, and the blue-green algae are often primary colonizers of exposed soil surfaces under extreme conditions. Soil algae are notoriously difficult to identify, often showing aberrant morphology in soil, but members of the Chlorophyta and Bacillariophyta are most commonly represented in neutral and acid soils, whereas blue-green algae such as *Anabaena*, *Calothrix*, *Oscillatoria* and *Nostoc* spp. are found under more alkaline conditions. In biomass terms the algae and protozoa are comparable and not very significant fractions of the microbial population, and protozoa probably spend a considerable amount of time encysted due to the unavailability of water (10 μm pores drain at ψ_m of about -0.1 bar).

All the major groups of fungi are represented in soil isolates, but imperfect fungi of the genera *Penicillium*, *Aspergillus*, *Cephalosporium*, *Cladosporium*, etc. are particularly easily isolated because conidiospores are copiously produced. However, many different ascomycetes and basodiomycetes are also present in soils, often showing pronounced geographical distribution, unlike the majority of the imperfect fungi, although their contribution to the total fungal biomass is obscure. It is probable that imperfect fungi constitute the major fungal group, particularly under dry conditions, but it should not be forgotten that soil also contains a large group of non-cultivable mycorrhizal fungi, including vesicular-arbuscular fungi (4.5) which may constitute a major part of the fungal biomass.

1.8 Microbial growth rates and energy flow

Enumeration and biomass data give some idea of the "standing crop" of microorganisms in any given soil, but they do not indicate how fast the microbial population is growing, or indeed if it is growing at all. There is no really satisfactory method of directly measuring microbial productivity in soils without producing disturbances and/or unnatural surfaces during the sampling procedures (1.3). There have nevertheless been many attempts to measure growth rates (usually of chemoorganotrophic bacteria) directly, both in the field, and under special conditions in the laboratory with sterile soils amended with known microbial populations. Although such measurements might be expected to overestimate rather then underestimate naturally-occurring growth rates, even in nutrient-amended soils the growth rates found never approach the growth rates commonly encountered with pure cultures in the laboratory. It is generally agreed that the mean doubling time of soil bacteria seldom falls below 12–15 h in nutrient-amended soils, and may be more than 10 d in unamended soils.

Confirmation of these findings has been obtained from calculations of possible growth rates based on the "standing crop" (microbial biomass) and the addition of substrate (litter) in certain soils. A certain proportion of the energy input utilized by microorganisms is used in maintaining vital functions rather than in growth. (Maintenance energy may reflect a great number of processes, for example, maintaining concentration gradients across membranes in non-growing cells.) The overall energy of consumption can be divided into that utilized for growth and that consumed for maintenance, thus:—

$$\begin{array}{c}\text{Overall rate of} \\ \text{energy consumption}\end{array} = \begin{array}{c}\text{Rate of energy} \\ \text{consumption for growth}\end{array} + \begin{array}{c}\text{Rate of energy} \\ \text{consumption for maintenance}\end{array}$$

i.e.

$$\frac{\mu x}{y} = \frac{\mu x}{y_g} + \frac{ax}{y_g}$$

where μ is the specific growth rate (h^{-1}); x is the microbial biomass (g); y is the observed growth yield (g biomass.g^{-1} substrate); y_g is the growth yield assuming no expenditure of energy in maintenance; a is the specific maintenance rate (h^{-1}). In certain systems it is possible to measure the input of energy substrate (dS/dt), by weighing the amount of leaf litter, etc., over a period, and the microbial biomass in a given soil can be estimated by a variety of procedures (1.3). If the term for maintenance is included in the familiar equation derived from chemostat studies relating growth rates (dx/dt) to rate of uptake of substrate, then

$$\frac{dx}{dt} + ax = y\frac{dS}{dt}$$

where S is the substrate available for growth. Estimates of y and a can be made from chemostat studies with pure cultures. In truth, we do not know how values derived from chemostat experiments relate to the specialized soil microflora in an inhomogeneous environment, but values of $0.001–0.003\ h^{-1}$ and $0.35–0.60\ g$ biomass g^{-1} substrate for a and y respectively, are commonly used in calculations of this kind. Such calculations support the view that the mean doubling time of the soil microflora is probably in excess of $10\ d$ in relatively fertile soils, and there are data which suggest that the energy input is only sufficient to support the maintenance energy requirement of the microflora, i.e. $dx/dt = 0$.

All of these calculations give a mean doubling time calculated over a long period, and it is possible that the soil population does indeed grow very slowly at a constant rate. However, the more widely accepted implication of these results is that the soil microflora spends most of its time in a dormant or quiescent state, and that none of the physiological groups is continually active. Bursts of activity presumably depend on the input of fresh substrate—the growth of microorganisms in the rhizosphere is a different situation, since substrate is continually available from root exudates (4.4).

1.9 The relationship of the soil microflora to that of the atmosphere

The atmosphere contains a large number of different types of small particulate biological entities ranging from microorganisms to pollens and other types of plant spore. The aerobiologist is as much concerned with the source, distribution and spread of pollens, as he is with the features of the microbial population. The atmospheric behaviour of small particles is clearly of great significance for the plant pathologist (and for governments concerned with the implications of germ warfare!), and there is an extensive body of work which seeks to explain the dispersion of clouds of particles in mathematical terms.

Most sampling techniques involve the separation of particles of different size classes by sedimentation or sieving, followed by impingement of the particles on a sticky trapping surface, or on the surface of nutrient media. Extensive sampling has produced no evidence for a real aerial plankton in the sense of a population of microorganisms living and reproducing at great heights, and there seems little reason to doubt that airborne microorganisms originate from the terrestrial and oceanic environments. The bacterial population over terrestrial areas largely reflects the microbial population of soils, and is composed of Gram-positive coryneform organisms (probably *Arthrobacter* spp.), *Bacillus* spp. and *Micrococcus* spp. In theory there should be a logarithmic decrease in microbial numbers with height, and in practice there are far more bacteria just above the ground (anything from 10^3–10^6 per m^3), than at 1000 m (10^2–10^3), but a steady state is seldom realized because weather conditions fluctuate rapidly. Bacterial loadings over oceans are on average lower (10^2–10^3 bacteria per m^3 above the ocean surface), and include significant numbers of Gram-negatives, reflecting both the composition and paucity of the mid-ocean bacterial flora. Local variations produced by activated sludge plants which generate aerosols of Gram-negative microorganisms seem to have had little effect in the long term. Protozoan and algal numbers are insignificant in the atmosphere, but the fungal population of the atmosphere usually outnumbers the bacterial population, particularly at height, and is probably derived from surface colonies of fungi on decaying vegetation or infected plants, rather than from soils *per se*. The spores of the imperfect fungi, especially *Cladosporium* spp., and basidiospores, dominate the fungal population over both terrestrial and oceanic areas, showing roughly the same variation in number as bacteria relative to height above oceanic or terrestrial habitats. At high altitudes ($> 5000\,m$) only small numbers of microorganisms are normally detected ($1-10\,per\,m^3$), and there is no evidence that the undoubted seeding of the upper atmosphere by passenger aircraft has had any noticeable effect to date.

REFERENCES

Books

Alexander, M. (1977) *Soil Microbiology* (2nd edition), John Wiley & Sons.

Burges, A. and Raw, F. (1967) *Soil Biology*, Academic Press.

Courtney, F. M. and Trudgill, S. T. (1976) *The Soil—An Introduction to Soil Studies in Britain*, Edward Arnold.

Griffin, D. M. (1972) *Ecology of Soil Fungi*, Chapman & Hall.

Litchfield, C. D. and Seyfried, P. L. (1979) *Methodology for Biomass Determinations and Microbial Activities in Sediments*, ASTM Special Publication 673, American Society for Testing and Materials, Philadelphia.

McLaren, A. D. and Peterson, G. H. (1967) (Editors) *Soil Biochemistry*, Vol. 1, Marcel Dekker.

Parkinson, D., Gray, T. R. G. and Williams, S. T. (1971) *Methods for Studying the Ecology of Soil Microorganisms*, IBP Handbook 19, Blackwell Scientific Publications.

Rosswall, T. (1973) *Modern Methods in the Study of Microbial Ecology*, IBP Bulletin from the Ecological Research Committee 17. NFR, Stockholm.

Walker, N. (1975) (Editor) *Soil Microbiology*, Butterworths.

Articles

Burns, R. G. (1979) Interactions of microorganisms, their substrates and their products with soil surfaces, in *Adhesion of Microorganisms to Surfaces*, editors D. C. Ellwood, J. Melling and P. Rutter, Academic Press, 109–138.

Dommergues, Y. R., Belser, L. W. and Schmidt, E. L. (1978) Limiting factors for microbial growth and activity in soil. *Adv. Microbial Ecol.* **2**, 49–104.

Domsch, K. H., Beck, T. H., Anderson, J. P. E., Soderstrom, B., Parkinson, D. and Trolldenier, G. (1979) A comparison of methods for soil microbial population and biomass studies. *Zeitschr. Planz. Bodenkunde*, **142**, 520–533.

Felbeck, G. T. (1971) Chemical and biological characterization of humic matter, in *Soil Biochemistry*, Vol. 2, editors A. D. McLaren and J. Skujins, Marcel Dekker, 36–59.

Gray, T. R. G. (1976) Survival of vegetative microbes in soil, in *The Survival of Vegetative Microbes*, editors, T. R. G. Gray and J. R. Postgate, Cambridge University Press, 327–364.

Gray, T. R. G. and Williams, S. T. (1972) Microbial productivity in soil, in *Microbes and Biological Productivity*, editors D. E. Hughes and A. H. Rose, Cambridge University Press, 255–286.

Griffin, D. M. and Luard, G. J. (1979) Water stress and microbial ecology, in *Strategies of Microbial Life in Extreme Environments*, editor M. Shilo, Dahlem Conference Report, **13**, Verlag Chemie, 49–64.

Haider, K., Martin, J. P. and Filip, Z. (1975) Humus biochemistry, in *Soil Biochemistry*, Vol. 4, editors E. A. Paul and A. D. McLaren, Marcel Dekker, 195–244.

Hissett, R. and Gray, T. R. G. (1976) Microsites and time changes in soil microbe ecology, in *The Role of Terrestrial and Aquatic Organisms in Decomposition Processes*, editors J. M. Anderson and A. Macfadyen, Blackwell Scientific, 23–40.

Holding, A. J., Collins, V. G., French, D. O., D'Sylva, B. T. and Baker, J. H. (1974) Relationship between viable bacterial counts and site characteristics in tundra, in *Soil Organisms and Decomposition in Tundra*, editors A. J. Holding, O. W. Neal, S. F. MacLean and P. M. Flanagan, IBP Tundra Biome Stockholm, 49–64.

Kuprevich, V. F. and Shcherbakova, T. A. (1971) Comparative enzymatic activity in diverse types of soil, in *Soil Biochemistry*, Vol. 2, Marcel Dekker, 167–201.

Lacey, J. (1979) Aerial dispersion and the development of microbial communities, in *Microbial Ecology—A Conceptual Approach*, editors J. M. Lynch and N. J. Poole, Blackwell Scientific, 140–170.

Lynch, J. M. (1979) The terrestrial environment, in *Microbial Ecology—A Conceptual Approach*, editors J. M. Lynch and N. J. Poole, Blackwell Scientific, 67–91.

Marshall, K. C. (1971) Sorptive interactions between soil particles and microorganisms, in *Soil Biochemistry*, Vol. 2, editors A. D. McLaren and J. Skujins, Marcel Dekker, 409–445.

Paul, E. A. and Voroney, R. P. (1980) Nutrient and energy flows through soil microbial biomass, in *Contemporary Microbial Ecology*, editors D. C. Ellwood, J. N. Hedger, M. J. Latham, J. M. Lynch and J. H. Slater, Academic Press, 215–238.

Rosswall, T. and Kvillner, E. (1978) Principal components and factor analysis for the description of microbial populations. *Adv. Microbial Ecol.* **2**, 1–48.

Stotzky, G. (1972) Activity, ecology and population dynamics of microorganisms in soil. *CRC Critical Reviews in Microbiology*, **2**, 59–138.

CHAPTER TWO

THE AQUATIC ENVIRONMENT

2.1 Physical and chemical properties of the aquatic environment

About 97 % of earth's water is in the oceans, 2 % in glaciers and polar ice, 0.009 % in lakes, 0.00009 % in rivers, and the residue in ground waters. As the oceans cover 71 % of the globe's surface, water is thus the dominant environment.

Water has a very high specific thermal capacity. Consequently, large bodies of water absorb or lose a great amount of heat energy without much change in temperature, and many aquatic organisms enjoy very stable climates, with 90 % of all oceanic water never reaching a temperature greater than 4°C. Because of its temperature–density relationship, fresh water approaching 4°C sinks, and the bottoms of large ponds, lakes and their sediments are rarely frozen. The solute content of sea water leads to an increase in density, lowering both the freezing point and the specific thermal capacity.

Other significant physical features of water include light absorption and hydrostatic pressure. The first regulates the distribution of phototrophs and primary production, and thus indirectly the distribution of many chemoorganotrophs. Light intensity in pure water decreases by 53 % in the first metre, and by 50 % in each subsequent metre of depth. Where it declines to 1 % of the incident light at the surface, the *compensation point* is reached, where photosynthesis is assumed to be balanced by respiratory losses. This point marks the base of the *euphotic* zone to which primary production is confined; its position ranges from 200 m depth in very clear lakes, to 100 m depth in the open ocean, and as little as 2 m depth in turbid estuaries. Hydrostatic pressure also relates to depth, rising by 1 atmosphere every 10 m, and over 90 % of oceanic water is at pressures exceeding 100 atmospheres. This has important consequences for the activities of the inhabitants and also affects the design of sampling equipment.

Table 2.1 Cation and anion composition in sea water of 35‰ salinity. (From Parsons, T., Takahashi, M. and Hargrave, B. (1977), *Biological Oceanographic Processes*, 2nd edn., Pergamon Press, Oxford.)

Cations	$g\,kg^{-1}$	Anions	$g\,kg^{-1}$
Na^+	10.76	Cl^-	19.35
Mg^{2+}	1.30	SO_4^{2-}	2.71
Ca^{2+}	0.41	Br^-	0.07
K^+	0.40	HCO_3^-	0.14
Sr^{2+}	0.01	H_3BO_3	0.03

Sea water contains an average of 35 parts per thousand (‰) dissolved salts (table 2.1), whereas soft fresh water has a salinity of 0.065‰, and hard water one of about 0.3‰. Buffering is chiefly regulated by the important equilibrium

$$CO_2 + H_2O \rightleftharpoons H_2CO_3 \rightleftharpoons HCO_3^- + H^+ \rightleftharpoons CO_3^= + H^+$$

The pH of the sea is maintained between 8.0 and 8.3, and most fresh waters between 6.0 and 9.0. As CO_2 is three times as soluble as oxygen, CO_2 deficits are rare, whereas the maximum concentration of O_2 in pure water at sea level of $14.6\,mg\,l^{-1}$ at $0°C$ is often significantly lowered by solutes, increases in pressure and temperature, and biological demand (8.3). The diffusion of O_2 from the atmosphere, between different water masses, and into sediments is slow, and where mixing is restricted, anoxic conditions can quickly be initiated in organic-rich waters and sediments due to depletion by decomposers (8.3). Once established, reducing conditions can be maintained by the formation of H_2S, reduced organic compounds, and reduced iron and manganese salts (7.1, 7.3).

2.2 The aquatic environment as a microbial habitat

The main zones of the sea are shown in figure 2.1, which excludes intermediate regions such as estuaries. Inland surface waters are separable into flowing (*lotic*) and still (*lentic*) environments. The lotic streams and rivers provide relatively uniform environments throughout their depths, whereas, in contrast, lentic lakes develop distinct water layers differing in temperature, density, chemistry and biology (figure 2.2). This stratification is also found at times in the sea, and commonly results from surface heating when turbulence is low enough to prevent mixing of the water column. It can also arise when ocean currents meet, or if very saline water is trapped in

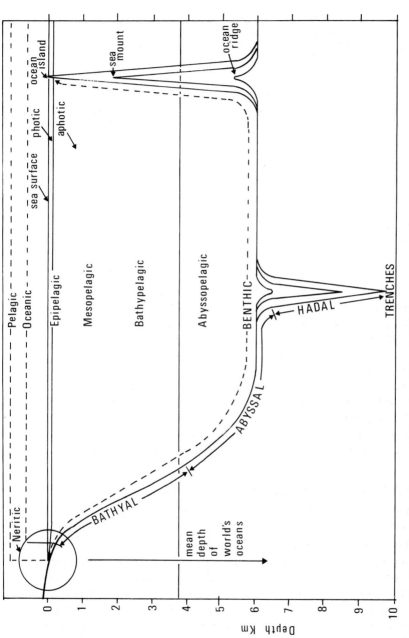

Figure 2.1   The major zones of the ocean (redrawn from Sieburth, 1979).

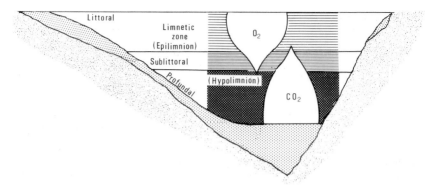

Figure 2.2 Zonation in a stratified eutrophic lake. The thermocline is positioned between the O_2-rich epilimnion and the O_2-depleted hypolimnion (redrawn from Cole, G. A. (1979), *Textbook of Limnology*, 2nd edn., The C. V. Mosby Co., St. Louis).

lake or ocean basins. The base of the warmed upper layer is indicated by an abrupt drop in temperature, the *thermocline*. In stratified waters, the vertical movement of solutes and gases across the thermocline is very slow. As a result, organic and inorganic nutrients including silicon released by decay below the thermocline are not returned to the euphotic zone to maintain production by diatoms (7.5) and other phototrophs, while the stratification remains. At the same time, decomposition in the deeper water can lead to O_2 depletion and the accumulation of fermentation products and of H_2S. The summer appearance of an O_2-limited lower zone (*hypolimnion*) is characteristic of nutrient-rich, relatively shallow *eutrophic* lakes (lakes producing 75–250 g fixed $C\,m^2y^{-1}$). Production in *oligotrophic* lakes (lakes producing < 25 g fixed $C\,m^2y^{-1}$) is nutrient-restricted, and they do not develop an anoxic hypolimnion. Re-entry of nutrients into the euphotic zone occurs when the thermocline is destroyed by autumn gales, and is often marked by an algal, often diatom-dominated bloom, as nutrients and silicon become available.

Aquatic habitats are listed in table 2.2. The air–water interface (neustonic habitat) is the most extreme and unusual. It is the site of a detergent-like film of hydrophobic hydrocarbons, fatty acids and esters overlying a layer of polysaccharide–protein complexes just below the interface. The dissolved organic matter in this surface skin may reach $2–9\,g\,l^{-1}$ compared with $1–5\,mg\,l^{-1}$ dissolved organic matter in many oceanic waters, and there may be as many as 10^8 bacteria ml^{-1}. Liquid–solid interfaces are also regions where nutrients and carbon sources may

Table 2.2 Microbial habitats

Habitat	Definition	Community terms	Sub-divisions
1. Neustonic	The surface film (air/water interface)	Neuston	
2. Planktonic	The water column; its free-floating inhabitants of limited motility	Plankton	Potamoplankton (= river plankton)
3. Benthic	In and on permanently submerged sediments	Benthos	(a) Psammon or Hydropsammon (interstitial water between sand grains) (b) Epipsammon (on sand grains) (c) Epipeplon (on mud)
4. Epibiotic	On living and non-living surfaces large enough to support a mixed microbial community	Periphyton (all attached organisms)	(a) Epiphyton (on plants) (b) Epizoon (on animals) (c) Epilithic (on rocks and stones)
5. Enteric-faecal sestonic	Within animal guts and continuing on faeces; also on any floating particulate organic matter	Enteric Faecal Seston	—

accumulate through sorption (1.5). Microorganisms can be attracted to such enriched surfaces and be retained there by sorption (1.5). However, fewer bacteria than would be expected appear attached to suspended particles in oceanic water, perhaps because of nutrient depletion by rapid temporal succession of microorganisms on newly-formed animal and plant residues.

2.3 The methodology

Detecting microorganisms and monitoring microbial activity is easier in water than in soil, and in principle most of the soil methodology can be applied in the aquatic habitat (1.3). Sediments create difficulties since like soils they are inhomogeneous environments. Also, sediments are frequently separated into oxic and anoxic layers over short distances, are perturbed by burrowers and have varying degrees of compaction.

A variety of containers, grabs and corers are used to sample waters and sediments. The chief problems are the need to examine large volumes of water for the often thinly-dispersed microbes, and the temperature and pressure differences that may exist between the sampling point and the surface. Thus an ideal sampler for deep-sea water should be able to take a relatively large uncontaminated sample, and maintain it at the original pressure and temperature during recovery (which may take hours) and in the laboratory. Samplers with these properties have been developed for use down to 6000 m, but such devices are expensive, requiring high technological and engineering standards. By contrast, samplers for use down to a few hundred metres have employed more conventional containers and are relatively simple in design. For many purposes, strict asepsis is not needed, and widely used samplers in lakes and the sea are designed to trap up to 5 l of water after being lowered open to a predetermined depth.

In order to culture and count relatively sparse aquatic microorganisms, they must be concentrated, and may have to be separated from other groups in the water samples, for example, by size fractionation. This is most easily achieved by trapping cells on graded filters. The estimation of microbes in water follows the same principles as, and suffers similar defects to, the approaches used with soil (1.3). Membrane-filtered samples can be stained to provide direct total microscopic counts (staining with fluorescent dyes, and examination using epifluorescence microscopy have proved particularly useful), or can be placed on nutrient media for microcolony development. Most Probable Number (MPN) techniques (1.3) can be used to enumerate certain groups. Direct counts of bacteria are often two or three orders of magnitude greater than colony counts, raising the question of how many of the visible bacteria are viable. One approach to this question is to add yeast extract and the antibiotic nalidixic acid to seawater samples in order to stimulate the growth of viable cells, but to delay their division so that they elongate and become easily recognizable after a few hours' incubation. The numbers of bacteria so counted in one experiment were three orders of magnitude larger than colony counts, but still one order less than the total direct count.

Concentrated samples can be specifically enriched to yield particular physiological groups (1.3). Bacteria with low specific growth rates and high substrate affinities (2.6, 4.2) cannot be isolated by conventional enrichment procedures, since they are outgrown by more common microorganisms with high specific growth rates. However, such bacteria can often be isolated by enrichment in chemostats run at very low dilution rates (2.6, 4.2). Buried or suspended slides or peloscopes (1.3) have also been used to detect and enrich particular groups of microorganisms with unusual growth characteristics.

The ATP assay (1.3) has been widely used to measure total biomass, and is particularly suited to the homogeneous aquatic habitat. Membrane filtered samples can be readily lysed in an appropriate buffer, and an appropriate luciferin–luciferase system used to assay the ATP. Sediment samples present the same problems as soil samples, and appropriate extraction procedures for ATP have to be employed. Biomass estimates of specific groups of microorganisms can be made based on total counting procedures, but an alternative approach is to assay biochemical markers specific to a group, usually cell wall components such as muramic acid for bacteria, or chlorophyll a for algae (although both eukaryotic and blue-green algae possess chlorophyll a) (1.3).

Microbial activity is most easily assessed by measuring the uptake of specific substrates, or measuring respiration rates (1.3). Uptake studies have been largely based on Michaelis–Menten kinetics applied to the short-term transport of labelled compounds into the natural microflora. If respiratory CO_2 output is too low to be used as an index of organotrophic activity, respiratory activity can be measured through the reduction of tetrazolium salts.

Growth rates have been followed by measuring changes in biomass, macromolecular synthesis (stable RNA) or organotrophic CO_2 uptake, while autoradiography has been applied to growths on solid surfaces. Estimates of rates *in situ* have been obtained indirectly from the frequency of dividing cells in samples. Another approach has been to separate a population from the main water mass by enclosure within permeable membranes, and measuring the response to diurnal fluctuations in dissolved carbon while the apparatus is submerged. Changes in growth rates can be monitored by periodic recovery for biomass determinations.

2.4 The microbial population

The bacteria most commonly isolated from the aquatic environment are Gram-negative rods, and indeed, 90% of all isolates fall into this category, usually including species of *Vibrio*, *Pseudomonas* and *Flavobacterium* or related organisms. Rivers and streams frequently have larger numbers of Gram-positive types, presumably due to wash-in from the surrounding terrestrial environment, but Gram-negative types nevertheless predominate. Numerous small ($0.2\,\mu m–0.5\,\mu m$) unidentified marine planktonic bacteria also show Gram-negative cell wall structure. Sediments contain a much higher proportion of Gram-positive types, especially *Bacillus* spp. In view of the requirement of microorganisms for water, we may ask whether there is such a thing as a truly "aquatic" microorganism. In general the frequency of occurrence and the ability to survive and grow in the aquatic environment are regarded as appropriate pointers to a strictly aquatic mode of life. Unfortunately, it is rare to have this information about most of the more common isolates from fresh water and it is possible that many of these simply outlast other microbial types after being washed in from elsewhere. Bacteria commonly isolated from mid-ocean environments are less likely to be simply in transit, but there are no clearly defined marine genera, and it is equally reasonable to question whether specifically marine bacteria exist. The only general characteristic of most marine isolates is their ability to survive and grow in sea water; many also have a requirement for NaCl at marine concentration, particularly when first isolated, and most marine isolates are noticeably psychrotrophic or even psychrophilic (3.1). It is however likely that the majority of sheathed and appendaged bacteria are essentially aquatic, having a benthic or epibiotic habitat. Some of these are particularly important in element cycling (7.1, 7.3) and in polluted environments (8.3). Phototrophic bacteria are also clearly truly aquatic, planktonic bacteria, and these may be important primary producers in certain unusual environments (7.1).

Microscopic examination of natural waters, particularly those with low nutrient content which have been left undisturbed for long periods, often reveals morphologically distinct forms which can seldom be maintained in culture. Organisms with unusual morphologies, including the production of prosthecae, or the formation of filamentous, ring-shaped, network or sheet-like micro-colonies often constitute a significant proportion of the microflora of such water masses.

The problem of buoyancy in the water column is sometimes solved by small size, motility, or the possession of gas vesicles. Gas vesicles occur in many blue-green algae, and in aquatic phototrophic and chemoorganotrophic bacteria, particularly those found in the hypolimnion of eutrophic lakes. Analogous structures maintain halobacteria (3.2) at the surface of brine pools. Another possible positional mechanism is found in motile, sediment-inhabiting bacteria which contain axial arrays of iron particles.

These organisms show magnetotactic movements in the direction of the magnetic poles.

Fungi appear more prevalent in fresh water than in the sea, and feature most prominently in the decay of introduced higher-plant residues. Lower fungi with flagellated zoospores, such as chytrids, are regarded as primarily aquatic, and include freshwater and inshore marine parasites of planktonic algae, as well as fermentative species capable of growth in anoxic sediments (some of these are also found in the rumen—see 9.4). Oomycetes are poorly represented in the sea, though widespread in lakes and common in rivers, streams and ponds. The Thraustochytridiales are exclusively marine, though often coastal, and are related to the Labyrinthulales, another marine group. Septate higher fungi that may have reverted to permanent life in water are mainly ascomycetes and imperfect fungi. In fresh water they are largely associated with leaf decay in rivers and streams. Here, in common with some basidiomycetes, they have evolved branched, tetraradiate (four-armed), or sigmoidally curved asexual spores which, in running water, impact efficiently on potential substrates. Marine ascomycetes have mainly been studied in submerged timber or in mangrove swamps, and while some decompose large algae, a few have lichen-like associations with these plants. The wood-decaying species often have radiating appendages on their ascopores, which may aid contact with timber or flotation.

Planktonic yeasts have been found in oceans down to depths of 3000 m in low numbers (usually $< 100 l^{-1}$) but are more common in coastal waters associated with dinoflagellate blooms. Species of *Debaryomyces, Torulopsis* and *Rhodotorula* are widespread, while unusual psychotrophic basidiomycetous yeasts (*Leucosporidium* spp. and *Rhodosporidium* spp.) are found in the Antarctic (3.1). The copepod parasite *Metschnikowia* is mainly coastal, and also attacks freshwater cladocerans.

2.5 The distribution and activity of the microbial population

The distribution of chemoorganotrophs in the water column broadly follows that of the active primary producers (figure 2.3). Bacterial numbers also follow seasonal primary production maxima, and range from below $10^3-10^4 \, ml^{-1}$ in oligotrophic waters to $10^7-10^8 \, ml^{-1}$ in eutrophic waters. The largest numbers below the neuston habitat (2.2) are often associated with phytoplankton maxima near the base of the euphotic zone, or where there is a high density of grazers. Exceptions to this pattern include H_2S-rich anoxic bottom waters, where chemolithotrophic production

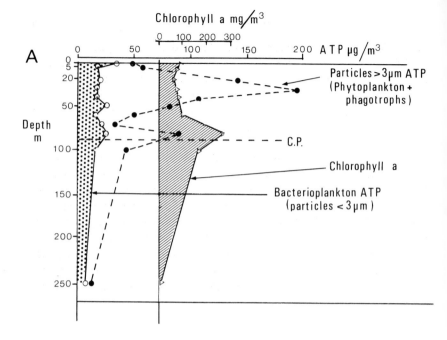

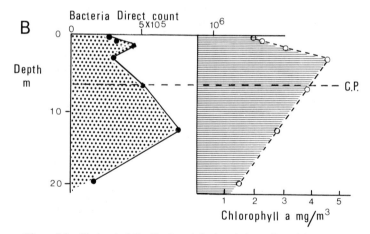

Figure 2.3 The vertical distribution of planktonic bacteria and phytoplankton.
A. In the Atlantic near the Azores. Bacteria estimated as ATP in particles <3 μm, phytoplankton as chlorophyll *a*.
B. In Lake Biwa, Japan. Bacteria as a direct count, phytoplankton as chlorophyll *a*. C.P. = compensation point, where light intensity is 1% of the surface illumination. (A, redrawn from Sieburth (1979); B, redrawn from Tanaka, N., Nakanishi, M. and Kadota, H. (1974), *Effect of the Ocean Environment on Microbial Activities*, eds. R. R. Colwell and R. Y. Morita, University Park Press, Baltimore, pp. 495–509.)

occurs. Very high local concentrations of S oxidizers are supported by the H_2S from deep sea hydrothermal vents. In lakes, much of the detritus reaches the sediment surface where microbial activity and bacterial numbers can be high ($10^9 g^{-1}$). The situation is presumed similar in many littoral marine sediments, but less so in mid-ocean sediments, where little detritus reaches the ocean floor, and bacterial numbers are lower ($10^4–10^5 g^{-1}$).

The concentration of dissolved organic carbon (DOC) in oceanic water is generally $1–5 mg l^{-1}$, but can exceed $40 mg l^{-1}$ inshore, and fall to $0.5 mg l^{-1}$ or less below 300 m. Lakes have $1–50 mg l^{-1}$ DOC; particulate organic carbon (POC) is about one-tenth of these values. Between 60% and 90% of oceanic DOC is of unknown composition, and may be several hundred years old in deep water. Only about 10% represents assimilable bacterial substrates, and most of this is cycled within the euphotic zone. The transfer of 25% of aquatic primary production to bacterial biomass may occur. Estimates for the Baltic and Black Sea approach this figure,

Table 2.3 Growth rates of planktonic bacteria in natural water

Location	Observation period	Doubling or generation times (h)	Method
Oligotrophic lake[1] (Mirror Lake, New Hampshire)	Yearly average	60–188	Biomass estimation by $^{35}SO_4^{2-}$ uptake
	September	29	
	February (under ice)	> 2 400	
Brackish water[2] (Baltic, Swedish coast)	Over 1 year	10–100	Frequency of dividing cells
Brackish water,[3] inshore (Baltic, Kiel Fjord)	July–October	70–111	Diffusion culture (in laboratory)
	November–June	0–1980	
Brackish water,[3] offshore (Baltic, Kiel Bight)	July–October	105–1510	Diffusion culture (in laboratory)
	November–June	0–3040	

1. Jordan, M. J. and Likens, G. E. (1980) Measurement of planktonic bacterial production in an oligotrophic lake. *Limnol. & Oceanogr.* **25**, 719–732.
2. Hagstrom, A., Larson, U., Horstedt, P. and Nomark, S. (1979) Frequency of dividing cells, a new approach to the determination of bacterial growth rates in aquatic environments. *Appl. Env. Microbiol.* **37**, 805–812.
3. Meyer-Reil, L. A. (1977) Bacterial growth rates and biomass production. From Rheinheimer (1977) pp. 223–236.

but it is likely that only about half this level of transfer occurs in oligotrophic lakes.

In the relatively warm (15°–20°C) euphotic zone near the Azores, *in situ* diffusion cultures of bacterioplankton indicate that three doublings occur per day, with the shortest generation time (4 h) during daylight. Clearly, in relatively warm, nutrient-rich waters, there can be quite rapid microbial activity in the vicinity of phytoplankton concentrations. Other measurements on natural waters give much slower growth rates (table 2.3). Long doubling times agree with estimates of up to 200 h for doubling times obtained in chemostat cultures of single isolates growing on filtered sea water. Indirect kinetic measurements of microbial activity mirror summer/winter growth rate fluctuations.

2.6 Oligotrophy

Certain aquatic bacteria are said to be *oligotrophic*, which in this context means that the organism has the ability to grow under very low nutrient concentrations. One definition of an oligotrophic bacterium is that it is capable of growth on media containing as little as $1–15\,mg\,Cl^{-1}$. These concentrations are comparable with carbon levels in oceanic waters (2.5), but are a thousand times less than the available C content of many laboratory media. Bacteria normally grown on rich media show loss of viability in chemostat cultures at very low growth rates (figure 2.4). This phenomenon could partially explain differences between total and viable counts from low nutrient natural environments. Low nutrient supply and slow growth rates also produce abnormal morphologies (2.4) and dwarfing. Thus, it is not clear whether the small size of some of the marine bacterioplankton (2.4) is a taxonomically useful feature, or merely a phenotypic response.

Perhaps the most important characteristic of oligotrophs is a high substrate affinity (i.e. low K_s) coupled with a low maximum growth rate (μ_{max}) (4.2). Such bacteria persist as metabolically active cells whereas bacteria with low substrate affinities and high maximum growth rates are unable to compete (4.2). Appendaged bacteria appear to be examples of oligotrophs and their production of appendages may be a response to low nutrient conditions in some instances (2.4). It is possible to isolate oligotrophic microorganisms by running chemostats under low nutrient conditions with very slow dilution rates, and one might expect appendaged bacteria to become enriched in these cultures. However, in practice, probably because technical problems preclude slow enough dilution rates,

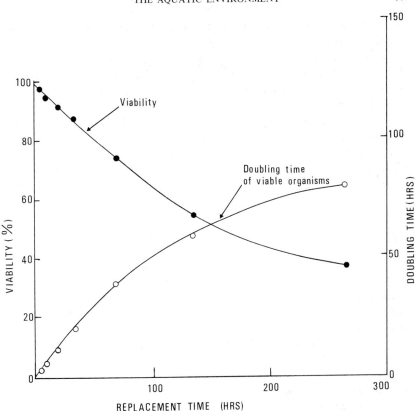

Figure 2.4 The loss of viability with increasing doubling time of *Klebsiella aerogenes* cells in a glycerol-limited chemostat culture (redrawn from Tempest, D. W. and Neijssel, O. M. (1978), *Adv. Microbial Ecology* **2**, 105–153).

rather unexceptional organisms such as *Pseudomonas* and *Spirillum* spp. are usually isolated by these procedures, although there is no means of knowing if their morphology might change under very low nutrient conditions.

2.7 Barophily and bioluminescence

Hydrostatic pressure, averaging 380 atm on the ocean floor, significantly affects the behaviour of marine organisms, as most biological reactions are slowed at pressures greater than 300 atm. If there is appreciable microbial activity near the ocean floor and in its sediments, the participants must be either *barophilic* (more active at high pressure) or *barotolerant* (most active at 1 atm but withstanding high pressure). Early tests on decompressed sediments suggested that certain deep-sea bacteria were barophilic, since samples from 10 000 m in the Philippines trench gave MPN counts of 10^4–10^6 bacteria per ml when incubated at 1000 atm, but only 10^2 ml^{-1} at 1 atm.

The concept of an active barophilic abyssal microflora was however severely jolted by the accidental sinking of the submersible *Alvin* in 1968. On recovery, after 11 months in sea water at 1540 m, a lunch box containing bologna sandwiches and apples was found. The food was remarkably well-preserved, but spoiled rapidly at atmospheric pressure, prompting a re-examination of decomposition near the sea abyssal floor, since the oceans have long been considered to have almost unlimited capacity to decompose or detoxify discarded material.

The use of pressure-retaining samplers, permitting the study of un-decompressed bacteria for the first time, suggests the absence of true barophiles amongst planktonic bacteria. The restricted decomposition by deep sea bacteria has been shown to be a function of both the prevailing high pressures and low temperatures. It has been suggested that barophilic bacteria might exist only in the guts of scavenging animals such as amphipods, and recently a barophilic spirillum has been isolated from such a source. However, it is clear that barophily is not a general feature of the deep-sea microflora, and that most processes go on very slowly compared with surface waters, except, presumably, in the intestinal contents of scavengers where there would be considerable advantage in having a barophilic microflora.

The gut contents and bodies of marine animals are among the habitats of another largely marine group, the luminous bacteria. Light is produced through the luciferase-mediated oxidation of reduced flavin mononucleotide ($FMNH_2$) coupled to the oxidation of a long-chain aliphatic aldehyde, probably tetradecanal—this system differs from that of the firefly (1.3). Marine luminescent bacteria are classified in the genera *Photobacterium* (four species) and the vibroid *Beneckea* (two species). Certain *Photobacterium* spp. can be free-living in marine waters, and are also found in crustacean tissues, and in specific light organ symbioses in numerous mid-water fishes and some squids. Bacteria cannot be cultured from all light organs, but luciferase extracts produce the relatively fast kinetics of the *Photobacterium* system, except in the flash-light fishes (anomalopids). Luciferase from the latter resembles that of *Beneckea* spp., which are presently not known as symbionts, although otherwise are as versatile as *Photobacterium* spp.

Although the biochemical advantages of luminescence are largely unknown, the bacteria presumably benefit in some way which justifies the commitment of up to 5% of cell protein to luciferase. One suggested advantage of light emission is the attraction of potential hosts to heavily colonized food fragments, thereby ensuring entry of the bacteria into a protected, nutrient-rich habitat. Luminescent bacteria epitomize many attributes of marine bacteria, following both oligotrophic and eutrophic strategies for survival.

REFERENCES

Books

Litchfield, C. D. (ed.) (1976) *Marine Microbiology*, Benchmark Papers in Microbiology V. II, Dowden, Hutchinson and Ross, Stroudsbury.

Litchfield, C. D. and Seyfried, P. L. (eds.) (1979) *Methodology for biomass determinations and microbial activities in sediments*, ASTM Special Technical Publication **673**, American Society for Testing and Materials, Philadelphia.

Jones, J. G. (1979) *A Guide to Methods for Estimating Microbial Numbers and Biomass in Freshwater*, Scientific Publication No. 39, Freshwater Biological Association, Ambleside.

Gareth Jones, E. B. (ed.) (1976) *Recent Advances in Aquatic Mycology*, Elek Books, London.

Lovelock, D. W. and Davies, R. (eds.) (1978) *Techniques for the Study of Mixed Populations*, Society for Applied Bacteriology, Technical Series II, Academic Press.

Rheinheimer, G. (1980) *Aquatic Microbiology*, 2nd edn., John Wiley & Sons, London.

Rheinheimer, G. (ed.) (1977) *Microbial Ecology of a Brackish Water Environment*, Springer-Verlag, Berlin.

Rosswall, T. (ed.) (1973) *Modern Methods in the Study of Microbial Ecology*, Bulletin of the Ecological Research Committee (Stockholm), **17**.

Skinner, F. A. and Shewan, J. M. (eds.) (1977) *Aquatic Microbiology*, Society for Applied Bacteriology Symposium Series **6**, Academic Press, London.

Sieburth, J. M. (1979) *Sea Microbes*, Oxford University Press, New York.

Sorokin, Y. I. and Kadota, H. (eds.) (1972) *Techniques for the Assessment of Microbial Production and Decomposition in Fresh Waters*, IBP Handbook **23**, Blackwell Scientific Publications.

Articles

Blakemore, R. P., Frankel, R. B. and Kalmijn, A. J. (1980) South seeking magnetotactic bacteria in the southern hemisphere, *Nature*, **286**, 384–385.

Caldwell, D. E. (1977) The planktonic microflora of lakes, *CRC Critical Reviews in Microbiology*, **5**, 305–370.

Collins, V. G., Jones, J. G., Hendrie, M. S., Shewan, J. M., Wynn-Williams, D. D. and Rhodes, M. E. (1973) Sampling and estimation of bacterial populations in the aquatic environment. In *Sampling—Microbiological Monitoring of Environments*, R. G. Board and D. W. Lovelock, eds., Society for Applied Bacteriology, Technical Series **7**, Academic Press, London, pp. 77–110.

Fenchel, T. M. and Jørgensen, B. B. (1978) Detritus food chains of aquatic ecosystems: the role of bacteria, *Adv. Microbial Ecol.* **2**, 1–58.

Hirsch, P. (rapporteur) (1979) Life under conditions of low nutrient concentrations (Group report). In *Strategies of Microbial Life in Extreme Environments*, ed. M. Shilo, Dahlem Konferenz, Berlin, pp. 357–372.

Jannasch, H. W. (1979) Microbial ecology of aquatic nutrient habitats. In *Strategies of Microbial Life in Extreme Environments*, ed. M. Shilo, Dahlem Konferenz, Berlin, pp. 243–260.

Jannasch, H. W. and Wirsen, C. O. (1977) Microbial life in the deep sea. *Scientific American*, **236**, 42–52.

Kuznetzov, S. I. and Lepeteva, O. N. A. (1979) Biology of oligotrophic bacteria, *Ann. Rev. Microbiol.* **33**, 377–388.

Marquis, R. E. and Matsumara, P. (1978) Microbial life under pressure. In *Microbial Life in Extreme Environments*, ed. D. J. Kushner, Academic Press, London, pp. 105–158.

Marshall, K. C. (1980) Reactions of microorganisms, ions and macromolecules at interfaces. In *Contemporary Microbial Ecology*, eds. D. C. Ellwood, J. N. Hedger, M. J. Latham, J. M. Lynch and J. H. Slater, Academic Press, London, pp. 93–106.

Nealson, K. H. and Hastings, J. W. (1979) Bacterial bioluminescence: the control and ecological significance, *Microbiol. Rev.* **43**, 496–518.

Norkrans, B. (1980) Surface microlayers in aquatic environments. *Adv. Microbial Ecol.* **4**, 51–86.

Sieburth, J. M. (1976) Bacterial substrates and productivity in marine ecosystems, *Ann. Rev. Ecol. & Systematics*, **7**, 259–285.

Walsby, A. E. (1978) The gas vesicles of aquatic prokaryotes. In *Relations between Structure and Function in the Prokaryote Cell*, eds. R. Y. Stanier, H. J. Rogers and B. J. Ward, Society for General Microbiology, Symposium **28**, Cambridge University Press, Cambridge, pp. 327–357.

Yayanos, A. A., Dietz, A. S. and Van Boxtel, R. (1979) Isolation of a deep sea barophilic bacterium and some of its growth characteristics, *Science*, **205**, 808–810.

CHAPTER THREE

EXTREME ENVIRONMENTS

Growth and multiplication are the decisive parameters for successful competition in any environment. Many parts of the world, such as geothermal regions, polar regions, acid and alkaline springs, and the cold pressurized deeps of the ocean, are unsuitable environments for most forms of life; nevertheless, organisms are to be found surviving and growing under these conditions. It can be argued that extreme environments are simply those in which some organisms can grow whereas others cannot, and therefore the definition of an extreme environment is a taxonomic one. In virtually all examples of extreme environments it is found that as conditions become more and more demanding, microorganisms predominate, and certain prokaryotic microorganisms may exclusively occupy the more extreme niches.

The most immediately obvious and therefore the most commonly considered extreme environments are those produced by extremes of temperature, pH, and water activity, but given the definition of an extreme environment alluded to above, it is worth remembering that other less often considered stresses such as low nutrient conditions, low redox potential and high radiation levels may impose selective pressures just as great.

3.1 Temperature as an environmental extreme

Extremes of temperature impose a unique stress on very small organisms. Such organisms have no means of preventing their internal temperatures from equalizing with the exterior, whereas the internal environment of the cell can generally be maintained in a relatively equable condition in the face of most other types of stress. Thermophilic organisms are usually classified as having a temperature optimum for growth greater than the

upper limit of the mesophilic range (40°C). High-temperature environments often contain several overlapping groups capable of growth under
these conditions, and the terminology can become unwieldy if attempts are
made to categorize each group succinctly with an appropriate descriptive
term. The same semantic problems surround attempts to categorize
organisms from any extreme environment whether it be determined by
temperature, pH or salinity. There are organisms that fit the description of
a thermophile above but which are incapable of growth in the mesophilic
range (*obligate thermophiles*). Organisms with a temperature optimum in
the mesophilic range, but capable of growth at high temperatures are
usually referred to as *facultative thermophiles* or thermotrophic organisms.
Occasionally, further subdivision within a category is made, e.g. organisms
with temperature optima greater than 65°C are sometimes called *extreme
thermophiles* or caldoactive organisms. At the other end of the temperature
spectrum, psychrophilic organisms are considered to be those unable to
grow at temperatures above 20°C, usually growing well at 0°C. Organisms
capable of growing at low temperature that do not meet the rest of this
description are therefore considered to be *facultative psychrophiles* or
psychrotrophic organisms.

High-temperature environments

Those high-temperature environments which concern the microbiologist
do not generally exceed the temperature of boiling water (91°C–101°C
depending on altitude), and include hot springs, areas heated by high-
intensity solar radiation, and self-heating piles of organic material.
Although it may be less immediately obvious, cold environments are much
more common, since 70% of the Earth's surface is ocean, and more than
90% (by volume) of the oceans never exceeds 5°C (2.1). However, the
diversity of microorganisms that have been cultured at high temperatures
is considerable—a brief list of eukaryotic and prokaryotic thermophiles is
given in table 3.1.

The economic damage caused by the self-heating of a wide variety of
different types of stored organic material has provided some impetus to
the study of thermophilic microorganisms. In municipal garbage and
stored cereals, a succession of thermotrophic and thermophilic fungi
occurs, contributing significantly to heating. Thermotrophic fungi such as
Geotrichum candidum and *Aspergillus fumigatus* are succeeded at 50–60°C
by the thermophiles *Mucor pusillus* and *Humicola lanuginosa*. At temperatures above 65°C, numbers of such fungi diminish, and further heating is

Table 3.1 Thermophilic microorganisms (adapted from Brock, 1978).

Genus	Approximate optimum temperature (°C)	Approximate maximum temperature (°C)
Eukaryotes		
15–20 genera of fungi including *Rhizopus, Penicillium, Coprinus, Humicola, Dactylaria,* etc.	40–50 depending on species	50–60 depending on species
A few genera of protozoa including *Cercosulcifer, Naegleria*	40–45	50–55
*Cyanidium** (red algae)	45	55
Prokaryotes		
8–10 genera of blue-green algae including *Synechococcus, Mastigocladus, Oscillatoria*	40–65 depending on species	50–75 depending on species
15–20 genera of bacteria and actinomycetes including *Chloroflexus, Bacillus, Thiobacillus*, Thermoplasma*, Thermus, Sulfolobus*, Thermomicrobium, Thermoactinomyces*	40–70 depending on species	50–85 depending on species

* Genus contains acidophilic thermophiles.

due to bacterial and actinomycete growth and exothermic chemical reactions. Coal waste tips, which commonly reach temperatures exceeding 60°C, also contain thermophiles including the unusual acidophilic mycoplasma-like thermophile *Thermoplasma acidophilum*, which seems to be restricted to coal tips, probably as a consequence of a requirement for a particular growth factor. Many thermophiles commonly encountered in compost heaps can also be isolated from temperate soils (1.6).

Geothermal environments have provided fruitful sources of thermophiles, particularly thermophilic chemolithotrophs. Hot springs tend to be either acid (pH less than 4 due to oxidized sulphur compounds) or alkaline (pH more than 8 due to metal carbonates and bicarbonates, usually Na^+, occasionally Ca^{2+}). In hot (> 60°C) sulphurous acid springs, prokaryotic chemolithotrophic sulphur oxidizers such as *Sulfolobus acidocaldarius* and *Thiobacillus* spp. are to be found. Boiling acid springs do not harbour microbial populations and seem to be devoid of life, but *Sulfolobus acidocaldarius* has been shown to be capable of growth at 85°C, the highest recorded temperature for growth of a pure culture. Hot acid springs at lower temperatures (50°C to 60°C) often contain eukaryotes including the characteristic red alga *Cyanidium caldarium* which forms mats with certain thermophilic fungi and thermophilic *Bacillus* spp. In alkaline hot springs at temperatures up to 70°C, mats of algae are commonly found, but in this case these are quite characteristically prokaryote, composed of a sandwich of blue-green algae (usually *Synechococcus lividus*, occasionally *Mastigocladus laminosus* depending on geographical location), with the unique gliding thermophilic prokaryotic phototroph *Chloroflexus aurantiacus*. Other bacteria described from such environments include *Bacillus* spp., thermophilic methanogens similar to *Methanobacterium thermoautotrophicum*, and the ubiquitous *Thermus aquaticus* which has extensively colonized domestic hot-water systems. Protozoa such as *Cercosulcifer* spp. and *Vahlkampfia* spp. are found at temperatures below 55°C, but appear to be absent at higher temperatures. In contrast to boiling acid springs, boiling alkaline springs have been shown by slide colonization experiments to have growing populations of filamentous and rod-shaped bacteria, but these organisms have not yet been cultured.

Low-temperature environments

Temperate soils and waters, as well as oceans and polar soils, yield large numbers of organisms capable of growing at 0°C–5°C, but the vast majority of such isolates seem to be psychrotrophic rather than psychrophilic. True psychrophiles appear to be particularly sensitive to temperatures above 20°C, and many are killed by exposure to such temperatures for relatively short periods. This clearly has practical consequences for their isolation and enumeration, and stable cold environments such as the cold depths of the oceans and permanently frozen soils would therefore be expected to harbour the greatest number of such organisms. Psychrophilic algae such as *Raphidonema nivale* are found in polar regions in association with psychrophilic fungi such as *Sclerotina borealis*, and are also commonly associated with frozen soils and subterranean caves. Terrestrial psychrophilic bacteria are generally chemoorganotrophic Gram-negative organisms of the genera *Pseudomonas*, *Cytophaga* and *Flavobacterium*, although Gram-positive bacteria, notably *Arthrobacter glacialis*, *Micrococcus cryophilus* and *Bacillus psychrophilus* may be the dominant types in certain subterranean caves. Marine isolates are almost always of the genera *Pseudomonas*, *Vibrio* and *Spirillum*, and the best known example is *Vibrio marinus* which is widely distributed below the thermocline in the oceans of the world. Considerable biochemical activity is detectable below the thermocline at 0–5°C, in contrast with frozen soils where activity is extremely low presumably due to lack of liquid water.

Deep sea isolates have the additional stress of high pressure, and some appear to be barophilic as well as psychrophilic (2.7).

Certain cold dry valleys in the Antarctic have been extensively examined over the last few years, as they have been considered the closest terrestrial analogues to the Martian environment, although recent findings suggest that the supposition may not be as valid as was once thought. These valleys seldom achieve temperatures above freezing (except occasionally in direct sunlight), and the humidity is extremely low. Primary productivity seems to be entirely due to a small psychrophilic blue-green alga which may be a *Gleocapsa* sp., found at a depth of 1–2 mm in the porous translucent rocks of the area. Characteristic psychrophilic yeasts such as *Cryptococcus vishniacii*, *Leucosporidium antarcticum*, and a range of as yet uncharacterized filamentous fungi and bacteria make up a highly specialized ecosystem.

Biochemical adaptations to life at extremes of temperature

There is now considerable support for the view that the maintenance of membrane stability is an important aspect of life at extreme temperatures. It is suggested that domains of gel and liquid must coexist to maintain both the structural integrity and the functional capability of a membrane, and that therefore a larger proportion of high-melting temperature membrane lipids would be predicted in thermophiles, and conversely, a larger proportion of membrane lipids fluid at low temperatures would be necessary in psychrophiles. This prediction seems to be broadly correct; furthermore, bacteria are able to modulate the synthesis of the proportions of such lipids as the growth temperature changes. The thermophile *Thermus aquaticus* exemplifies these properties, as in addition to possessing a large proportion of high-melting point membrane lipids, it shows a decrease in C_{17} branched fatty acids, with a concomitant increase in higher melting point C_{16} straight-chain fatty acids as the growth temperature is increased. Psychrophilic bacteria have large amounts of unsaturated low-melting point fatty acids, and psychrotrophic mutants of mesophilic bacteria such as *Salmonella typhimurium* show altered fatty acid patterns, with fewer saturated fatty acids.

Early reports suggested that rapid resynthesis of heat-denatured proteins was necessary for survival and growth at high temperatures. There is now little support for this view, and the overwhelming body of evidence suggests that proteins and nucleic acids from thermophiles are intrinsically stable at high temperature. Precisely why obligate thermophiles fail to grow below a certain temperature is not clear, and there may be no one unifying explanation for obligate thermophily, although it has been suggested that enzymes from thermophiles are not particularly active at high temperature, and simply do not function well enough at lower temperatures as a reflection of this effect. Similarly, there is no unifying theme to explain the thermosensitivity of psychrophiles, and there may be a variety of key processes affected. Preliminary genetic experiments with psychrophilic and thermophilic mutants of mesophilic bacteria suggest that relatively few genes are involved in determining the conditions of psychrophily and thermophily. To date, these remarkable adaptations to the environment remain a fascinating challenge for the biochemist and the geneticist.

3.2 High solute concentration as an environmental extreme

High concentrations of salt (NaCl) and sugar have long been used as food preservatives, and the observation that microbial deterioration of treated foodstuffs was then inhibited originally stimulated interest in the effect of high solute concentrations on microbial growth and activity. Water activity (a_w) is generally used to describe the amount of available water in a particular habitat (1.4). Many different types of microorganisms capable of tolerating low a_w values have now been described (table 3.2). Undoubtedly, by far the most interest has been generated by those microorganisms growing at salt-induced low a_w values. Several classes of salt-tolerant microorganisms are recognized, although such classes are by no means clearly distinct from one another. Microorganisms capable of growth in the absence of salt, but tolerant of varying concentrations are considered to be *halotolerant*, and the group includes many yeasts, filamentous fungi, eukaryotic algae, blue-green algae and bacteria. Microorganisms with a specific requirement for salt are designated *halophiles*, and there are a number of overlapping subdivisions within this group. Marine microorganisms are considered to be slight halophiles requiring 0.2 M–0.5 M NaCl, moderate halophiles are considered to require 0.5 M–2.5 M NaCl, and extreme halophiles require at least 2.5 M NaCl for growth. As salt concentrations approach saturation (5.2 M, $a_w = 0.75$), a quite distinctive ecology is generated, and the environment becomes dominated by a few types of microorganisms, usually bacteria of the genera *Halobacterium* (halobacteria) and *Halococcus* (halococci) which possess certain C_{50} carotenoids called bacterioruberins that impart a red coloration to the environment. Red patches appear on salted fish and hides due

Table 3.2 Microorganisms capable of growth under high solute concentrations

Genus	Approximate lower limit of a_w for growth
Eukaryotes	
10–12 genera of fungi including *Mucor, Penicillium, Aspergillus, Saccharomyces, Xeromyces*	0.75–0.80 for most, 0.60–0.70 for *Xeromyces* and *Saccharomyces* spp. (in sugar)
a few genera of green algae including *Dunaliella**	0.75–0.80 (in salt)
Prokaryotes	
A few genera of blue-green algae including *Aphanothece**	0.75–0.80 (in salt)
12–15 genera of bacteria and actinomycetes including *Bacillus, Staphylococcus, Vibrio, Ectothiorhodospira*, Actinopolyspora*, Halococcus*, Halobacterium**	0.75–0.80 depending on species (in salt)

* Moderate or extreme halophiles.

to the growth of these bacteria, and the red coloration in solar evaporation ponds used for harvesting common salt from sea water is common in equatorial regions, and indeed was first reported by the Chinese some 5000 years ago. The halophilic eukaryote alga *Dunaliella salina* is also to be commonly found associated with halobacteria and halococci in the most saline environments.

In contrast, there are relatively few naturally-occurring environments in which a_w is low because of a high concentration of a non-ionic solute. Most of the microorganisms known to tolerate high concentrations of non-ionic solutes have been isolated from foods whose a_w is low. These environments are dominated by yeasts and filamentous fungi, and the general descriptive terms *xerotolerant* or *osmotolerant* are best applied to such organisms, since an obligate requirement for a specific solute has yet to be convincingly demonstrated.[1] The nature of the solute seems not to be important in most cases, but occasionally microorganisms react differently to ionic and non-ionic solutes, e.g. *Saccharomyces rouxii* has a limiting salt-induced a_w of 0.85, but will grow at an a_w of 0.62 in the presence of sugars. No higher plant or animal is capable of growth at a_w values even

[1] A possible exception is *Xeromyces bisporus* (figure 1.6).

remotely approaching those tolerated by certain of these xerotolerant fungi.

Biochemical aspects of life in high solute concentrations

It was formerly thought that microorganisms growing under high solute concentrations maintained a more dilute cell interior, but it is now clear that the a_w inside the cell is comparable to that of the growth medium. Halobacteria and halococci may be unique in that an appropriate a_w within the cells is achieved by excluding Na^+ and concentrating K^+. Enzymes and other proteins from halobacteria and halococci have a specific requirement for high levels of KCl for stability and maximum activity. High internal K^+ concentrations clearly act as an osmotic protectant, but the specific requirement for K^+ rather than Na^+ or any other solute indicates that proteins from halobacteria and halococci not only require a low a_w, but specifically react with K^+. In addition, the cell envelopes of halobacteria require 1–2 M NaCl for stability, and cells lyse when suspended in salt concentrations lower than this. It is thought that high concentrations of cations are required to shield the mutual repulsion of cell envelope subunits by like acid groups, and Na^+ is much more effective than K^+.

Under microaerophilic conditions most of the halobacteria have also been shown to synthesize substantial amounts of "purple membrane", i.e. areas of the cell envelope which contain bacteriorhodopsin, a light-sensitive pigment similar to vertebrate rhodopsin in that it contains a retinal moiety attached to a specific protein (bacterioopsin) by a protonated Schiff base linkage (figure 3.1). In the presence of light, bacteriorhodopsin undergoes a reversible change in its absorption peak from 560 to 415 nm, and protons are released and excreted, producing a proton flux which creates an electrochemical gradient across the cell membrane, and this can be harnessed for phosphorylation. This is the only known example of non-chlorophyll-mediated photophosphorylation, and presumably confers considerable selective advantage in the natural environment where high light intensity prevails.

Halobacteria and halococci share a number of other unique properties including the possession of ether- rather than ester-linked lipids in the cell membrane, but these properties are probably unrelated to halophily and reflect a more fundamental evolutionary grouping briefly discussed at the end of this chapter (3.5). Probably all other halophiles, and the xero-tolerant group of organisms, exclude the external solute and maintain

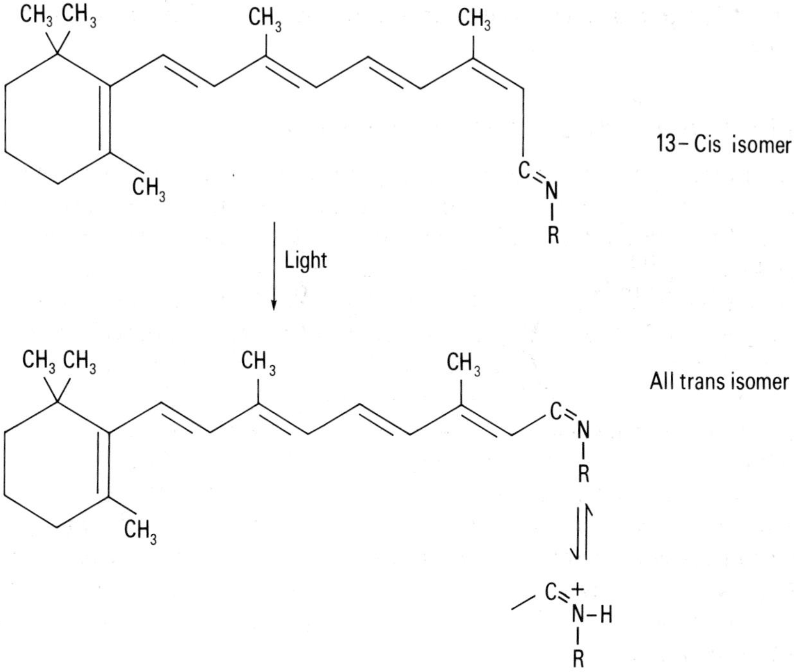

Figure 3.1 The structure of retinal. In halobacteria, the 13 cis-isomer is converted by light to the all-trans isomer. R represents the protein, bacterioopsin. The protonation reaction is shown for the all-trans isomer.

a similar a_w inside the cells by synthesizing high concentrations of osmotically-active polyols, usually glycerol, occasionally arabitol or mannitol. Enzymes from these organisms are stable and active in the presence of these polyols, which have come to be known as "compatible solutes". It is likely that these mechanisms also apply in less well-studied examples of halotolerant and moderately xerotolerant organisms. There is also some evidence to suggest that proline acts as a compatible solute in certain other microorganisms.

The genetic basis of halophily and extreme xerotolerance remains to be elucidated. Useful mutants of halophiles have not yet been obtained but xerotolerant mutants of fungi have been studied. The available evidence suggests that a few genes confer xerotolerance through a wide variety of pleiotropic effects.

3.3 pH as an environmental extreme

Very high (> 10) and very low (< 3) pH values are inhibitory to most microorganisms, but some are nevertheless to be found growing in environments where pH values approach 0, and indeed at pH values of 11 and above. Table 3.3 illustrates the range of microorganisms found at extremes of pH.

Fungi tend to dominate moderately acid (pH 3–5) environments, and many common soil fungi such as *Cephalosporium* spp. and *Fusarium* spp. are acid-tolerant, although the pH optima of such isolates are closer to neutrality. Extremely acid environments are commonly associated with areas of high sulphide concentration and include mine effluents (7.2), leach pile effluents (7.8), and geothermal springs. The low pH (pH 0–2) is produced by the oxidation of metal sulphides to H_2SO_4 by sulphur bacteria (7.1). Not surprisingly, these habitats are dominated by chemo-lithotrophic sulphur-oxidizing bacteria, generally of the genus *Thiobacillus*. Many of the thiobacilli are acidophiles, in that they have pH optima between 2 and 4 and are unable to grow at neutrality. Acid production by these bacteria can cause serious pollution problems (7.2, 8.4). The self-heating interiors of coal tips harbour thermophilic acidophiles

Table 3.3 Microorganisms capable of growth at extreme pH

Growth under acid conditions (pH < 3)	*Growth under alkaline conditions* (pH > 10)
Eukaryotes 6–8 genera of fungi including *Saccharomyces, Cephalosporium, Penicillium*	**Eukaryotes** A few genera of fungi including *Aspergillus, Fusarium, Penicillium*
Cyanidium (red algae), *Chlorella, Chlamydomonas, Euglena* (green algae)	diatoms including *Nitzschia*
Prokaryotes	**Prokaryotes** Blue-green algae including *Anabaenopsis, Spirulina, Microcystis, Plectonema*
8–10 genera of bacteria including *Thiobacillus*, Metallogenium, Sulfolobus*, Bacillus*, Sulfobacillus*, Thermoplasma*, Thiomicrospira, Leptospirillum*	A few genera of bacteria including *Flavobacterium†, Agrobacterium, Ectothiorhodospira†, Bacillus†*

* Genus contains acidophiles.
† Genus contains alkaliphiles.

such as *Thiobacillus thermophilica* and *Thermoplasma acidophilum*. Acid sulphurous thermal springs contain the thermophilic acidophile *Sulfolobus acidocaldarius*, mats of the acidophilic thermophilic red alga *Cyanidium caldarium* associated with *Bacillus acidocaldarius*, and certain filamentous fungi such as *Dactylaria gallopava*. Blue-green algae seem not to be found under acid conditions.

Far less information is available about alkaline habitats, presumably because these are rather more rare. Man-made environments above pH 10 include cement factory effluents which may exceed pH 12, and certain alkali-containing food processing wastes. The most alkaline naturally-occurring environments in the world are soda lakes and soda deserts, which are now uncommon and are in any case in relatively inaccessible areas. The more dilute soda lakes have a characteristic population of blue-green algae, usually *Anabaenopsis arnoldii* and *Spirulina platensis*. Phototrophic bacteria of the genus *Ectothiorhodospira* also uniquely occupy these lakes, and the more concentrated saline soda lakes harbour populations of characteristic halobacteria. Many organisms from these lakes appear to be true alkaliphiles, in that they have pH optima about pH 9, and are unable to grow at neutrality. Certain *Bacillus* spp. do seem to be alkaliphiles despite being readily found in ordinary soils, but examples of other alkaliphiles are rare.

Biochemical aspects of life at extremes of pH

Organisms that grow under extreme conditions of pH have to contend with effects other than high or low concentrations of H^+ or OH^-. Metal ions are much more soluble at low pH, and microorganisms colonizing acid mine drainage waters or coal tips tolerate high concentrations of metals such as copper and molybdenum which would be toxic to most other microorganisms. Microorganisms growing at high pH exist in an environment essentially devoid of divalent cations such as Mg^{2+} and Ca^{2+} (which precipitate as carbonates) and presumably such micro-organisms must have very efficient systems for concentrating such metals. In addition, NH_4^+ at high pH converts to free NH_3, which is inhibitory to many cells, and this may be the primary inhibitory effect experienced by many microorganisms on exposure to high pH. The internal pH of acidophiles and alkaliphiles never deviates from neutrality by more than 2 pH units or so, and in general, intracellular enzymes from such cells do not function at extremes of pH, although extracellular enzymes generally have pH optima similar to the pH optimal for growth. The difference in pH between the outside and inside of the cell is presumably accomplished by exclusion mechanisms for OH^- or H^+, or there may be specific pumping mechanisms. Alkaliphiles have particular problems in generating energy by the chemiosmotic process since the normal pH gradient across the cell membrane is reversed. Evidence for clear differences between the cell walls of acidophiles, alkaliphiles and other microorganisms is lacking. There is some evidence that acidophiles contain unusually large amounts of cyclized lipids, and a preponderance of amino-containing phospholipids which might function in a H^+ exclusion mechanism has also been reported, but little real biochemical insight into acidophily has been obtained. Alkaliphiles are virtually unexplored biochemically, and nothing is known about their cell walls to date.

Recent work has concentrated on the thermophilic acidophiles *Sulfolobus acidocaldarius* and *Thermoplasma acidophilum*. It has become clear that these bacteria do differ significantly from other bacteria, but although cyclized lipids are again in evidence, the differences seem mainly to be unrelated to acidophily. These organisms contain ether-linked lipids (figure 3.2) and in addition, *Thermoplasma acidophilum* has a mycoplasma-like outer envelope that requires high concentrations of H^+ to maintain this structure, presumably by blanketing the repulsion of like charge groups on the surface. The possession of ether-linked lipids and the requirement for H^+ as a cell envelope stabilizing factor in *Thermoplasma acidophilum* indicates certain similarities with the halobacteria. Undoubtedly these organisms are fundamentally different from other thermophiles, and deserve to be considered as a separate case (3.5).

3.4 Other environmental extremes

Many different environments are "extreme" in the taxonomic sense discussed at the beginning of this chapter; precisely what constitutes such an environment is mainly a matter of opinion. We discuss elsewhere those organisms capable of overcoming the stress imposed by low nutrient conditions (2.6, 4.2), and the effect of barometric pressure as a stress was assessed as a feature of the habitat of certain marine microorganisms (2.7). The anoxic environment is a less obvious candidate for discussion.

Anoxic environments

Obligate anaerobes are capable of generating energy and synthesizing cell material in the absence of oxygen, but are unable to grow in the presence of oxygen. Certain obligate anaerobes are so highly sensitive to oxygen that they are rapidly killed in its presence, and special procedures are required for their isolation and enumeration (9.4). Such anaerobes are not a homogeneous group by any morphological criteria, and include methanogenic bacteria, certain phototrophic bacteria, and a variety of unrelated Gram-positive and Gram-negative bacteria. However, they all appear to share one biochemical feature, namely the lack of certain defence mechanisms necessary to protect against oxygen.

The toxic effects seen in the presence of oxygen are due to a number of oxygen derivatives produced by the interaction of oxygen with cell components, rather than to oxygen itself. Hydrogen peroxide (H_2O_2) is invariably produced by reactions catalysed by flavoproteins, and the toxic effects of peroxide anion are well documented. Nearly all aerotolerant organisms possess the enzyme catalase which decomposes hydrogen peroxide. Superoxide anion ($O_2^{\cdot-}$), an extremely reactive and damaging free radical, is generated in aqueous solutions by procedures effecting a one-electron reduction of oxygen, including the interaction of oxygen with reduced compounds such as flavins, and also by the action of certain oxidases. Further toxicity problems are generated by the reaction of hydrogen peroxide with superoxide anion, which may produce singlet oxygen ($^{\cdot\cdot}O_2$) wherein the two unpaired valence electrons are antiparallel in spin, and also hydroxyl radical ($HO^{\cdot}$) by the following reactions:

$$O_2^{\cdot-} + H_2O_2 + H^+ \rightarrow O_2 + H_2O + HO^{\cdot}$$
$$O_2^{\cdot-} + HO^{\cdot} \rightarrow OH^- + {}^{\cdot\cdot}O_2$$

Both of these molecular species are indisputably damaging to cells. Singlet oxygen may also be generated by the exposure of cells to light in the presence of certain photosensitizers such as cytochromes or chlorophylls. Protection against these damaging substances is conferred by certain enzyme systems. All aerotolerant organisms possess one or more members of a family of metalloprotein enzymes collectively known as superoxide dismutase, whose function is to catalyse the dismutation of superoxide anion by the reaction

$$O_2^{\cdot-} + O_2^{\cdot-} + 2H^+ \rightarrow H_2O_2 + O_2$$

To date, no obligate anaerobe has been found which contains significant amounts of either catalase or superoxide dismutase, and the possession of these enzymes may be the principal biochemical determinant of aerotolerance. However, it is generally recognized that even the total exclusion of oxygen may not ensure the growth of certain obligate anaerobes, and a low redox potential is also required to provide sufficient "reducing power" commensurate with that required for energy generation and biosynthesis.

3.5 Common features of microorganisms from extreme environments

The majority of microorganisms isolated from extreme environments appear to have little in common apart from the capacity to grow and survive under unusual circumstances. However, recent investigations into the phylogenetic origins of eukaryotes and prokaryotes have revealed hitherto unexpected similarities between a few types of organisms found in extreme environments. An organism's genome may be the ultimate record of its evolutionary history, and recent efforts have concentrated on comparative analyses of certain nucleic acid sequences in order to determine evolutionary relationships (4.9). Ribosomal RNA, which we predict should be highly conserved, has been considered a suitable molecule for investigation. Any major differences between rRNA sequences or base modifications in rRNA's from different sources might be expected to indicate a very ancient evolutionary divergence. The 16S rRNA's of a variety of different prokaryotes and that of eukaryote chloroplasts have now been compared with the equivalent 18S rRNA's of eukaryote cytoplasms, and instead of the two predicted major groupings corresponding to eukaryotes and prokaryotes/eukaryotic organelles, three major groupings have emerged. One of these encompasses the majority of prokaryotes and also includes the eukaryote chloroplast. A second major grouping encompasses all the eukaryotic 18S rRNA's so far analysed. However, unexpectedly, another major prokaryote grouping of equivalent hierarchial rank exists which contains a few specialized prokaryotes, namely the methanogens, the halobacteria and halococci, and the thermophiles *Sulfolobus acidocaldarius* and *Thermoplasma acidophilum*.

It has been suggested that these three groupings are at a hierarchical level above the currently recognized kingdoms, and should accordingly be designated "Primary Kingdoms" or "Urkingdoms". The designation Urkingdom *Eubacteria* is given to the grouping that includes the vast majority of prokaryotes and the organelles of eukaryotes (supporting the endosymbiont theory of the origins of such organelles) (4.9). The Urkingdom *Urkaryota* is represented by the cytoplasm of eukaryotes (the remains of the engulfing species in the primary composite eukaryote), and the group encompassing the methanogens, halobacteria and halococci, and certain thermophiles is designated Urkingdom *Archaebacteria*.

The name "archaebacteria" is designated to denote antiquity, and

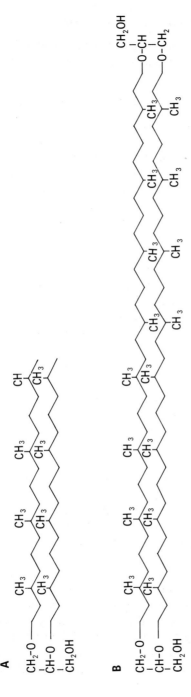

Figure 3.2 The lipids of archaebacteria. C_{20} diphytanyl glycerol diether (A), found in all archaebacteria, is an analogue of the fatty acid ester-linked glycerol lipids possessed by all other bacteria. C_{40} bidiphytanyl diglycerol tetraether (B) is found in certain methanogens, and the thermophilic genera *Sulfolobus* and *Thermoplasma*. Free OH groups may be linked to carbohydrate, sulphate or phosphate residues. One or more of the phytanyl limits may be cyclized.

characteristically the bacteria in this group occupy environments that are extreme by present-day standards, but would have been common in Archaean times (3760–2500 million years B.P.). Life is imagined to have arisen in concentrated, warm pools in a totally anoxic environment, and the properties of some of the present-day archaebacteria are suggestive of the kinds of properties predicted for very early microorganisms. It could be argued that each type of present-day archaebacterium, namely methanogen, halophile and thermophile, enshrines an adaption to one of the major stresses experienced by the original archaebacteria. Certain other individual peculiarities of these bacteria have been re-examined and a general unified biochemical pattern is beginning to emerge which makes it clear that these bacteria differ fundamentally from all others. In particular, peptidoglycan is absent from the cell walls of archaebacteria, and archaebacterial cells contain negligible amounts of ester-linked lipids, having functionally analogous diether-linked lipids unrelated to other bacterial lipids (figure 3.2).

A number of interesting questions remain to be answered, not least whether the engulfing urkaryote line has completely disappeared apart from its ubiquitous vestigial presence as the cytoplasm of eukaryotes. Accordingly, extreme environments present a fascinating challenge, both as an ecological and biochemical insight into the extraordinary conditions under which life can flourish, and also in terms of what certain inhabitants of extreme environments may have to tell us about major phylogenetic relationships.

REFERENCES

Books

Brock, T. D. (1978) *Thermophilic Microorganisms and Life at High Temperatures*, Springer-Verlag, Berlin—Heidelberg—New York.

Heinrich, M. R. (ed.) (1976) *Extreme Environments. Mechanisms of Microbial Adaptation*, Academic Press.

Kushner, D. J. (ed.) (1978) *Microbial Life in Extreme Environments*, Academic Press.

Shilo, M. (ed.) (1979) *Strategies of Microbial Life in Extreme Environments*, Dahlem Conference Report, Verlag Chemie, Weinheim—New York.

Articles

Axelunxen, R. E. and Murdock, A. L. (1978) Mechanisms of thermophily. *CRC Critical Reviews in Microbiology* **6**, 343–393.

Bayley, S. T. and Morton, R. D. (1978) Recent developments in the molecular biology of extremely halophilic bacteria. *CRC Critical Reviews in Microbiology* **6**, 151–205.

Brown, A. D. (1976) Microbial water stress. *Bacteriol. Rev.* **40**, 803–846.

Imhoff, J. F., Sahl, H. G., Soliman, G. S. H. and Truper, H. G. (1978) The Wadi-Natrum: chemical composition and microbial mass developments in alkaline brines of eutrophic desert lakes. *Geomicrobiol. J.* **1**, 219–234.

Morita, R. Y. (1975) Psychrophilic bacteria. *Bacteriol. Rev.* **39**, 144–167.

Morris, J. G. (1976) Oxygen and the obligate anaerobe. *J. Appl. Bacteriol.* **40**, 229–244.

Woese, C. R., Magrum, L. J. and Fox, G. C. (1978) Archaebacteria. *J. Molecular Evolution* **11**, 245–252.

CHAPTER FOUR

INTERACTIONS

4.1 Definitions

Pure cultures are largely a laboratory artefact. In nature, microorganisms interact with plants, animals and other microorganisms in a bewildering variety of ways. Table 4.1 attempts to depict and define some of these interactions in a simplified form in terms of the behaviour of two distinct populations. Interactions most often involve exchange of, or competition

Table 4.1 A classification of interactions involving microorganisms

Interaction	Population A	Direction of determinant activity	Population B
Neutralism	No effect	nil	No effect
Competition	Increased or decreased	External ←－－nutrients－－→	Decreased or increased
Amensalism	No effect or increased	──────────→ Inhibitors	Decreased
Parasitism	Increased	Contact and ────────→ entry ←－－nutrients－－－	Decreased
Predation	Increased	──Capture──→ ←－－nutrients－－－	Decreased
Commensalism	Increased	Nutrients ←－－－－－－－	Not affected
Mutualism	Increased	Contact in some ────────→ ←－－nutrients－－→	Increased

for particular nutrients, but sometimes the presence of inhibitory substances may be an important feature of a particular relationship. Superimposed on these exchanges is the phenomenon of specificity—an additional important factor in whether or not a particular organism will react with another.

A number of interactions can be grouped under the general heading of *antagonism*, including *competition, amensalism, parasitism* and *predation* (table 4.1). Competition implies an indirect effect of one population upon another, whereas in amensalism one population produces an inhibitor that directly affects the other. In practice, it is often difficult to distinguish competition and amensalism, since the common boundary of the two interactions is by no means clearly defined. Parasitism and predation are other examples of antagonistic effects which are not sharply separated; in both cases, one participant is nutritionally dependent upon the other, which may be damaged or killed as a result.

Any discussion of microbial interactions must contain a large section dealing with those interactions described as examples of *mutualism*. In such interactions, benefits of varying degree accrue to both participants, and presumably such associations have evolved from *commensalism* where only one of the participants benefits. Mutualistic interrelationships range from those where physical contact between the partners is not necessary, to those best exemplified by root nodule associations between higher plants and bacteria, where intimate physical metabolic integration is ensured within specialized tissues and organs. The term *symbiosis* has been used to describe a variety of different types of mutualistic associations. In its most literal sense it means "having a common life", and thus most kinds of interactions can be included in this broad definition, but in this chapter its use is restricted to mutualistic interactions.

Parasitism clearly overlaps the domain of pathogenicity to some extent. The particular characteristics of pathogens, and the associated features of the host response, constitute extensive topics in their own right, and are considered to be outside the scope of this text.

4.2 Competition/amensalism

Two situations which illustrate the overlap of competition and amensalism are the induction of fruiting body formation in the cultivated mushroom (*Agaricus brunnescens*), and *mycostasis*, the widespread failure of viable fungal spores to germinate in unmodified soils; *bacteriostasis* is also known but less studied.

The vegetative mycelium of *A. brunnescens* is usually grown on horse-manure-based composts rich in cellulose, lignin and microbial residues. Very limited sporophore production occurs unless the well colonized compost is covered with a shallow "casing" layer of soil or peat buffered to near neutrality. Axenic cultures with sterile casing fail to fruit unless a small amount of non-sterile soil is added before the casing is colonized. Fruiting is then accompanied by a marked restriction in hyphal growth into the casing, suggesting that the soil microflora is inducing fruiting. The inductive microorganisms have been identified as bacteria of the genus *Pseudomonas*. However, no "inducing substances" have as yet been implicated, and it is possible that the inductive capabilities arise because the organisms efficiently remove fungal metabolites from the vicinity of the hyphae; indeed, axenic fruiting of *A. brunnescens* can be initiated by activated charcoal.

Mycostasis has attracted attention because it produces a form of exogenous dormancy, potentially prolonging the survival of fungal spores, including those of plant pathogens. There are two main hypotheses as to the cause of germination inhibition in soil. One hypothesis postulates the production of inhibitors—if so, mycostasis would be an example of amensalism. This view arose from the early finding that agar discs placed in contact with soil became inhibitory, suggesting active diffusible substances. Unfortunately, such compounds have not consistently been isolated, although more recently, stronger evidence has accumulated for the presence of volatile inhibitors. Ammonia has been identified as the inhibitor in an alkaline clay loam, whereas ethylene has been reported to be effective against sclerotia of *Sclerotium rolfsii* in Australian acidic soils. The hydrocarbon allyl alcohol is another candidate, inhibiting conidial germination of *Arthrobotrys oligospora* at 4 ppm. The second hypothesis proposes competition by other microorganisms for nutrient materials exuded by hydrated spores. It is supposed that these substances must exceed a threshold level before germination can proceed in the nutritionally limited soil environment. At present the causes of soil mycostasis appear complex, with nutrient competition as the likely general basis upon which the effects of inhibitors are superimposed.

Antibiotic production may be one of the factors involved in amensalism, but it has proved hard to demonstrate this in a natural situation. However, fungal synthesis of penicillin, patulin, gliotoxin and griseofulvin has been shown in plant debris, while some streptomycetes have been found to produce antibiotics in sterile, glucose-supplemented soil. Circumstantial evidence pointing to the natural presence of antibiotics includes the wide distribution of producers, especially actinomycetes, and the equally common occurrence of inactivating enzymes. The β-lactamases, acting on penicillins and cephalosporins are a good example of the latter. These have been detected in cultures derived from *Bacillus* spp. endospores present in dried soil on 300-year-old herbarium specimens, and suggest the presence of penicillin in the environment long before its clinical use.

Competition is of general interest since it constitutes one of the mechanisms which operates in the process of natural selection. One of the simplest forms of competition occurs when two populations share dependence on a particular growth factor. This kind of competition is amenable to study in liquid cultures, where one particular nutrient is limiting, and the kinetics of free competition have been extensively studied and mathematically modelled in closed batch culture and open continuous culture systems. In essence, in continuous culture, the growth rate of a particular population is restricted by the input rate of the growth-limiting substrate (dilution rate). The relationship can be described by an equation which is similar to the Michaelis–Menten equation for enzyme kinetics, thus:

$$\mu = \mu_{max} \frac{S}{K_s + S}$$

where S is the concentration of the limiting nutrient ($g\,l^{-1}$), μ the specific growth rate (h^{-1}), μ_{max} the maximum possible specific growth rate on that particular substrate, and K_S a constant (the saturation constant), which is defined as the substrate concentration allowing the population to grow at half the maximum possible growth rate ($g\,l^{-1}$). K_S values for many soluble nutrients such as sugars and amino acids vary considerably, but are generally very low ($<0.1\,g\,l^{-1}$), and a consideration of the above equation indicates that under high nutrient conditions organisms with high maximum growth rates (high μ_{max}) have a considerable selective advantage. Under very low nutrient conditions, however, low μ_{max} organisms with a greater affinity for substrate (low K_S values) have the selective advantage. Many microorganisms living in oligotrophic waters (2.6) exploit this advantage and accordingly survive, presumably representing the indigenous population of such environments, although they are difficult to isolate because they are outgrown by high μ_{max} organisms in most kinds of culture media.

4.3 Parasitism/predation

The beneficiary in *parasitism* is normally smaller than its host and makes casual contact with it. If the parasite obtains most of its nutrition after causing the death of the host cells it is *necrotrophic*; if nutrient exchange occurs during intimate contact with the living host cells, then the parasite is *biotrophic*. Intermediate patterns of nutrition can occur and facultative necrotrophs may be able to grow *saprotrophically* on organic residues. Microbial *predators* are essentially necrotrophs, but have developed structural or behavioural modifications to capture, or improve contact with, their living nutrient sources.

There are numerous examples of prokaryotic and eukaryotic microorganisms parasitic on other eukaryotes, and these include many pathogens. Examples of microorganisms which parasitize or prey on other microorganisms are also common—many of the protozoa are predators on bacteria, but prokaryote/prokaryote examples are rare. Gliding nectrotrophic myxobacteria constitute one example of prokaryote parasites/predators, since these bacteria are capable of hydrolyzing many microbial structural polymers.

The curious bacteria of the genus *Bdellovibrio* uniquely invade the cells of other prokaryotes. Although these were originally considered predators, *Bdellovibrio* spp. are better described as intra-mural parasites. The small (0.2–0.4 μm $\times$ 1–2 μm) comma-shaped cells are propelled by a single, thick, polar flagellum at speeds of up to 100 cell lengths per second, making violent random contact with their Gram-negative host bacteria. Bdellovibrio cells become attached end-on to the host cell via fine stiletto-like filaments. A hole is then made through the host wall accompanied by rapid rotation of the bdellovibrio, penetration being completed in 5–20 min. Once within, the bdellovibrio occupies an intramural position between the host's wall and its invaginated plasmamembrane, elongating into a large spiral structure (figure 4.1). This finally divides into motile daughter vibroid cells which are released, 3–4 h after contact, by lysis of the residual host cell envelope, the number of progeny ranging from about 5 if the host is *Escherichia coli*, to 20 in *Spirillum serpens*. A motile host ceases to move within a few seconds of bdellovibrio attachment, and rapid changes in the host include the cessation of protein and nucleic acid synthesis and increased membrane permeability to small molecules, enabling degradation products to pass rapidly to the parasite.

Features of bdellovibrios relevant to parasitism include high endogenous respiration rates, the inability to utilize carbohydrates, strong and invariable proteolytic ability, and unusual permeability to host-derived nucleoside monophosphates. Bdellovibrios without hosts rapidly lose viability as a result of their unusually high endogenous respiration. This raises the question of their survival in natural habitats, where bacterial

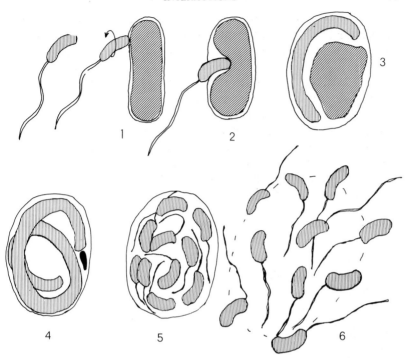

Figure 4.1 The developmental cycle of *Bdellovibrio*. 1. Contact with host with rotation by the attached bdellovibrio. 2. Entry to an intramural position. 3, 4. Growth of a large spirillum in the swollen bdelloplast. 5. Production of small vibrios. 6. Rupture of bdelloplast membrane.

numbers fluctuate rapidly and potential hosts may be unevenly distributed. However, they are readily isolated from soil (10^3–10^5 g^{-1}), sewage (10^5 ml^{-1}) and sea water (50 ml^{-1}). Cells resembling bdellovibrios have also been described from transmission electron micrographs of the rhizosphere.

Various mathematical models have been derived describing predator/prey dynamics in both limited and unlimited systems. For instance, the behaviour of bdellovibrios growing on certain hosts has been mathematically modelled, while a considerable body of work describes protozoan predation on bacteria under various conditions. In essence, in an unlimited environment

$$\begin{array}{c}\text{rate of change}\\\text{of prey biomass}\end{array}\left(\frac{dH}{dt}\right)=\begin{array}{c}\text{rate of prey}\\\text{biomass production}\end{array}(\mu H)-\begin{array}{c}\text{rate of prey}\\\text{biomass removal}\end{array}(fP)$$

where H is the prey biomass concentration (g 1^{-1}); μ is the prey's specific growth rate (h^{-1}); P is the predator biomass concentration, and f is a constant known as the specific rate of predation (g prey biomass g^{-1} predator biomass h^{-1}).

A similar equation for predators can be derived:

$$\underset{\text{predator biomass}}{\text{rate of change of}} \left(\frac{dP}{dt}\right) = \underset{\text{biomass loss (death)}}{\text{rate of predator}} - (dP) + \underset{\text{biomass production}}{\text{rate of predator}} (f'P),$$

where d is the specific death rate of the predator and f' is the specific growth rate of the predator (g predator biomass g^{-1} prey biomass h^{-1}). Clearly, the growth rate of the predator is related to both the concentration of the prey and the specific rate of predation. These equations describe the related changes in predator and prey populations, and the numerical solution shows that both prey and predator oscillate in concentration in a damped fashion, the predator lagging behind (figure 4.2). Appropriate

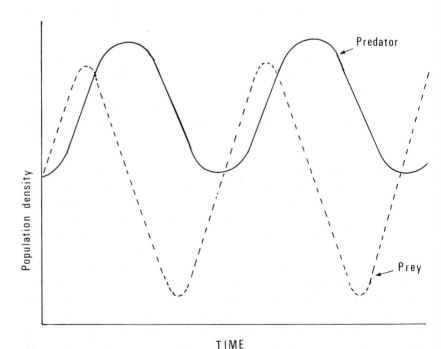

Figure 4.2   Predator/prey dynamics in a closed unlimited environment (redrawn from Slater (1979)).

terms can be included to depict an environment of a finite size, or to allow for "wash out" of cells such as occurs in continuous culture systems like the activated sludge process. It is to be expected that predictive modelling of this kind will prove more and more important in the practical sense in the description of the vastly important parasitism/predation interactions in sewage treatment processes, and other complicated mixed culture environments.

Fungi are particularly successful plant parasites and can also invade invertebrates and vertebrates, including man; some parasitize their own kind. This last group are sometimes called *mycoparasites*. Both necro-trophs and biotrophs are found among the fungi attacking other fungi, but they are less diverse taxonomically and in adaptations to parasitism than plant pathogenic fungi, presumably reflecting the smaller size and lower complexity of their hosts. *Verticillium malthousei* and *Mycogyne perniciosa* appear early in the development of the cultivated mushroom, and are likely to be true parasites, but other moulds on agaric fruitbodies may be saprotrophic on moribund tissues. Necrotrophs usually have wide host ranges, and show few morphological adaptations. *Trichoderma viride*, facultatively necrotrophic on the important plant pathogen *Gaeuman-nomyces graminis* and many other fungi, combines a rapid rate of hyphal extension with the production of diffusible and volatile antibiotics, and also possesses inducible polysaccharases that rapidly degrade fungal cell walls. Many nectrotrophs grow readily on simple media or plant debris, and so the nutritional advantages of parasitism are obscure; oomycetes such as *Pythium acanthicum* might for instance gain sterols needed for sexual reproduction.

Biotrophic fungi are usually ecologically dependent on their hosts, although some have been axenically cultured on complex media. So-called contact biotrophs, which do not invade other cells, mostly belong to a very small group of hyphomycetes requiring a water-soluble factor, *mycotrophein*, which is presumably obtained by their short, specialized lateral hyphae that are closely appressed to those of the host, an example being *Gonatobotrys simplex* associated with *Alternaria* spp. The biotrophs that have received most attention are characterized by their production of *haustoria* (figure 4.3) within host hyphae. Haustoria are modified, some-times much branched, intracellular hyphae, usually surrounded by an altered, invaginated host plasmalemma, forming the extrahaustorial membrane. Haustorial parasites of other fungi belong to two families of the Mucorales, the Dimargaritaceae and the Piptocephalidaceae. Most attack other members of the Mucorales, exceptions being *Dispira simplex*

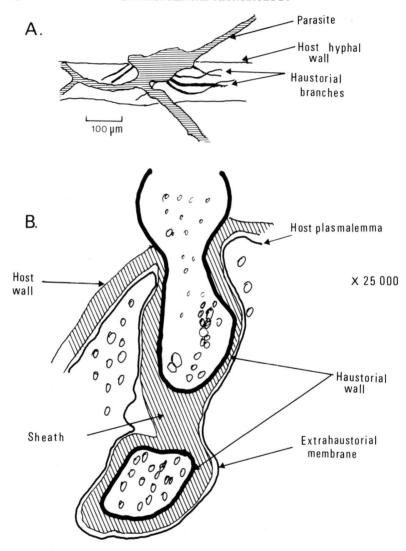

Figure 4.3 Haustoria of *Piptocephalis virginiana*. A. Haustorium developing from a swollen region (appressorium) of the parasite hypha. B. An old haustorium showing host penetration. The host plasma-lemma is invaginated to form an extra-haustorial membrane and a sheath of host wall material between this membrane and the haustorial wall. (A, redrawn from Webster, J. (1980), *Introduction to Fungi*, 2nd edn., Cambridge University Press, Cambridge; B, traced from an electron micrograph in Manocha, M. S. and Letourneau, D. R. (1978), Structure and composition of host-parasite interface in a mycoparasite system, *Physiol. Pl. Pathol.* **12**, 141–150.)

Table 4.2 Predatory fungi

Prey	Capture method*	Fungal group	Predatory genera
Amoebae (and some testaceous rhizopods)	Adhesive hyphae	Zoopagales	Acaulopage, Stylopage, Zoopage
		Hyphomycetes	Dactylaria, Pedilospora, Tridentaria
Loricate rotifers	Short, adhesive hyphal branches	Oomycetes (Pythiaceae)	Sommerstorfia, Zoophagus
Nematodes	1. Adhesive main hyphae	Zoopagales	Stylopage
	2. Adhesive lateral branches	Hyphomycetes	Triposporina, Monacrosporium
	3. Adhesive knobs	Hyphomycetes Basidiomycetes	Monacrosporium Nematoctonus
	4. Adhesive network, (a) Two dimensional	Hyphomycetes	Monacrosporium
	(b) Three dimensional	Hyphomycetes	Arthrobotrys
	5. Non-constricting ring	Hyphomycetes	Dactylaria
	6. Constricting rings	Hyphomycetes	Arthrobotrys Dactylaria

* Individual species usually have only one type of trap.

found on the ascomycete genus *Chaetomium*, and *Piptocephalis xenophila* which grows on *Penicillium janthinellum*, and on other hyphomycetes and ascomycetes. A characteristic feature of biotrophic parasites is that host damage is minimized and mucoralean parasites have little effect on host growth.

Besides exploiting their own kind, fungi have evolved the capacity to obtain nutrition from rotifers, nematodes, and amoebae. This has been achieved either by modifying hyphae as capture organs (a form of predation) or by producing spores that germinate after adhering to an animal's surface or following ingestion (regarded as endoparasitism). In practice these distinctions become blurred, since in both cases the animals are immobilized before or during colonization by nectotrophically grow-ing hyphae. *Nematoctonus*, a basidiomycetous genus attacking nematodes, includes both predatory and endoparasitic species.

Examples of predators are given in table 4.2, the best known group being nematode trappers, which are mostly hyphomycetes. Six different nematode capture mechanisms are known (figure 4.4), and four of these depend on adhesive surfaces, a method also used by fungi preying on amoebae and rotifers. The adhesive may be produced after prey contact with undifferentiated hyphae, as in *Stylopage* spp., or be continuously present but localized on the trapping organs. The adhesive of *Arthrobotrys oligospora* is equally effective dry or in water and has recently been identified as a lectin, a class of carbohydrate-binding proteins implicated in a wide range of recognition systems (4.6). Non-constrictive rings, as found in *Dactylaria candida*, depend on the worm becoming tightly wedged and, like the commoner adhesive knobs, remain viable and potentially invasive after detachment. One of the most fascinating and enigmatic of all fungal structures is the three-celled constricting ring possessed by species of *Arthrobotrys*, *Monacrosporium* and *Dactylaria*. Those of *D. brochopaga* close in 0.1 s, after a brief lag following contact on their inner, luminal surface. Closure is effected by expansion of the four-layered luminal walls of the trap cells, presumably driven by rapid water uptake. The trap cells increase threefold in volume, and the net effect is to tightly grip the worm, often by the tapering tail, nearly bisecting it. Hyphae originating from the trap then invade the prey, a feature shared by the other capture mechanisms. Nematode-trapping fungi also synthesize immobilizing toxins, and nematodes are often killed after only minimal contact with the hyphae. There is also some evidence for the production of nematode attractants by the fungi, and of chemo-induction of trap formation by the prey (amino acids are probably involved). Corpses invaded by nematode-

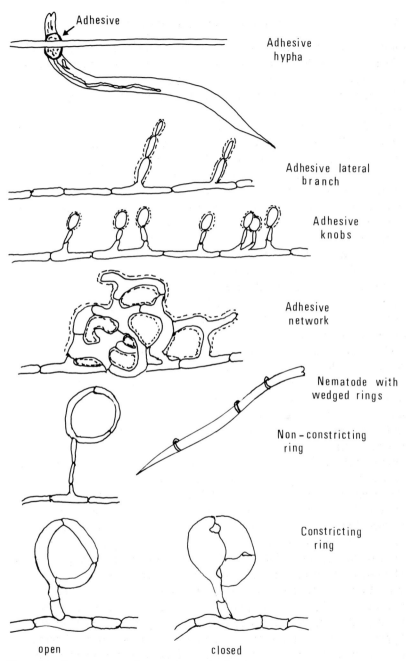

Figure 4.4 Capture organs of nematode trapping fungi.

trapping fungi seem relatively free of other bacteria or fungi, and some of the endoparasitic fungi such as *Harposporium* and *Meria* spp. show anti-fungal activity, presumably through antibiotic production. Hopes of using these fungi for the biological control of plant pathogenic nematodes have however been disappointed, partly by the susceptibility of the spores to mycostasis.

4.4 Mutualism/commensalism: the rhizosphere

The surfaces and environs of young, physiologically active, vascular plant organs possess a selected and often enriched microflora, and this can be viewed as an example of commensalism. The special nature of the microbiota around roots was recognized early, and in 1904 Hiltner introduced the term *rhizosphere* for the soil region biologically affected by plant roots. The apical growing region of roots are sites of considerable material loss, with possibly up to 20% of photosynthetic production being passed into the soil from cereal roots. Sources for this loss include polysaccharide mucigel production by root cap and epidermal cells, sloughed-off root cap, epidermal and cortical cells, and root exudates from the thin-walled expanding cells behind the apex. Not all exudates are necessarily stimulatory; very young pea roots, for example, produce inhibitors of *Rhizobium leguminosarum*.

A consequence of this export of plant products into the soil is an increase in microbial numbers and biomass by factors of two, three or even greater orders of magnitude compared with non-rhizosphere populations. The effect varies with plant species, age and physiological state; the greatest effect of dwarf beans, *Phaseolus vulgaris*, on fungal biomass is between the onset of flowering and maturation of the pods, the period of maximum photosynthetic activity. The selection of distinct physiological and taxonomic groups occurs, and an increased proportion of rhizosphere bacteria degrade cellulose, ferment sugars, solubilize phosphates, produce extra-cellular polysaccharides and synthesize growth factors. Taxonomic-ally there is a high proportion of Gram-negative bacteria, particularly *Pseudomonas* spp. Fungi closely associated with root surfaces include pathogens such as *Phytophthora cinnamoni*, *Fusarium solani* and *Gaeumannomyces graminis*, as well as saprotrophs like *Trichoderma koeningii* and *Penicillium nigricans*.

Treating the rhizosphere as a commensalistic community, with the microbes the only beneficiaries, is an oversimplification, as there are usually beneficial effects on the plants. The potential benefits to plants from the rhizosphere have recently received renewed attention, arising from the discovery of rhizosphere nitrogen-fixing bacteria such as *Azotobacter paspali* and *Azospirillum brasiliense* (6.5). The uptake of phosphate and other ions has also been examined, prompted by the effect of bacterial contaminants on these processes in water-cultured plants. In both these cases any improved transfer of nutrients to plants is uncertain, and any improvement in yield may be due to plant growth-promoting substances which are known to be synthesized by rhizosphere micro-organisms (4.5, 6.5).

4.5 Mutualism: mycorrhiza

The formation of mycorrhizal symbioses between fungi and roots, an extension of the rhizosphere effect, produces certain ecologically important partnerships. These are obligatory to many of the fungi, but often facultative to the plants, which do not necessarily develop them if grown in high nutrient conditions. The term *mycorrhiza* (literally "fungus root") was introduced by Frank in 1885, following his observations on the fungus-ensheathed feeder roots of temperate forest trees such as the European beech, *Fagus sylvatica*. This type of mycorrhiza, where the fungal tissues form a sheath external to the root, is classed as an *ectomycorrhiza* (figure 4.5A). Where there is intercellular and intracellular penetration of root tissues by the fungus, the association is described as an *endomycorrhiza* (figure 4.5B), this includes vesicular-arbuscular mycorrhiza, those in the hair roots of the Ericales, and those in orchids. (Orchid mycorrhizae are exceptional, as they represent a state of balanced parasitism between plant and fungus in which the normal direction of carbon transfer is reversed, the plant being the recipient. In most other mycorrhizal associations the fungus obtains carbon from the plant.)

Sheathing or ectomycorrhizae are formed by many agaric basidiomycetes (*Amanita, Boletus, Lactarius, Russula, Suillus, Tricholoma,* etc.), some gasteromycetes (*Pisolithus, Rhizopogon* and *Scleroderma*), ascomycetes (*Tuber*), and imperfect fungi (*Cenococcum*). Some of these fungi are obligate symbionts, although some are also decomposers such as *Paxillus involutus* and many have been cultured axenically. Host specificity is often low. For many gymnosperms (*Abies, Larix, Picea* and *Pinus*), and some angiosperms (*Carpinus, Fagus* and *Quercus*), mycorrhizal development is essential. The external sheath of fungal pseudoparenchyma originates from spores or hyphal cords, and develops in response to root exudates. A connected mesh of fungal tissue, the Hartig net, forms between

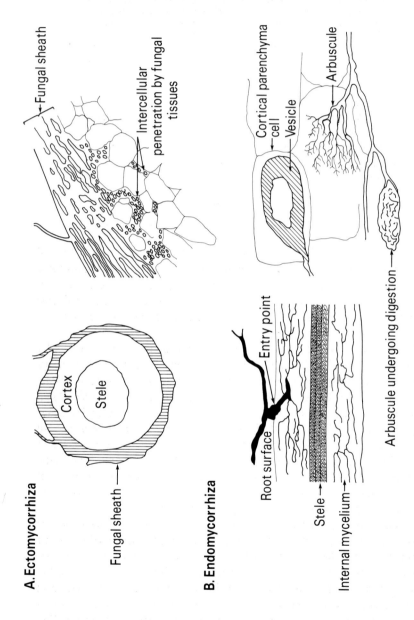

Figure 4.5 Mycorrhizae—the general (left) and detailed (right) distribution of the fungi in the plant roots. A. Ectomycorrhiza on Scots pine. B. Endomycorrhiza (vesicular–arbuscular type) in onion.

Table 4.3 Effect of inoculation with ectomycorrhizal fungi on *Pinus strobus* seedlings. (From Bowen, G. D. (1973) Mineral nutrition of ectomycorrhizae. In *Ectomycorrhizae: their Ecology and Physiology*, eds. G. C. Marks and T. T. Kozlowski, Academic Press.)

	Inoculated	Uninoculated
Dry weight (mg.)	405	303
Root/shoot ratio	0.78	1.04
N % dry weight	1.24	0.85
N per seedling (mg)	5.00	2.69
P % dry weight	0.196	0.074
P per seedling (mg)	0.789	0.236
K % dry weight	0.744	0.425
K per seedling (mg)	3.02	1.38
Uptake mg/mg dry root		
N	0.029	0.016
P	0.0045	0.0014
K	0.017	0.008

hypertrophied cortical cells, and there is often an extensive system of mycelial cords ramifying into the soil or litter. The plant second and third order roots exhibit markedly altered morphology and anatomy, due in part to the production of auxin and cytokinin analogues by the fungi. The fungi exist biotrophically on the roots, and transfer of photosynthate to the fungus occurs.

The functional importance of ectomycorrhizal associations is shown by the improved growth and enhanced mineral content of infected seedlings (table 4.3). Understanding of the underlying mechanisms is incomplete, although P uptake has received considerable attention—mycorrhizal roots of *F. sylvatica* incorporate P as phosphate at rates two to five times those of uninfected roots, most of the P accumulating as an inorganic pool within the fungal sheath, and then being transferred to the plant when external P levels are low. This improvement in P uptake may be due to the increased volume of soil tapped by the external mycelium. Additional benefits conferred by ectomycorrhizal fungi may include protection against pathogens, and increased longevity of feeder roots.

Vesicular-arbuscular endomycorrhizae, unlike ectomycorrhizae, do not produce gross distortions of root morphology, which may partly account for the delay in realizing their significance. Named after their characteristic structures within or between root cortical cells (figure 4.5B), they are the most widespread of all mycorrhizae, being found among bryophytes and many vascular plants including ferns, trees of tropical and southern hemisphere forests, grasses and many crop plants. Structures resembling these distinctive fungi appear in fossil rhizome tissues of the Devonian plant *Rhynia*, some 4×10^8 y old. The fungal symbionts are unusual zygomycetes of the family Endogonaceae, often collectively referred to as *Endogone*, although eight genera have now been described. They have not yet been axenically cultured, laboratory stocks being maintained in pot cultures with a host.

These fungi have an extraordinarily wide host range; for example *Glomus mosseae*, used extensively in laboratory experiments, invades monocotyledons such as maize as readily as it does dicotyledons like tomato and strawberry. Infection is from the enormous (up to $200 \mu m$ diameter) resting spores, via the development of an appressorium, from which the intercellular mycelium spreads into the root cortex with or without intracellular entry, to produce haustorium-like arbuscules. Lipid-rich vesicles form either within or between the cortical cells. Both seasonal factors and the availability of P help to determine the incidence of this endomycorrhiza. Functionally, there is a broad resemblance to ectomycorrhizae, and infected plants gain P, other minerals and possibly water, showing improved growth where these are naturally limiting. Mycorrhizal plants tap the same soil P pool as uninfected plants, but they gain because the external hyphae act as an extended substitute for, or supplement to the root hairs. Although procedures are limited by the inability to grow the fungi axenically, there is evidence that field inoculations of appropriate strains produce beneficial effects in areas where the indigenous population is deficient.

4.6 Mutualism: nitrogen-fixing root nodule systems

Angiosperms have evolved nitrogen-fixing symbioses with two groups of prokaryotes which become located in root nodules unique to the associations. These prokaryotes are either members of the Gram-negative genus *Rhizobium*, found in nodules of the Leguminosae (legumes), or filamentous actinomycetes provisionally named *Frankia*, occurring in non-leguminous tree and shrub genera, mostly found as part of pioneering communities in marginal habitats and on newly exposed soils (6.5). In the last decade *Rhizobium* has been found to nodulate a tropical member of the elm family (Ulmaceae), now recognized to be a *Parasponia* sp., although first identified as *Trema*. Realization of the agronomic and ecological importance of biological nitrogen fixation (6.5) has led to increasing research on symbiotic systems. This section is concerned with the development of the interactions and exchanges between the partners.

Rhizobium spp. are classified according to the host range they infect. There are two physiologically distinct groups of *Rhizobium*; fast-growing, peritrichously-flagellated, acid-producing strains, including *R. leguminosarum*, *R. phaseoli*, *R. trifolii* and *R. meliloti*; and slow growing, polarly-flagellated, alkali-producing strains that include *R. japonicum*, *R. lupini*, and the tropical "cow-pea" rhizobia. The second set are not closely interrelated, are regarded as relatively primitive, and include isolates from *Parasponia*.

Nodule initiation follows the sequence shown in figure 4.6 in *Trifolium* (clovers) for most legumes with fast-growing rhizobia. Entry through wounds caused by lateral root emergence occurs in the peanut (*Arachis hypogaea*), and probably with other hosts of primitive rhizobia. The nodules arise from a meristematic region initiated in the inner cortical cells well ahead of the advancing infection thread. Vascular traces from the stele run around the central mass of bacteria-filled cells, indicating that the nodule is a novel structure, not a modified lateral root. Rhizobia released from infection threads on reaching the dividing nodule cells multiply, and are transformed into swollen, pleomorphic *bacteroids* by the nutrient-rich environment. Leghaemoglobin, a pigment unique to the symbiosis, is produced in effective nodules, probably located between the bacteroid envelope and the surrounding host membrane. The protein portion of leghaemoglobin is host-specified whereas the haem derives from the bacteria. This pigment is concerned in O_2 transfer, and in the protection of the enzyme responsible for N_2 fixation, nitrogenase (6.5). Bacteroids eventually become the site of nitrogenase synthesis and activity, losing at the same time the ability to reproduce when removed from the nodule. Successful production of an effective nodule clearly involves complementary activities of plant and prokaryote at each stage; mutations in either the rhizobia or the legume can alter the onset, size and effectiveness of the nodules.

Lectins are considered to be involved in determining the specificity of the attachment of rhizobia to root hairs. Lectins are mainly glycoprotein tetramers which bind to carbohydrates in a manner analogous to antigen–antibody reactions. Soya bean seed lectin has been found to bind to homologous *R. japonicum* cells but not to those of heterologous, noninfective rhizobia, except for a few "cow-pea" strains. The surface of *R. trifolii* is thought to bind to the clover root lectin *trifoliin*, through 2-deoxyglucose residues in the rhizobial exopolysaccharide. However, lectins may not be the sole determinants of specificity.

Nodule activity is closely related to photosynthetic activity. In the pea,

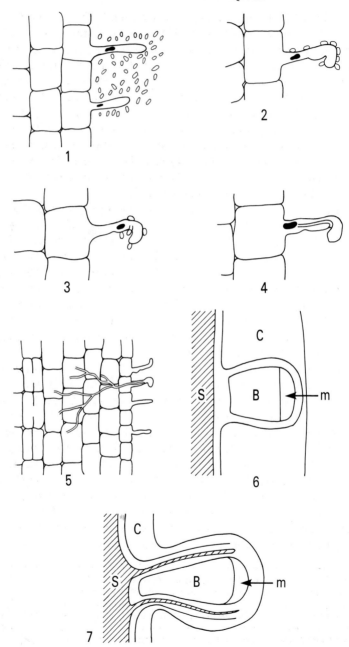

nodules receive 32% of photosynthetically fixed carbon, while 15% is returned to the shoot as amino acids, 12% is lost in respiration, and 5% is used in nodule growth and maintenance. The high respiratory loss reflects the energy requirement for nitrogen fixation. Rhizobia release more NH_4^+ than non-symbiotic nitrogen fixers, up to 90% in the case of axenic *R. japonicum* cultures. Leghaemoglobin helps provide the high O_2 flux needed for ATP generation in the bacteroids, and at the same time the pigment's high O_2 affinity maintains a sufficiently low concentration of O_2 for nitrogenase to function (6.5). Early attempts to show nitrogenase activity in cultures of *Rhizobium* spp. were unsuccessful due to the failure to realize that N_2 fixation was sensitive to O_2. Cultures of *Rhizobium* spp. do, however, fix N_2 under microaerophilic conditions.

Legumes obviously gain the additional nitrogen supplied by the nodules; where there is adequate soil nitrogen nodule formation is suppressed. The main cost to the plant is a reduced growth efficiency arising from photosynthate consumption by the nodule, but the success of the symbiosis is determined by the establishment and survival of the plant. The advantages for the bacteria are less evident. When nodules disintegrate, the only viable rhizobia within are residual untransformed cells of the original invaders. The real advantage for the rhizobia may be in the selective stimulation of the rhizosphere rhizobia by increased root exudation from effectively nodulated plants.

Much less is known about the interactions of *Frankia* and non-legumes, as the infective actinomycete has defied most attempts at isolation. Species based on cross-inoculation groups comparable to those of the *Rhizobium* groups have been proposed, using crushed nodules as inocula. However, infective cultures of the actinomycete have recently been obtained by microdissection of enzymically disrupted, cultured nodule tissue of *Comptonia peregrina*. The *Comptonia* isolate is a slow-growing, microaerophilic filamentous organism. Three species of the closely related genus *Myrica* have been shown to be nodulated by the *Comptonia* isolate, as well as five species of the unrelated *Alnus*, including the geographically separated European *A. glutinosa*. The infection process has been largely studied with inocula from crushed alder nodules. As in legumes, there is root hair

Figure 4.6 The induction of a clover (*Trifolium*) root nodule by *Rhizobium* spp. 1. Multiplication of rhizobia. 2. Attachment of rhizobia associated with root-hair curling. 3. Start of infection thread (root-hair nucleus in black). 4. Growth of infection thread. 5. Spread of infection thread into cortex and induction of plant cell division. 6. Nodule developing in root cortex. 7. Developed nodule with vascular strands. B, bacteroid-containing tissue; C, root cortex; m, nodule meristem (dividing cell zone); s, vascular stele (transport system).

distortion and infection thread development. However, unlike legumes, once within the cortex the ramifying actinomycete hyphae, enclosed by host membranes, induce cell divisions which result in the development of an adventitious lateral root. The young lateral root then develops into a nodule when its cortical cells are invaded. Actinomycete-induced nodules are persistent, branched, coralloid structures, and those of *Myrica* spp. may have upward growing roots that aid the entry of oxygen. Their overall function parallels that of legume nodules, but there is no pigment equivalent to leghaemoglobin. Presumably nitrogenase in this system has to be protected against oxygen, but how this is achieved is not known.

4.7 Mutualism: lichens

These composites of a fungus (the mycobiont) and an alga (the phycobiont) inspired De Bary's original conception of symbiosis. There are between 15 000 and 18 000 described species of lichen. In the majority the mycobiont is an ascomycete, although a few are septate imperfect fungi, a very small number are basidiomycetes, and a few rather atypical forms are aseptate lower fungi. Lichen associations account for roughly half of all known species of the Ascomycotina. While numerous mycobionts have been cultured separately they often do not occur naturally without their algal partners; yet only two lichens have ever been reconstituted in the laboratory. Although specific identification of the phycobionts is difficult, 26 genera are known. Most lichens contain green algae (Chlorophyta), common genera being *Trebouxia*, *Coccomyxa*, *Myrmecia* and *Trentepholia*, blue-green algae are found in about 10 % of all lichens, *Nostoc* being the most frequent genus. Many of the algae are capable of independent existences, although *Trebouxia* seems confined to lichens. Lichens are prevalent on sites subject to cycles of wetting and drying, such as rock surfaces, bark, and poorly vegetated soils.

Typical lichens have highly ordered structures. The three main types, foliose (leaf-like), fruticose (shrub-like, filamentous) and crustose (encrusting) are shown in figure 4.7. In such lichen thalli, the algae occupy a restricted region in the medulla, just under the compact tissue of the outer cortex. The mycobiont usually dominates, and in *Peltigera* spp. only 3–10 % of the dry weight is algal. Lichen morphology is not entirely determined by the fungus: the foliose *Sticta* is transmuted into the fruticose *Dendriscocaulon* if instead of the green alga (*Coccomyxa* sp.), the phycobiont is a blue-green algae (*Nostoc* sp.).

Studies on lichen physiology are bedevilled by the need to use field

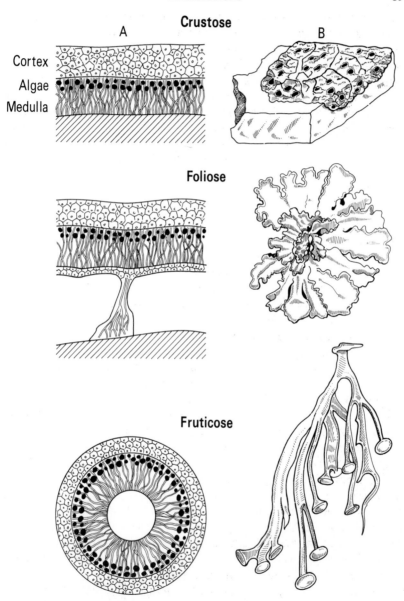

Figure 4.7 Main types of lichen. A. Diagrammatic sections to show the fungal cortex and medulla, and the position of the algal layer. B. Sketches of generalized forms.

material, and by the excruciatingly slow growth rates of their subjects. The radial expansion of lichen thalli is often only 1 mm y^{-1}; crustose lichens on rocks may be several hundred years old, with extremes of $1–4.5 \times 10^3$ y old in the Canadian tundra. Ironically, although lichens were the original model for symbiosis, the mutualistic basis, particularly the benefits accruing to the algae, is not fully understood. Phycobionts have been shown to release characteristic forms of soluble carbohydrate peculiar to the lichenized state. *Nostoc* sp. produce glucose; the green algae liberate polyols—ribitol from *Trebouxia*, *Myrmecia* and *Coccomyxa*, erythritol from *Trentepholia*, and sorbitol from *Hyalococcus*. The algae export a very high proportion of total fixed carbon, perhaps as much as 90%. Why contact with the mycobiont should cause such a large efflux, or promote synthesis of novel forms of photosynthate is a mystery. Very little photosynthate is incorporated into structural components, and much is lost through respiration or leakage, particularly during rewetting. It is possible that such a large commitment to the synthesis of polyols reflects the necessity for a compatible solute (3.2) as a consequence of low a_w levels during periods of desiccation, and thus contributes to low growth rates by diverting carbon and energy. It is certainly clear that this algal–fungal partnership is able to survive severe fluctuations in water activity that would be lethal to the separated bionts. Although carbon transfer is a central feature of the lichen symbiosis, lichens containing the blue-green algal phycobionts *Nostoc*, *Calothrix* or *Stigonema* receive an additional bonus of fixed nitrogen. Many lichens produce secondary metabolites unique to the symbiosis, mostly aromatic substances which form the basis for lichen chemotaxonomy. Such substances have chelating properties and may be implicated in the accumulation of cations that occurs in lichens, and in the decomposition of aluminosilicates (1.1., 7.5).

4.8 Mutualism: the rumen

Ruminants such as domesticated cattle, sheep and goats possess a large expansion of the oesophagus, the *rumen*, in which the ingested, masticated vegetation is subjected to an anaerobic fermentation to yield volatile fatty acids (acetate, propionate and butyrate), CO_2, methane (CH_4), microbial cells and lignin/cutin-rich plant residues. The volatile fatty acids are absorbed by the animal through the wall of the rumen and lower parts of the alimentary tract, and are used as primary sources of carbon and energy. Further digestion of microbial cells in the stomach and small intestine supplies all the animal's amino-acid and growth factor needs.

Ruminants are thus able to survive on fibrous vegetation rich in structural carbohydrates. The relationship between a cow and its rumen microflora can be viewed as an example of mutualism, in response to which the animal has evolved specialized anatomical, physiological and metabolic features.

Mutualistic cross-feeding interactions between rumen bacteria have been demonstrated. Three such examples illustrate how the overall fermentation may be influenced by such interactions. The non-cellulolytic *Selenomonas ruminantium* is important as one of the few producers of propionate, the volatile fatty acid mainly used by the animal in gluconeogenesis. With cellulose as the carbon source in a defined medium, it grows only if the cellulolytic *Bacteroides succinogenes* is present. In addition to this example of cross-feeding, *S. ruminantium* decarboxylates the succinate generated by *B. succinogenes* to propionate. *S. ruminantium* does not seem to gain from the decarboxylation of exogenous succinate, but the step is critical to the fermentation balance in the rumen as other species which produce succinate are unable to convert it to propionate, perhaps because of the high concentration of CO_2.

The transfer of H_2 in methanogenesis (9.4) is the third key interaction because, despite a potential daily production of 800 litres H_2 by a 500 kg cow, the partial pressure of H_2 in the rumen is maintained at 10^{-4} atm. Essentially, fermentative organisms are H_2 donors for CH_4 production by *Methanobrevibacter* and *Methanomicrobium* spp. (see table 5.3), the H_2

Table 4.4 The effect of H_2 transfer to CH_4 by *M. ruminantium* on the fermentation products derived from cellulose by *R. flavefaciens*. (From Latham, M. J. and Wolin, M. J. (1977) Fermentation of cellulose by *R. flavefaciens* in the presence and absence of *M. ruminantium*. *Appl. Envir. Microbiol.*, **34**, (3), 297–301).

Product	mol/100 mol hexose units fermented to products	
	R. flavefaciens alone	R. flavefaciens plus M. ruminantium
Acetate	107	189
Succinate	93	11
Formate	62	1
H_2	37	0
CH_4*	0	83
CO_2*	−48	94

*Calculated assuming 1 mol CO_2 was used to form 1 mol of succinate, and that moles of 1 C compounds equal moles of acetate *minus* formate *plus* methane.

originating from the ferredoxin-mediated re-oxidation of NADH produced during glycolysis. If H_2 is not rapidly removed by methanogenesis, another route of NADH oxidation is followed, consuming pyruvate in the production of electron-sink compounds such as ethanol, lactate or succinate. The formation of such electron-sink compounds is disadvantageous to the H_2 donors since pyruvate freed from electron acceptor duties can be oxidized via acetyl CoA to yield ATP. Table 4.4 illustrates this theme, showing how the fermentation products of *Ruminococcus flavefaciens* grown on cellulose change in the presence of *Methanobrevibacter ruminantium*. The rumen differs from most other anaerobic systems in that whereas about 70 % of the CH_4 produced in digesters (9.4), or in swamps, is derived from acetate, most of the CH_4 produced by the rumen is derived from CO_2 reduction. This presumably reflects the difference in the objectives of the systems in that the rumen has a short retention time (1 d) and has evolved to maximize production and absorption of volatile fatty acids, whereas sewage digesters have a long retention time and are designed to maximize gas production.

4.9 Mutualism and the origins of the eukaryotic cell

Microorganisms have established mutualistic (symbiotic) relationships with a bewildering array of plants, animals and other microorganisms. The degree of intimacy in symbiosis ranges from the non-contact consortial relationships exemplified by interspecies H_2 transfer (4.8, 9.4) and sulphur transfer (7.1) through associations where one partner lives on the surface of the other (*ectosymbiosis*), to the extreme case where one of the partners lives within the tissues or cells of the other (*endosymbiosis*).

Considerable attention has been focused on microbe/microbe endosymbioses, largely because these are considered by some to represent present-day examples of the kind of endosymbioses which originally gave rise to the eukaryote cell. Such endosymbioses are exemplified by certain freshwater protozoa such as *Cyanophora* spp. which harbour blue-green algal endosymbionts known as cyanellae, other protozoa such as *Pelomyxa* spp. and *Paramecium* spp., which harbour endosymbiont bacteria, and the remarkable anaerobic protozoan *Myxotricha paradoxa* which, in addition to harbouring endosymbiont bacteria, has spirochaetes attached to the cell wall, apparently with a locomotory function. Often the endosymbionts in these microbe/microbe associations have not been cultured outside the host, and studies, mainly of the *Paramecium* system, have shown that genetic compatibility is necessary to establish a stable symbiosis. The nutritional advantages to the partners are obvious, particularly in the case of an association between a phototrophic and a non-phototrophic organism. Occasionally, benefit accrues to one of the partners in other than nutritional terms—the bacterial endosymbionts of *Paramecium* spp. for instance, are responsible for the liberation of toxins which are lethal to other strains of *Paramecium*.

The currently favoured hypothesis relating to the organelles of the eukaryotic cell invokes a symbiotic origin for mitochondria, chloroplasts and perhaps flagella, and present day microbe/microbe symbioses have attracted a considerable amount of attention as possible models for the original proto-eukaryote. A discussion of this topic forms an appropriate finale to consideration of mutualism, subject to the caveat that any attempt to adduce evidence from extant organisms is highly speculative in view of the origins of eukaryotes some 1.5×10^9 years ago under quite different environmental conditions.

The original proto-eukaryote host is usually considered to have been a large anaerobic cell wall-less organotrophic prokaryote capable of engulfing other prokaryotes. The steps leading to a eukaryote with a full complement of organelles are imagined to be

(1) incorporation of a small aerobic prokaryote—the protomitochondrion;
(2) the acquisition of enhanced mobility through the attachment of spirochaetes to its surface, and the eventual evolution of these into flagella;
(3) incorporation of phototrophic oxygen-evolving prokaryotes, originating the choroplast.

The second stage is the most controversial, largely because of the lack of success in finding the characteristic ninefold microtubule pattern of eukaryote flagella in any present-day spirochaete. However, a present-day descendant of the original protomitochondrion is considered to exist in the bacteria *Paracoccus denitrificans*, which contains an electron transport chain very similar to that of mitochondria. Blue-green algae are imagined to be descendants of the original protochloroplasts of red algae, which contain phycobilins and chlorophyll *a*. The recently described prokaryotic algae which live in symbiotic association with certain didemnids (or sea squirts), the so-called *Prochloron* group (which lack phycobilins and contain chlorophyll *a* and chlorophyll *b*) may be descendants of the original protochloroplasts of green algae and higher plants. However, no known present-day prokaryote contains chlorophyll *c*, an accessory pigment in the complex group of eukaryotic algae known as the Chromophyta.

Recent attempts to shed some light on the evolutionary relationships of prokaryotes and eukaryotes have concentrated on the analysis of cell components that are of such vital importance to the maintenance of a cell that they might be expected to be highly conserved. The ribosome is considered to be such a component, and ribosomal RNAs in particular have been examined in detail, with the hypothesis that major differences in sequences or base modifications between organisms might indicate major and ancient evolutionary divergencies. Such techniques have revealed that organellar rRNAs do indeed resemble the rRNAs of certain present-day prokaryotes (but less so the archaebacteria—see 3.5), whereas the cytoplasmic rRNA of eukaryotes is quite different and distinct, being largely unrelated to any prokaryotic rRNAs examined so far. The question then arises whether an ancestor of the original engulfing prokaryote exists somewhere in some odd environments (apart from its ubiquitous presence as the cytoplasm of eukaryotes)—it would presumably be an anaerobic cell wall-less prokaryote with the usual prokaryotic features except for its eukaryote-like ribosomes.

The success of present-day mutualistic associations is evident—if the endosymbiont hypothesis for the origin of eukaryotic cells is correct, we are all proof of ancient success.

REFERENCES

Books

Barron, G. L. (1977) *The Nematode-Destroying Fungi*, Canadian Biological Publications, Guelph.

Cooke, R. (1977) *The Biology of Symbiotic Fungi*, John Wiley & Sons, London.

Dommergues, Y. R. and Krupa, S. V. (editors) (1978) *Interactions between Non-Pathogenic Microorganisms and Plants*, Elsevier, Amsterdam.

Hale, M. E. (1974) *The Biology of the Lichens*, 2nd edition, Edward Arnold, London.

Margulis, L. (1970) *Origin of Eukaryotic Cells*, Yale University Press, New Haven.

Marks, G. C. and Kozlowski, T. T. (1973) *Ectomycorrhizae*, Academic Press, New York.

Richmond, M. H. and Smith, D. C. (Organizers) (1979) *The Cell as a Habitat*, The Royal Society, London (also published in *Proceedings of the Royal Society, London, Series B*, **204**, 113–286).

Sanders, F. E., Mosse, B. and Tinker, P. B. (editors) (1976) *Endomycorrhizas*, Academic Press, London.

Subba Rao, N. S. (editor) (1980) *Recent Advances in Biological Nitrogen Fixation*, Edward Arnold, London.

Articles

Barnet, H. L. and Binder, F. L. (1973) The fungal host-parasite relationship. *Ann. Rev. Phytopathol.* **11**, 273–292.

Farrar, J. F. (1976) The lichen as an ecosystem: observation and experiment, in *Lichenology: Progress and Problems*, editors D. H. Brown, D. L. Hawksworth and R. H. Bailey, Academic Press, London, 383–406.

Lockwood, J. L. (1977) Fungistasis in soils, *Biol. Rev.*, **52**, 1–43.

Lynch, J. M., Fletcher, M. and Latham, M. J. (1979) Biological interactions, in *Microbial Ecology: A Conceptual Approach*, editors J. M. Lynch and N. J. Poole, Blackwell Scientific Publications, 171–190.

Rovira, A. D. and Davey, C. B. (1974) Biology of the rhizosphere, in *The Plant Root and its Environment*, editor E. W. Carson, University of Virginia Press, Charlottesville, 153–204.

Slater, J. H. and Bull, A. T. (1978) Interactions between microbial populations, in *Companion to Microbiology*, editors A. T. Bull and P. M. Meadow, Longman, London, 181–206.

Slater, J. H. (1979) Microbial population and community dynamics, in *Microbial Ecology: A Conceptual Approach*, editors J. M. Lynch and N. J. Poole, Blackwell Scientific Publications, 45–66.

Symbiotic Nitrogen Fixation in Actinomycete-Nodulated Plants. *Bot. Gaz.*, **140**, (1979) Supplement.

Van Valen, L. M. and Maiorana, V. C. (1980) The Archaebacteria and eukaryotic origins. *Nature*, **287**, 248–250.

Woese, C. R. and Fox, G. E. (1977) Phylogenetic structure of the prokaryotic domain: the primary kingdoms. *Proc. Nat. Acad. Sci. U.S.A.*, **74**, 5088–5090.

Wolin, M. J. (1979) The rumen fermentation: a model for microbial interactions in anaerobic systems. *Adv. Microbial Ecol.*, **3**, 49–77.

PART 2—MICROORGANISMS AS ENVIRONMENTAL DETERMINANTS

CHAPTER FIVE

THE CARBON CYCLE

5.1 General aspects of the carbon cycle

The global carbon cycle (figure 5.1) involves both biological and geochemical components, with the bulk of the carbon locked away in an oxidized state as the carbonates in limestone and other rocks, or as dissolved bicarbonates in oceanic waters. The carbon in living cells, and in the fossil fuels derived from them is mainly in the reduced form, and originates from CO_2 fixation, mostly via the photosynthetic activities of eukaryotic algae, bryophytes and vascular plants. Blue-green algae participate in this primary reduction step and may account for a significant fraction of marine production, but their overall contribution on land is small. By contrast, chemoorganotrophic bacteria and fungi are responsible for the major part of the oxidation of biologically reduced carbon back to CO_2. Biological decomposition is essentially this latter process; it is inextricably linked to the carbon and energy metabolism of the participating organisms, and is more complex in detail than the corresponding stages of other elemental cycles.

In a broad sense, decomposition encompasses the loss of structure and organization in a dead organism, and the release of inorganic minerals from the moribund tissues. While it is easy to envisage the disintegration of a leaf, insect, or mammal, tracing the fate of their organic constituents presents a difficult problem because of their complexity, compounded by the delays in recycling caused by their partial incorporation into the cells of the decomposers. Carbon from relatively simple sources such as acetate or glucose may be immobilized for months in microbial cells; other molecules are inherently resistant to microbial attack, so complex residues derived from polyphenols, carotenoids or waxes may persist for thousands of years.

This chapter is concerned with the overall relationship between decom-

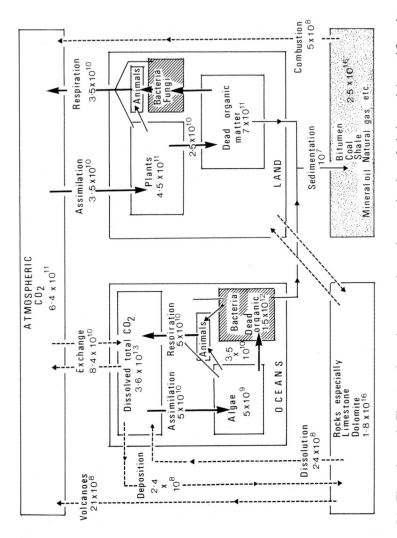

Figure 5.1 The carbon cycle. Figures are in metric tonnes, and are only approximations of relative pool sizes and fluxes between pools (modified from Fenchel and Blackburn, 1979).

position and other parts of the biological carbon cycle, and will concentrate on the nature and fate of the remains of terrestrial vascular plants. Only limited reference will be made to the breakdown of animal and microbial residues, partly because they have received relatively little attention; as the authors of a textbook on soil microbiology remarked, "the study of decomposing animal corpses in soil has never been a popular pastime". It will become apparent that we have only a rudimentary knowledge of some of the activities and interactions of the bacteria and fungi participating in decomposition; at present we cannot completely and fully answer the question, "What happens to a leaf when it falls?"

5.2 General aspects of the generation and decay of detritus

The total amount of carbon initially reduced by photosynthesis is referred to as *gross primary production*; that remaining after loss of respiratory CO_2 represents *net primary production*, and it is this latter parameter that is most readily measured, for example on a dry weight basis. Attempts have been made to estimate global net primary production and related parameters (figure 5.1), although clearly this involves many approximations (global primary production estimates range from 8.5×10^{10} tonnes to 1.8×10^{11} tonnes), and sparse reliable data are available from regions like the tropics.

On land, the primary producers are chiefly macroscopic, multicellular angiosperms and gymnosperms. Much of their assimilated carbon is transformed into biomass in the form of wood and related supportive and conductive tissues, with the consequences that terrestrial primary producers account for most of the world's plant biomass. Only about 5% of the terrestrial net primary production is consumed by herbivorous secondary producers (see table, p. 3) and most of the remainder forms a particulate component of the biological carbon cycle known as *detritus* or litter, utilized eventually as carbon and energy sources by bacteria and fungi. By contrast, the main oceanic primary producers are microscopic unicellular algae, particularly diatoms and dinoflagellates, which occur scattered through the upper euphotic zone. Total net primary production in oceans is roughly comparable to that on land, although the seas contain only about 0.2% of the global plant biomass. A much higher proportion of marine primary production is grazed by herbivores, particularly small copepods and other crustaceans, and phytoplankton may excrete 20% to 30% of its assimilated carbon in soluble form.

Various terrestrial ecosystems differ widely in the proportion of detritus biomass to total plant biomass and annual net primary production. Tropical forests represent one extreme, with the litter comprising less than 1% of the plant biomass and about 10% of net annual primary production; at the other extreme are tundra/alpine environments where the equivalent percentages are 150% and 800% respectively. These variations reflect differences in rates of decay; leaf litter decomposition in tropical forests has been estimated to potentially represent 485% of the annual input, compared with only some 20% in tundra soils. Decay rates are affected by the identity of the litter-producing plants, the pH of the underlying soil type, and by temperature and moisture regimes. The last is particularly important since waterlogging of litter can arrest decomposition, and lead to development of fossil fuels (5.6). Terrestrial litter decomposition generally includes an element of mechanical disintegration by soil animals. In European soils their overall contribution to decay has been estimated at 10%–20%, leaving the predominant role to microorganisms.

World-wide, the reduction and the oxidation of carbon are in balance (figure 5.1). In practice, a proportion of organic carbon, particularly the products of lipid and aromatic metabolism, escapes oxidation. Persistent residues, including soil humus and similar dissolved or particulate matter in the sea, exceed the living biomass five-hundredfold or more (figure 5.1); a roughly similar amount is found in fossil fuels. These reservoirs of organic carbon are thought to be greatly exceeded by other insoluble residues found dispersed throughout sedimentary rocks. This long-term accumulation of reduced carbon has contributed towards the maintenance of an oxygen atmosphere, which would be rapidly consumed if all fossil carbon was re-converted to CO_2.

5.3 The composition of terrestrial detritus

Angiosperm and gymnosperm litter on and above the soil surface consists of the aerial parts of these plants; the decay of the sub-surface parts has received less attention. Fragmentation by the soil fauna may reduce the size of the residues, usually with the more resistant components undergoing little chemical modification, although some invertebrates possess gut enzymes or microbial symbionts able to degrade certain structural polysaccharides.

Water-soluble metabolites are important in supporting the early bacterial and fungal colonizers of senescent and moribund tissues. Some of these may become unavailable to invading microorganisms through com-

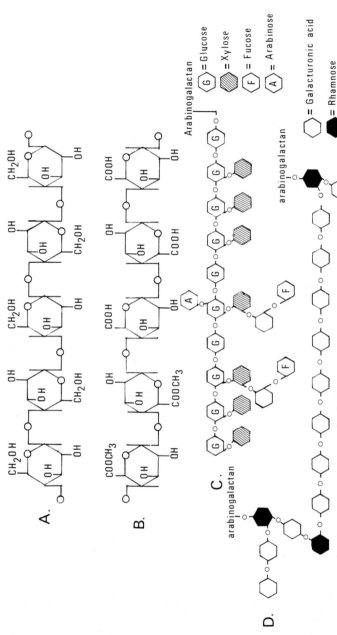

Figure 5.2 Examples of structural polysaccharides from plant cell walls.
A. Cellulose (β1-4 linked glucan).
B. "Pectin" (partly methylated α1-4 polygalacturonic acid).
C. Monomer arrangement in xyloglucan.
D. Monomer arrangement in rhamnogalacturonan.
(C and D redrawn from Albersheim, P. (1975), *Sci. Amer.* **232**, 80–95.)

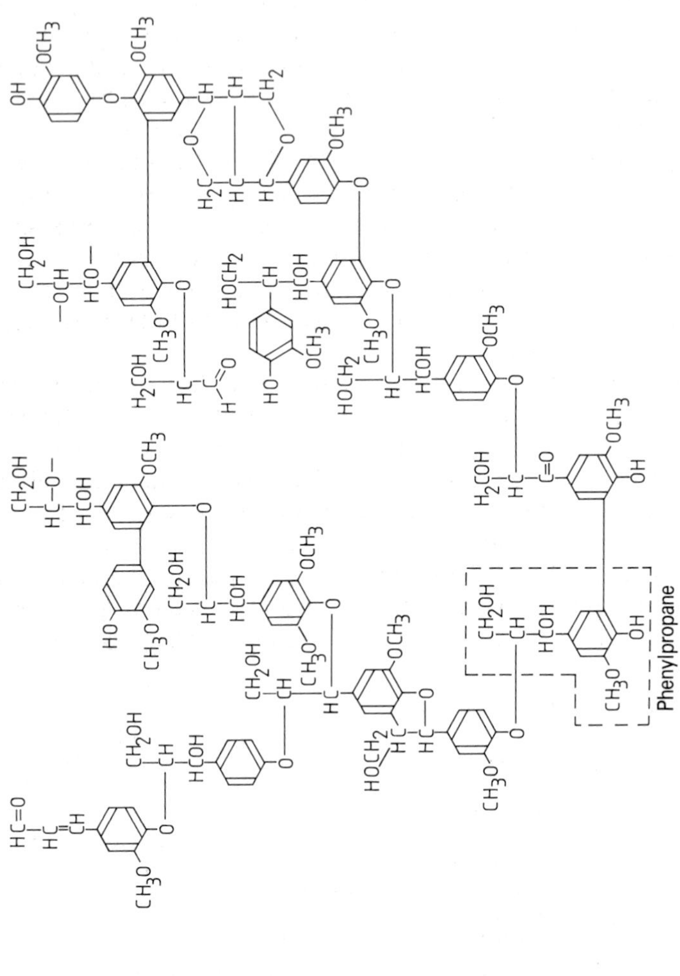

Figure 5.3   Lignin structure—phenylpropane-derived monomer indicated. Note varied inter-monomeric linkages.

plexing with recalcitrant phenolic constituents such as tannins, a process exploited in the preparation of leather.

Animal residues deserve brief mention before the composition of plant residues is discussed. Vertebrate and invertebrate corpses are frequently fragmented by predators and scavengers, and their decomposition may be partly effected by autolysis, and partly through invasion by bacteria present as gut and surface commensals. Collagen, and more particularly keratin, may show some resistance to this essentially proteolytic attack. Keratin, located in skin, hair, feathers and claws, has a fibrous, helical structure and numerous disulphide cross-linkages which make it resistant to many proteases. In and on soil, keratin is attacked by a group of specialist fungi such as *Arthroderma curreyi*, *Ctenomyces serratus*, *Keratinomyces* sp. and *Trichophyton* sp., which are related to the causal agents of such skin diseases as ringworm and athlete's foot. Biochemical details of keratin decomposition have proved difficult to establish in pure culture as the substrate is denatured when subjected to heat, irradiation, or chemical sterilization.

The structural polymers of plant cell walls which form the major part of terrestrial litter are perhaps the most abundant organic molecules in the biosphere, and it is appropriate to examine their characteristics and distribution in more detail. Two classes of structural polymers predominate, the regularly ordered polysaccharides (figure 5.2), and the randomized polyphenolic *lignin* (figure 5.3). A small amount of hydroxyproline-rich structural protein is also present in primary walls. Polysaccharides form the main structure of the wall and consist of hexose and/or pentose monomers linked by glycosidic bonds. The molecules

Table 5.1 Features of plant cell wall polysaccharides

Wall component	Monomers	Combinations	Glycosidic linkages
Cellulose	Glucose	—	$\beta1$–4
Hemicellulose	Arabinose Xylose Glucose Galactose Mannose	Arabinoxylans Xylans Xyloglucans Galactomannans Glucomannans	Main chain $\beta1$–4 Some $\beta1$–3
Pectins (contain uronic acids)	Galactose Galacturonic acid Rhamnose Arabinose	Rhamnogalacturonans Arabinogalactans	Main chains can be $\alpha1$–4, $\beta1$–4, $\beta1$–3 Some others $\beta1$–2

fall into three classes: *cellulose*, the predominant fibrillar element, *hemicelluloses* and *pectins*, the principal characteristics of which are given in table 5.1. There are extensive cross-linkages among these components, with hydrogen bonding between cellulose and hemicelluloses, and covalent bonding between hemicellulose chains, pectins and structural protein, so that the wall could be considered a giant molecule. As microbial substrates, these polysaccharides have the disadvantages of large size, a low degree of hydration, and the absence of nitrogen; these features are counterbalanced by the ordered regularity of the molecules, the possession of largely similar linkages between the monomers, and the ease with which any released monosaccharides can be absorbed and metabolized. Lignin (figure 5.3), in respect of order, uniformity of inter-monomeric linkages, and the ease with which its components are utilized by microbes, is the antithesis of the wall polysaccharides. Aptly described as a biological plastic, it is formed by the random, non-enzymic polymerization of free aromatic radicals. These are produced by the peroxidase-mediated dehydrogenation of units based on phenylpropane, such as coumaryl, coniferyl and sinapyl alcohols. The proportions of monomers derived from these precursors varies between different groups of plants. In the resultant three-dimensional molecule, not only are the phenylpropane units irregularly arranged, but there are permutations in the linkages between them; in addition, the entire lignin complex can be covalently linked to cellulose. The lack of repetitive structure and the multiplicity of inter-monomeric linkages, coupled with hydrophobic properties and potentially toxic degradation products, mean that only a restricted group of microorganisms can degrade this polymer efficiently.

5.4 Ecological aspects of the decomposition of land plant litter

In the United Kingdom, oak leaves disappear after 2 years in the litter layer and pine needles after 6 years, while bracken (*Pteridium aquilinum*) petioles may persist for 10 years. Mycological studies during the decay of all these examples have established the succession of fungi that can be recovered from the tissues or be induced to sporulate upon them. However, it is still not possible to quantify the contributions of the different species to the process, and furthermore, the activities of other groups, particularly bacteria, remain largely unknown. An inherent problem in any microbiological investigation of plant debris is the development of a very diverse microflora within a large number of microhabitats. Perhaps for this reason, many recent studies on plant decomposition have focused on overall changes in organic matter and minerals, while the microbiological details have received less attention.

Decomposers can be placed in two broad groups relating to their specificity for a given *resource*, a term which has been advocated for morphological entities like leaves, branches and fruits in order to avoid the biochemical connotations of the use of "substrate" for such materials. Certain fungi can be classed as either *resource specific*, examples being *Fusicoccum bacillare* on pine needles, and *Piptoporus betulinus* on birch wood, or as *resource nonspecific*, which includes such ubiquitous imperfect fungi as *Aureobasidium pullulans*, *Botrytis cinerea*, *Epicoccum nigrum* and *Trichoderma viride*, as well as the litter-decomposing basidiomycete *Mycena galopus*. The basis for resource specificity is generally unknown but may be determined by the presence of secondary metabolites such as terpenes or phenolics in wood. Other features which may determine an organism's place in a succession are its ability to utilize cell wall polymers, the efficient use of nitrogen or minerals when in short supply, tolerance of low oxygen and high carbon dioxide concentrations in decomposing tissues, and competitiveness with other decomposers.

Cellulose can be degraded by a small number of bacteria and a much greater variety of fungi. Aerobic bacterial genera with cellulytic members include *Pseudomonas*, *Erwinia*, *Bacillus*, *Cellulomonas*, *Cytophaga*, *Sporocytophaga*, *Streptomyces*, *Microbispora* and *Thermoactinomyces*; among the anaerobes are *Clostridium*, *Ruminococcus* and rumen-inhabiting isolates of *Bacteroides*. Among the fungi, cellulose decomposers include a large number of wood-rotting imperfect fungi and basidiomycetes; in addition chytrids such as *Rhizophylctis rosea* and oomycetes, mainly species of *Pythium*, appear on cellulose baits in water and soil. Zygomycetes are rarely reported to be cellulytic, one exception being *Mortierella ramanniana* from Alaskan tundra soils. The ability to hydrolyse partly degraded cellulose may be widespread in soil fungi. It was found that 47 species out of 300 isolated from a German wheatfield soil produced cellulytic activity when tested with the soluble carboxymethyl cellulose, including species of *Fusarium*, *Trichoderma*, *Cephalosporium*, *Truncatella*, *Gliocladium*, *Paecilomyces*, *Chaetomium*, *Rhizoctonia*, *Myrothecium*, *Humicola*, *Aureobasidium*, *Penicillium* and *Verticillium*.

The capacity to depolymerize hemicelluloses and pectins is probably commoner than cellulytic activity, but has been studied less in decomposers. Xylan was hydrolysed by many of the German wheatfield soil fungi, with species of *Phoma*, *Monilia*, *Penicillium*, *Oidiodendron*, *Cephalosporium*, *Fusarium*, *Plectosphaerella*, *Trichocladium*, *Scopulariopsis*, *Conio-*

thyrium and *Cylindrocarpon* being especially active. In the same survey, 54 species, mostly belonging to the genera *Penicillium* and *Fusarium*, cleaved pectin, an ability that is widespread among plant pathogenic bacteria and fungi as well as among the leaf surface (phylloplane) microflora; bacteria that might be active in soil in this respect include *Erwinia carotovora* and *Bacillus macerans*. A rather similar picture emerged from an IBP study on tundra decomposers, with the added complication that some isolates utilized both cellulose and pectin at room temperature but only cellulose at 2°C and 5°C.

Lignin appears to be decomposed mainly by the "white-rot" basidiomycetes (see table 5.2), and also by the less studied litter-decomposing basidiomycetes such as members of the genera *Mycena*, *Collybia*, *Marasmius* and *Clavaria*. The "white-rot" basidiomycetes can be extremely efficient in lignin removal; isolates of *Coriolus versicolor* for instance can cause up to a 97% decline in the lignin content of sweet-gum wood test blocks. Some ascomycetes such as species of *Hypoxylon* and *Xylaria* may also produce white-rots; however, most wood-rotting ascomycetes and imperfect fungi have relatively little lignolytic ability. Lignin may also be altered by the activities of decomposers on other substrates, although only a small amount of carbon is released. "Brown-rot" basidiomycetes for instance owe their name in part to the production of oxidized demethylated lignin residues which remain after cellulose has been destroyed.

A large question mark hangs over the ability of bacteria to degrade lignin, although many are capable of ring cleavage and other transformations of aromatic compounds. In nature, bacteria appear to take little part in the breakdown of lignin in wood, although species of *Streptomyces* and a few other genera may eventually decompose lignin *in vitro*.

Table 5.2 groups microorganisms according to their effects on exposed wood. Bacteria are often overlooked and are the least understood group, though they are among the first colonizers, and remain through all subsequent phases. In the lignified vessels and fibres they break down the pectin-containing membranes of the wall pits interconnecting the lumens of adjacent cells, thus facilitating the movement of both decomposers and water into the wood. Cellulose may be locally degraded by bacteria, and subsequent fungal growth may be affected by the changes they produce in permeability and nitrogen status. The first three fungal groups in table 5.2 overlap somewhat (both moulds and staining fungi are sometimes capable of producing soft-rots) but the predominantly basidiomycete "brown-rot" and "white-rot" fungi produce the greatest weight losses in laboratory tests. Brown-rotting basidiomycetes belong mainly to the Aphyllophorales,

Table 5.2 Organisms growing on wood

| Group | Main resource utilized | Polymers degraded | | | Examples of genera involved |
		Cellulose	Other poly-saccharides	Lignin	
Bacteria	Probably cell contents, walls also modified	+	+	?	*Pseudomonas* *Bacillus* *Clostridium* *Streptomyces*
Moulds (ascomycetes, Fungi Imperfecti)	Cell contents, also products of other decomposers	(+)	(+)	−	*Phialophora* *Coryne* *Cladosporium*
Blue-stain fungi (ascomycetes, Fungi Imperfecti)	Cell contents	(+)	(+)	−	*Alternaria* *Bispora* *Chloridium* *Ceratocystis*
Soft rots (ascomycetes, Fungi Imperfecti)	Lignified cell walls, storage materials in cells	+	+	− (some alteration)	*Chaetomium* *Sordaria* *Cytospora* *Phoma* *Pestalotia* *Chloridium* *Fusarium*
Brown rots (basidio-mycetes)	Lignified cell walls, lignin remains as a brown residue	+	+	−	*Piptoporus* *Coniophora* *Serpula* *Coriolellus* *Daedalea* *Poria* *Lenzites*
White rots (basidio-mycetes, some ascomycetes)	Lignified cell walls, some white cellulosic residues remain for some time	+	+	+	*Fomes* *Coriolus* *Stereum* *Phanerochaete* *Panus* *Phellinus* *Pleurotus* *Pholiota* *Armillaria* *Xylaria* *Hypoxylon*

+ = degraded
(+) = possibly degraded
− = not degraded

and modify but do not significantly depolymerize lignin, leaving it as a characteristic residue. In a strict sense, white-rotting fungi attack lignin before utilizing cellulose, but some, for example *Coriolus versicolor*, simultaneously degrade cellulose and lignin. Taxonomically this is a more diverse group than the "brown rots" including some members of the Aphyllophorales, Agaricales and Gasteromycetales, as well as a few ascomycetes.

Following the deposition of herbaceous litter, phylloplane organisms are largely replaced after contact with the ground by a microflora which is richer in cellulytic and lignolytic members. Using the example of bracken petioles, the resultant fungal succession is summarized in figure 5.4. The greatest weight loss occurs during the second year on the ground, coinciding with the presence of basidiomycete hyphae, and with the maximum production of the fruiting bodies of these fungi. The complex interactions that can occur in decomposition are suggested by the presence after three years of the nematode-trapping fungus *Dactyella megalospora*. This example of fungal colonization of plant debris indicates a quantitatively important role for basidiomycetes relating to their capacity to depolymerize woody plant cell wall constituents. In contrast, these higher fungi have not been recorded in most examinations of decomposing nonwoody plant remains, and this may accurately reflect a dominance of ascomycetes and imperfect fungi on tissues low in lignin, but it is also possible that the apparent absence of basidiomycetes may result through use of methods that do not lead to their recovery or identification.

Not surprisingly, fungal successions on wood vary considerably according to the tree species, the moisture, mineral and secondary metabolite content, the resistant reactions of any living plant cells, the degree of ground contact, and the interactions among the decomposer populations. Furthermore, if the occurrence of macrofungi is determined by recording fruiting bodies, then the sequence reported may relate more to their reproductive physiology than to the period of their activity in wood. In an investigation in Japan, beech logs developed staining fungi and moulds after 10 days' exposure, and the first basidiomycetes were detected within 1 to 2 months from cutting (these included *Stereum purpureum*, a rather weak "white-rot", and *Trametes sanguinea*) so lignin attack commenced quite early; agarics, *Pleurotus ostreatus* and *Pleurotus japonica* were noted after a year. Observations in England showed that the agaric *Hypholoma fasciculare* can colonize beech, birch and oak stumps within 6 to 12 months, particularly if the wood has been treated with ammonium sulphate to prevent tree regrowth.

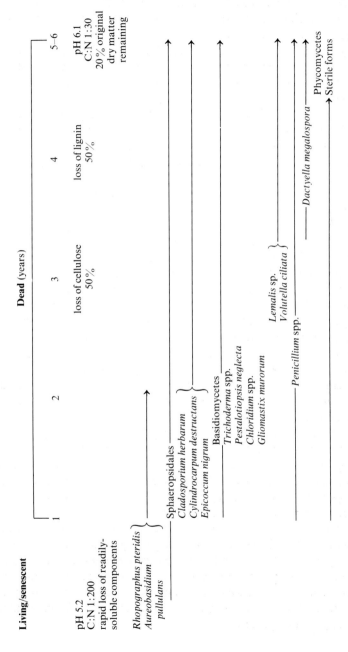

Figure 5.4 Succession of common fungi on detached bracken petioles (modified from Frankland, J. C. (1966) Succession of fungi on decaying petioles of *Pteridium aquilinum*, *J. Ecol.* **54**, 41–63).

The aerobic decay of terrestrial plant detritus is thus clearly a complex synergistic process. Primary decomposers are accompanied by secondary decomposers that utilize some of the released molecules, and may also degrade the primary decomposers in their turn, and so on.

5.5 Biochemical aspects of the microbial depolymerization of land plant litter

Many of the bacteria and most of the fungi active in the decomposition of higher plant detritus are aerobic chemoorganotrophs whose intracellular dissimilation of organic molecules follows common pathways, the critical factor determining the varied roles of the different species being the ability to depolymerize components of the plant cell wall. Much of our knowledge of microbial attack on plant cell walls stems from studies on timber decay, cotton fibre spoilage, and the entry of plant pathogens into living host cells. The assumption that decomposers of leaf-litter and other forms of plant debris deploy similar tactics is probably valid, although much of the screening of isolates from natural sources has employed tests that may not reflect the ability to degrade polymers in their native state.

Cell wall-degrading enzymes

Any organism that efficiently utilizes plant cell walls as carbon and energy sources clearly must produce a co-ordinated battery of extracellular enzymes capable of degrading most or all of the polymers present. Not the least of a student's problems when reading about polysaccharide breakdown is the terminology applied to the enzymes involved. Briefly, *polysaccharase* is a collective term for any enzyme cleaving polysaccharide chains into shorter units. Two terms are applied generally to enzymes hydrolysing glycosidic linkages; *glycanases* act on polymers but have little effect on dimers and trimers, which are the substrates of *glycosidases*; the term *hydrolase* may also be applied to all these enzymes. *Glucanases* are glycanases acting on polysaccharides with glucose as their monomeric unit; *glucosidases* are the equivalent glycosidases. The prefixes *exo-* and *endo-* respectively specify whether the enzymes hydrolyse glycosidic bonds at the ends of the polysaccharide chains or at intervals along their length. The stereospecificity of the glycosidic bond under attack is often stated, e.g. $\alpha 1$–4 or $\beta 1$–6. Other cases where the monomer composition is reflected in the enzyme name include *arabinases* for glycanases acting on arabans, and *polygalacturonases* for similar enzymes hydrolysing the

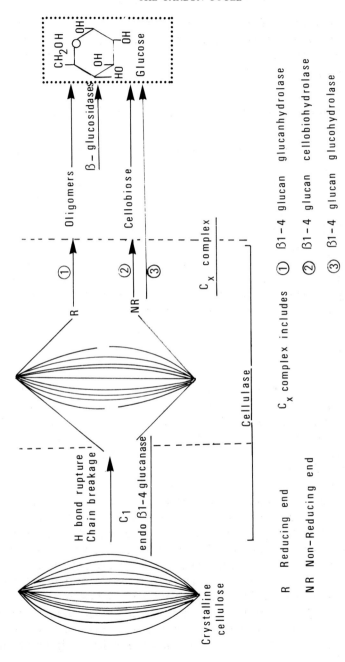

Figure 5.5 The mechanism of cellulose breakdown.

polygalacturonic acid chains of pectin. In some instances the trivial name of the polymer is adopted, e.g. amylase for starch- (amylose)-degrading glucanases, and laminarinases for laminarin-degrading glucanases.

Cellulose breakdown

Early studies on cellulose breakdown by species of *Trichoderma* and *Myrothecium* led to the proposal of the tripartite scheme shown in figure 5.5. In this scheme native crystalline cellulose is considered to be transformed into a structurally weakened form by what is termed the C_1 part of cellulase; the products of this preliminary action were then further decreased in chain length by the C_x components of the cellulose complex, to yield the disaccharide *cellobiose*, from which glucose was released by the action of $\beta1$–4 glucosidases. The C_1 component has been identified as an endo-$\beta1$–4 glucanase, and rather similar enzymes have been shown to occur in the C_x complex, which can contain ten or more endo- and exo-glucanases.

The enzyme concerned with the first step in cellulose degradation acts by breaking the covalent linkages of the glycosidic bonds, to expose the reducing and non-reducing ends of the ruptured cellulose molecules to the exo- and endo-glucanases of the C_x complex; equally importantly, unlike other endo-glucanases, it destroys the hydrogen bonds between the adjacent polysaccharide chains, the overall effect being to open up the cellulose crystals from the outside. The other enzymes, themselves unable to cleave crystalline cellulose, serve to remove oligomers and shorten $\beta1$–4 glucan chains from the broken cellulose molecules, probably improving access for the C_1 enzyme to the intact polysaccharides within the opened crystals.

It is not clear whether this sequential scheme (proposed for fungi such as *Trichoderma*) is more widely applicable, particularly to bacteria whose cellulases may be wall-bound, and to white-rot basidiomycetes where cellulase may be found mainly in extracellular mucilage around the hyphae; these locations seem anomalous given the difficulty of gaining access to the crystalline substrate. Anaerobic cellulose breakdown in the rumen probably involves interspecies synergism among the bacteria present (4.8). The brown-rot basidiomycetes, more mysteriously, do not appear to have cellulases that attack native cellulose, although they cause widespread weakening of walls and effect removal of the polymer at the same rate as do other cellulose-utilizing fungi. One feature of the early attack in wood by brown-rots is a loss of mechanical strength without a decrease in dry weight, which suggests chain breakage without any significant removal of sugar residues. This may be effected through random oxidation of inter-monomeric linkages by peroxide radicals in the presence of ferric iron. Brown-rot fungi have been found to produce H_2O_2, and there is sufficient iron in wood to act as a catalyst, although how these fungi convert it to the ferric state and how they generate substrates for H_2O_2 production is unknown.

Hemicellulose and pectin polysaccharide breakdown

The degradation of the hemicellulose and pectin polysaccharides is understood in less detail. Once again, extracellular inducible polysaccharases hydrolysing inter-monomeric glycosidic linkages are implicated. In the case of the galacturonic acid chains of pectin, three types of enzyme capable of altering their structure have been found in culture filtrates of many plant pathogenic bacteria and fungi. These are considered important both in effecting cell separation through disruption of the middle lamella, and in aiding the direct penetration of fungi through plant cell walls. Of these, the *polygalacturonases* are typical glycosidases cleaving the $\alpha 1-4$ links between monomers. However, the *pectin transeliminases* deploy an unusual mechanism to the same end, breaking the glycosidic bond through proton transfer from the C_5 of one galacturonic acid unit to the C_1 of the next monomer, followed by formation of a double bond between the depleted C_5 and the adjacent C_4 (figure 5.6). Enzymes of the third type, *pectin methylesterases*, remove methyl groups attached to the C_6 carboxyl, but it is not clear how this reaction relates to loss of wall structure.

Fungal cell walls, which constitute a large part of the microbial biomass of soils (1.7) like plant cell walls, are predominantly polysaccharide. Walls in the majority of taxa are comprised of chitin ($\beta 1-4$ poly-*N*-acetylglucosamine) variably associated with glucans and protein. In the laboratory, such walls can be degraded by a mixture of inducible polysaccharases produced by species of *Streptomyces* and *Trichoderma*. Successional studies on hyphae added to soil also implicate bacteria such as *Pseudomonas* spp., *Nocardia* sp., and fungi, including *Mortierella marburgensis* and *Verticillium* sp.; members of this last genus can also be aggressive parasites on cultivated mushrooms. It is likely that thin-walled unpigmented hyphae are rapidly decomposed in soils, but the presence of the phenolic derivative melanin in hyphal walls, along with the carotenoid derivative sporopollenin in some spores has a markedly protective effect. Chitin, a homologue of cellulose, is of broader interest as it is a widespread

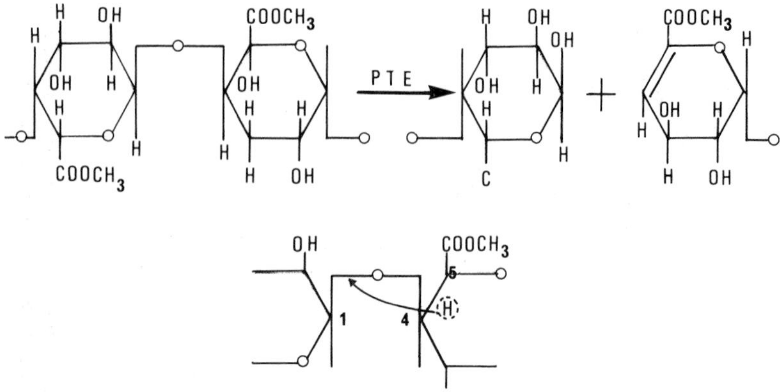

Figure 5.6 Pectin transeliminase (PTE) action. The lower diagram shows proton transfer from C_5 of the right-hand monomer.

component of arthropod exoskeletons, and also occurs though to a lesser extent in other phyla. Because it contains a nitrogen source in the form of an amino-acetyl group it is readily utilized by chitinase-producing bacteria and fungi, unless complexed with more refractory molecules as in insect cuticles. In this instance the associated polyphenols, waxes and insect cement can ensure its survival in soil for months or even years.

Lignin

Lignin decomposition presents many contrasts to microbial attack on polysaccharides. At present, neither the enzymes involved nor their products have been positively identified. The hypothetical process shown in figure 5.7 is mainly based on careful comparisons of the chemical properties of lignin extracted from wood before and after fungal attack, from chemical and physiological studies with ^{14}C-labelled synthetic lignins (sometimes called *dehydrogenative polymerizates* or DHP's), and model lignin products, and from genetic investigations. Many of the physiological and genetic studies have utilized *Phanerochaete chrysosporium* (synonym *Sporotrichum pulverulentum*), a white-rot basidiomycete which conveniently grows well at 40°C, and some confirmatory data have been provided by other basidiomycetes, including *Coriolus versicolor*. Lignin fragments isolated from rotted wood have been found to contain 8–10 aromatic

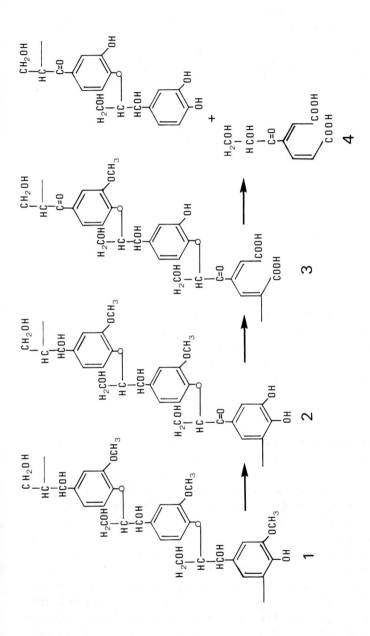

Figure 5.7 "Erosive" oxidative process of lignin depolymerization. Unmodified lignin (1) is partly oxidized and demethylated (2), followed by ring cleavage *in situ* (3), with further demethylation, terminated by breakage of the ether linkage between monomers (4), releasing an aliphatic fragment. This exposes another partly oxidized aromatic unit to attack.

units, and differ from similarly extracted lignin of sound wood in having an increased carboxyl oxygen content, fewer methoxyl and hydroxyl groups, and shorter propyl side-chains. Experiments with *P. chrysosporium* suggest that close contact between lignin and the hyphae is necessary. From the changes in chemical composition, the "erosive" oxidative process of figure 5.7 has been proposed, in which there is an initial cleavage *in situ* of the aromatic rings on the polymer and only limited release of phenolics. As an initial step, *mono-oxygenases* and possibly *phenoloxidases* demethylate and may further hydroxylate the phenolic units on the polymer surface, which are then susceptible to oxidative ring cleavage by *dioxygenases* (8.6), yielding carboxyl-rich aliphatic residues. The ether linkages between the latter are then attacked by an unknown mechanism producing shorter molecules which can enter the fungal cells, where oxidation is completed. The degradative system in *P. chrysosporium* has been shown to be constitutive, and strongly oxygen-demanding. Another feature, markedly contrasting with polysaccharide depolymerization, is that the process is non-specific for lignins of varied composition, cross-linkages and sources.

5.6 Arrested decomposition and fossil fuel accumulation

Most of the decomposers described in section 5.4 are aerobic chemo-organotrophs. If O_2 is absent, some decomposition can still proceed either through the adoption of fermentative energy metabolism by bacteria and some fungi, or by the use of inorganic compounds as terminal electron acceptors by bacteria (6.4, 7.1). However, decomposition is relatively inefficient. In the rumen, for example, the lignin of plant cell walls passes to the faeces with very little alteration. The failure of lignin to be utilized is a feature of anaerobic decomposition in other anoxic habitats such as water-logged soils, and lake, deltaic, or littoral sediments. As we have already seen, lignin breakdown is not only strongly oxygen-demanding, but is carried out most efficiently by basidiomycetes; these fungi appear to avoid these oxygen-deficient situations.

The development of peats

Peats, which contain about 55% carbon, represent an escape from the biological carbon cycle. Present-day peats develop in situations where waterlogging of the litter layer can occur for significant periods, either as a result of impeded drainage in upland regions, or in areas of low topography with an abundant but slow-moving water supply, including mature river valleys, deltas, estuaries and coastal mangrove swamps. Tropical coastal and lowland peats were much more important in the geological past, and were the progenitors of major lignite and coal deposits.

Developed peats often retain recognizable macroscopic plant remains, and traces of decomposers may also be present—indeed, persistent fungal hyphae are so abundant in some English upland peats that they thwart attempts at pollen analysis. Peats may contain up to 20% lignin, 30% cellulose and 36% hemicellulose on a dry weight basis, the relative proportion of polysaccharides usually being smaller than in undecomposed cell walls. Up to 80% humic acid (1.2) may be present in some river valley peats, but values of as low as 5% have been recorded, presumably reflecting the degree to which plant remains have been preserved. Fulvic acid (1.2) is also present, and peat contains many extractable phenolics, including tannins; other molecules of biological origin include lipids and both protein-derived and non-protein amino acids.

Profiles through peat often do not show increasing decomposition with depth, but instead reveal discrete layers of relatively undecomposed material sandwiched between more degraded plant remains; this suggests that the critical events determining peat formation occur at or near the surface of the deposit. Active decomposition of litter occurs on developing peats, and only a small proportion of the input from primary production need be spared for accumulation to occur; conservation of 7.5% of plant production was calculated to be sufficient for formation of an Everglades peat. It is far from clear why microbial activities should be selectively restricted, although studies of the microflora indicate that microbial numbers are highest at the surface, as determined by viable counts or by direct observation, and fungi, aerobic and anaerobic bacteria have all been reported to decrease in frequency down profiles, with very low recoveries of actively growing microorganisms at depth. Possible explanations for this decline include low oxygen tensions, the presence of inhibitory substances, and nutrient limitation, particularly the supply of inorganic nitrogen. Of these, poor oxygen availability may be the most significant factor; it is thought that the lower parts of deposits are permanently anaerobic. Inhibitory substances are not consistently found in peat extracts, which can equally often stimulate microbial growth, but strong circumstantial evidence for some preservative chemicals is provided by for instance the discovery of well-preserved human corpses, two millennia old, in Danish bogs. Conceivably, inhibitors operate only in waterlogged conditions, since it is noticeable that developed peats are rapidly decomposed if re-exposed at the surface. Much of the nitrogen content of peat may be locked away in organic complexes, and this might have a restrictive effect on microbial activity, although tropical peats often develop where inorganic nitrogen from blue-green algal blooms is available.

Clearly, given that peats develop in varied habitats with diverse vegetation, it is likely that no single factor makes a dominant contribution to their formation. Their conversion to coal follows burial by inorganic sediments; the cumulative effects of temperature and pressure in geological time then progressively increase the relative carbon content to 73% in lignites, 83% in bituminous coals, and 94% in anthracite.

Oil and natural gas deposits

These represent another departure from the biological oxidation of organic carbon, but the details of microbiological participation in their formation are even more speculative than in peat production. The biological origins of crude oil are now generally accepted. Crude oils contain many compounds such as alkanes, pristanes, isoprenoids and porphyrins which presumably originated in marine sediments deposited in ancient seas. It is thought that microbial activity initially degrades the remains of marine phytoplankton, leaving mainly the biolipids as the source material for oil. When this transformed organic matter is buried and subjected to enhanced temperatures and pressures, polymerization and condensation to an insoluble complex known as kerogen occurs. A polymeric, largely polymethylene material similar to kerogen is known to develop at the present time under blue-green algal mats on the tidal salt flats at Baja, California. Further geochemical changes and thermal cracking produce a range of hydrocarbons, including gases such as methane (CH_4), ethane (CH_3CH_3), propane ($CH_3CH_2CH_3$), and butane ($CH_3CH_2CH_2CH_3$). The composition and amount of crude oil generated depends on the composition of the original biomass. High temperature and pressure treatments of present-day biomass (algal mats etc.) generates a range of petroleum products comparable to those observed in various types of crude oil.

A different, more rapid route has recently been proposed for oil shale formation. This is based on the trapping of hypersaline water originating from artesian water flowing through salt-rich rocks and then discharging into relatively enclosed marine basins. This would lead to stratification of the water, with a marked boundary (halocline) between the underlying brines and the more normally constituted surface waters where a high level of primary production takes place. The presence of the halocline would maintain anoxic conditions in the concentrated brines, whose high salt content could have a selective effect on most anaerobic bacteria.

The hypothesis then involves patterns of carbon transformation by which low molecular weight compounds are turned into bacterial biomass, while high-molecular weight carbon compounds are only slowly decomposed, so that a combination of bacterial and plankton residues accumulates in the sediments beneath the brine, giving rise to crude oil precursors. Salt curing of the developing kerogen in the young oil shales then enhances its preservation and condensation. High temperatures are not a necessary part of this process of oil generation, which is based on conditions in the Black Sea and its sediments, and is thought to be applicable to oil deposits formed in earlier geographical periods in the Caspian region and under the North Sea.

Methane formation

Methane has a more direct biological origin in anoxic environments, although not all geological accumulations of this gas are due to biological activity. Methane formation occurs in aquatic sediments below the zone of SO_4^{2-} reduction, in sewage sludge (9.4), geothermal springs with volcanic H_2 and CO_2, the rumens (4.8) of cattle, sheep and goats, the gastrointestinal tracts of other mammals including man, and the slowly rotting wet heartwood of trees. Production of CH_4 in these habitats is thought to be effected by a unique group of strictly anaerobic methanogenic bacteria (table 5.3), all of which are capable of the reduction of CO_2 to CH_4 using H_2 as the electron donor (9.4). Methanogens can participate in interspecies hydrogen transfers, where H_2 is one of the dissimilative products of organisms higher in the decomposer chain. Interspecies H_2 transfer is now known to be a crucial feature of anoxic carbon transformations (4.8, 9.4).

The distribution of CH_4-producing bacteria in anoxic aquatic sediments reflects the inhibitory effects of SO_4^{2-} reduction, thermodynamically a more advantageous electron acceptor than CO_2; in Lake Vechten, it was found that methanogens were mostly present in the mud 2–3 cm below its surface, while SO_4^{2-} reducers were located between 0 and 2 cm. The inhibitory effects of SO_4^{2-} reduction reflect competition for H_2 and acetate as substrates both for methanogenesis and SO_4^{2-} reduction (8.3). Many

Table 5.3 Methanogenic bacteria (groupings based on Balch *et al.*, 1979)

Genus	Habitat	Comments
Methanobacterium	Sewage sludge, freshwater muds	Gram +ve rods with unusual cell wall structural polymer (pseudomurein)
Methanobrevibacter	Rumen, wet heartwood, sewage sludge	Gram +ve cocco-bacilli with pseudomurein
Methanococcus	Marine and freshwater mud	Gram +ve cocci with proteinaceous cell wall
Methanomicrobium	Rumen	Gram +ve, pleomorphic, no well-defined cell wall
Methanogenium	Marine mud	Gram +ve rods with proteinaceous cell wall
Methanospirillum	Sewage sludge	Gram +ve spirillum with sheath
Methanosarcina	Sewage sludge, freshwater mud	Gram +ve coccus with thick heteropolysaccharide cell wall

marine sediments are less significant sites of methanogenesis than fresh-water sediments, as a consequence of high SO_4^{2-} levels, but some methanogenesis does go on both in deep sea cores and in samples from shallower waters; in the latter, methane production occurs below 10–150 cm from the surface of the mud, a deeper location than in freshwater sites. In deeper waters, methanogens were found up to 3.5 m below the sediment surface in the Santa Barbara Basin, and two species of *Methanogenium* have been isolated from the Black Sea and the Cariaco trench; these latter situations are interesting as methane might form geologically stable hydrates under the high pressures that develop below salt water columns, providing an alternative route for natural gas accumulations to the thermal cracking process referred to earlier.

5.7 Microbial decomposition of fossil fuels

Lignites and coals do not provide readily-available carbon and energy sources compared with crude oil and natural gas. Crude oil is a highly complex and variable mixture, and can include straight-chain, branched and cyclic alkanes, aromatic residues, isoprenoid derivatives, traces of other organic molecules such as phenols, naphthenic acids and porphyrins, and complex larger molecules, the asphaltenes, which may be stacked condensed aromatic rings. These clearly constitute a heterogeneous set of microbial substrates whose diversity is emphasized by the detection of over 200 different hydrocarbons in some types of crude oil. Up to 7% sulphur may be present mainly either as attached thiol groups or as substituents in aromatic rings, and this can decrease biodegradability. Only a small (0.02%), but often toxic, fraction of crude oil is water-soluble, the bulk being hydrophobic, and this means that hydrocarbon utilizers, which require the presence of water, have contact and transfer problems. Oil decomposers are thus located near oil/water interfaces. Oil-degrading bacteria may have hydrophobic surfaces which would facilitate sorption, and bacteria certainly become bound to oil in some way. Another process, pseudosolubilization, involves direct cellular uptake of very small droplets; *Acinetobacter* spp. accumulate unmodified hydrocarbons as membrane bound inclusion bodies by this means. Oil–water emulsions are produced by yeasts and bacteria through the agency of cell-bound or extracellular glycolipids; peptide fatty acid mixtures may also be responsible.

The microbial decomposition of crude oil is currently receiving increased attention because of the threat of environmental pollution from oil spillages. Field studies support the laboratory finding that straight-chain n-alkanes, particularly those 11 to 19 carbon atoms long, are the most readily degraded fraction, the main pathway (figure 5.8) involving a mono-oxygenase mediated oxidation of the C_1 methyl group to a primary alcohol, then an aldehyde, and finally to a carboxylic acid which can then be cleaved to acetate units by the β-oxidative pathway. A similar but separate mechanism applies to simple methyl-branched alkanes, but it is not known how more complex branched chains are decomposed. Aromatic units can be metabolized following dioxygenation and ring scission (see figure 5.7), but are broken down more slowly than n-alkanes, particularly if multiple ring systems or sulphur substituents are also present. Cyclic alkanes may accumulate in the sea through the preferential use of n-alkanes by marine bacteria, and while these cyclic compounds can be microbially oxidized, it is not clear how they are incorporated and used as carbon or energy sources. It is likely that they are degraded through co-metabolic reactions by organisms growing on other more accessible substrates. This latter indirect mechanism is particularly important for synthetic (xenobiotic) molecules (8.6).

A variety of bacteria, yeasts and fungi has been found to grow on C11–C19 n-alkanes, promoting interest in these hydrocarbons as feedstocks for the production of single-celled protein. *Pseudomonas, Micrococcus, Corynebacterium, Nocardia* and *Mycobacterium* spp. are among the

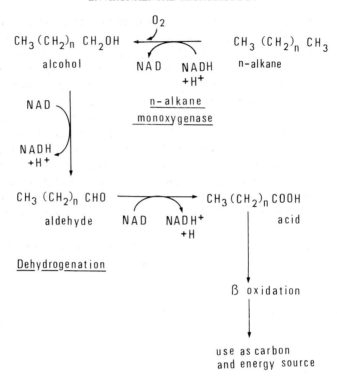

Figure 5.8   Microbial oxidation of straight-chain n-alkanes.

bacteria with this capacity. Yeasts include species of *Candida*, *Torulopsis*, *Rhodotorula*, *Pichia* and *Debaryomyces*, and filamentous fungi are represented by *Cunninghamella*, *Penicillium*, *Aspergillus*, *Fusarium*, and the interesting *Amorphotheca* (*Cladosporium*) *resinae*, which is very widespread and may be a dominant hydrocarbon utilizer in some situations. Long (C_{20} and above) n-alkanes tend to be solid at normal ambient temperatures, and are not easily available to microbial decomposers, but branched and cyclic alkanes are oxidized by specialist strains of *Mycobacterium* and *Pseudomonas*, and *Pseudomonas* spp. have also been studied extensively as oxidizers of aromatic compounds.

While oil-degrading microorganisms are widely distributed on land and in salt and fresh waters, very little is known of their activities on natural oil seepages, or other natural hydrocarbon sources such as the paraffinic components of plant and animal waxes. Microbially-modified hydrocarbons from natural petroleum flows are known from parts of Utah and Poland, where they have formed waxy deposits (ozokerite) which have been used as a source of paraffin. Anaerobic hydrocarbon-utilizing bacteria may be present in the ground water associated with sub-surface oil deposits, and SO_4^{2-} reducers are also present in marine sediments where anoxic oil decomposition occurs, although the process itself is a mystery. Refined petroleum products are subject to microbial decomposition with economically damaging results, although certain modifications can have a protective effect—growth of moulds in the water accumulating in aircraft fuel tanks and storage facilities has occasionally been disastrous, either through corrosion (7.2) or because of mycelial plugging of fuel lines. Not fatal, but probably more costly, is the microbial deterioration of the oil–water emulsions used as lubricants for machine tools and metal-rolling mills.

Natural gas contains between 50 % and 90 % methane, and also ethane, propane and other volatile hydrocarbons, decreasing in amount with

Table 5.4 Methane-oxidizing and methylotrophic bacteria

Genus or group	Comments
(1) Obligate CH_4-oxidizers (obligate methylotrophs)	
Methylomonas	RMP pathway; N_2 fixer
Methylococcus	RMP pathway: N_2 fixer
Methylosinus	Serine pathway; N_2 fixer; exospores
Methanomonas	Serine pathway; N_2 fixer
(2) Facultative CH_4-oxidizers (facultative methylotrophs)	
Methylobacterium	Serine pathway; N_2 fixer
Yeasts	Poorly described taxonomically; RMP pathway?
(3) Facultative methylotrophs unable to oxidize CH_4 (oxidize CH_3OH, $CH_3NH_3^+$, etc.) Many common soil eukaryotes and prokaryotes including:	
Arthrobacter	RMP pathway
Pseudomonas	Serine pathway
Bacillus	RMP pathway
Hyphomicrobium	Serine pathway; appendaged
Streptomyces	RMP pathway
Hansenula	RMP pathway?
Candida	RMP pathway?
Trichoderma	RMP pathway?

increasing chain length. Microbial growth on these alkanes occurs where gas diffuses from surface outcrops of reservoir rocks, and can be profuse enough to form deposits in soil of peat-like "paraffin dirt" composed of the remains of bacteria, yeasts and fungi. Detection of paraffin dirt and of ethane-utilizing bacteria (often species of *Mycobacterium* and *Pseudomonas*), has been used as a prospecting aid, but CH_4-utilizers are unreliable for this purpose because methane is widely produced biogenically.

The microbial oxidation of CH_4 has received most attention, perhaps because of its attraction as a cheap source for microbial protein production. An interesting group of bacteria and yeasts has been shown to use CH_4 as a carbon and energy source. Some bacteria are obligate users of CH_4, but some organisms can also grow on other carbon and energy sources (table 5.4). CH_4 oxidizers possess a mono-oxygenase which catalyses the oxidation of CH_4 to CH_3OH (figure 5.9); this enzyme has similarities to the oxygenase of NH_4^+-oxidizing bacteria (6.3). Formaldehyde (HCHO) is then generated, and this C_1 fragment is incorporated into biomass by either of two routes, the serine pathway, or the ribulose monophosphate (RMP) pathway (figure 5.9). These C_1 incorporation pathways are related to, but distinct from, the classic Calvin cycle which operates in CO_2 fixation. Organisms which "fix" C_1 fragments by either of these two routes are known as *methylotrophs*, and obligate CH_4 oxidizers are obligate methylotrophs, their CO_2 fixation mechanisms being insignificant. Certain other organisms unable to oxidize CH_4 also use methylotroph pathways for the fixation of C_1 fragments derived from carbon compounds which lack carbon–carbon bonds but are more reduced than CO_2 (CH_3OH, $CH_3NH_3^+$, etc.) (table 5.4).

As strict aerobes, bacterial CH_4 oxidizers occupy separate ecological niches from the methanogens. In one lake they were found to be widely dispersed in winter, when mixing of the water column made inorganic nitrogen sources available. When nitrogen was depleted by phytoplankton blooms in the warmer months, the CH_4 oxidizers became dependent on N_2 fixation, and became restricted to a microaerophilic zone near the thermocline of the now stratified lake. CH_4 oxidizers can also oxidize carbon monoxide (CO), probably utilizing the rather non-specific methane monoxygenase enzyme (which also oxidizes NH_4^+). CO is a major atmospheric pollutant ($\sim 2 \times 10^8$ tonnes yr^{-1} globally) partly derived from industrial activity, and partly from the decomposition of porphyrin derivatives. The mean residence time of atmospheric CO is about 20 days, and it is estimated that 50% of the total is removed via microbial activity. A diverse group of bacteria including *Pseudomonas*, *Seliberia* and

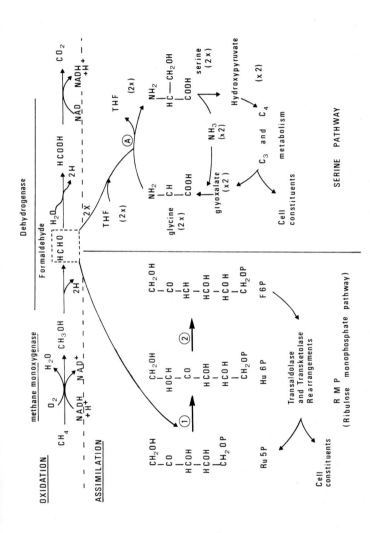

Figure 5.9 The oxidation of methane and assimilation of formaldehyde (HCHO). Key enzymes in the ribulose monophosphate pathway (RMP) (left) are (1) 3-hexulose phosphate synthase, which converts ribulose-5-phosphate (Ru-5-P) to hexulose-6-phosphate (Hu-6-P); (2) phospho-3-hexuloisomerase which converts H-6-P into fructose-6-phosphate (F-6-P). In the serine pathway (right) HCHO is incorporated as a 1C fragment from a tetrahydrofolate (THF) carrier into serine by serine transhydroxymethylase (A).

Achromobacter spp. ("carboxydobacteria") as well as CH_4 oxidizers are implicated in the aerobic oxidation of CO to CO_2, and its consequent removal from the system.

REFERENCES

Books

Anderson, J. M. and MacFadyen, A. (1976) (eds.) *The Role of Terrestrial and Aquatic Organisms in Decomposition Processes* (17th Symposium of the British Ecological Society), Blackwell Scientific Publications, Oxford.

Davis, J. B. (1967) *Petroleum Microbiology*, Elsevier, Amsterdam, London and New York.

Dickinson, C. H. and Pugh, G. J. F. (1974) (eds.) *Biology of Plant Litter Decomposition*, Vols. I and II, Academic Press, London and New York.

Fenchel, T. and Blackburn, T. H. (1979) *Bacteria and Mineral Cycling*, Academic Press.

Kirk, T. K., Higuchi, T. and Chang, H. (1980) *Lignin Biodegradation: Microbiology, Chemistry and Potential Applications*, Vols. I and II, Chemical Rubber Company Press, Boca Raton, Florida.

Swift, M. J., Heal, D. W. and Anderson, J. M. (1979) *Decomposition in Terrestrial Ecosystems* (Studies in Ecology Vol. 5), Blackwell Scientific, Oxford.

Whittaker, R. H. (1975) *Communities and Ecosystems*, Macmillan Publishing Co., New York.

Articles

Balch, W. E., Fox, G. E., Magrum, I. J., Woese, C. R. and Wolf, R. S. (1979) Methanogens: revaluation of a unique biological group. *Microbiol. Rev.* **43**, 260–296.

Colby, J., Dalton, H. and Whittenbury, R. (1979) Biological and biochemical aspects of microbial growth on C_1 compounds. *Ann. Rev. Microbiol.* **33**, 481–519.

Colwell, R. R. and Walker, J. D. (1977) Ecological aspects of microbial degradation of petroleum in the marine environment. *CRC Critical Reviews in Microbiology*, **5**, 423–445.

Crawford, D. L. and Crawford, R. L. (1980) Microbial degradation of lignin. *Enzyme and Microbial Technol.* **2**, 11–22.

Degens, E. T. and Paluska, A. (1979) Hypersaline solutions interact with organic detritus to produce oil. *Nature*, **281**, 666–668.

Given, P. H. and Dickinson, C. H. (1975) Biochemistry and microbiology of peats. In *Soil Biochemistry*, Vol. 3, eds. E. A. Paul and A. D. MacLaren, Marcel Dekker, New York, pp. 123–212.

Gutnick, D. L. and Rosenberg, E. (1977) Oil tankers and pollution: a microbiological approach. *Ann. Rev. Microbiol.* **31**, 379–396.

Hayes, A. J. (1979) The microbiology of plant litter decomposition. *Science Progr.* **66**, 25–42.

Reese, E. T. (1976) Degradation of polymeric carbohydrates by microbial enzymes. *Recent Adv. in Phytochem.* **11**, 311–367.

Zeikus, J. G. (1977) The biology of methanogenic bacteria. *Bacteriol. Rev.* **41**, 514–541.

CHAPTER SIX

THE NITROGEN CYCLE

6.1 General aspects of nitrogen cycling

Nitrogen has a crucial role to play in primary productivity, and indeed is the plant nutrient required in greatest quantity. In the biosphere it undergoes what is essentially a cyclical eight-electron shuttle between the most oxidized form at valence $+5$ (NO_3^-) and the most reduced form at valence -3 (NH_3). The main features of this cycle are outlined in figure 6.1.

Most nitrogen in biomass is in the most reduced form, and when organic N-containing compounds are catabolized, N is released, unchanged in valence, as NH_3. This process of *ammonification* (6.2) is central to the general mineralization process, whereby N immobilized in tissues is converted to mobile inorganic forms that provide plants with the major part of their N requirement. The ammonification process constitutes quantitatively the major flux in the N cycle. NH_3, in the ionized form NH_4^+, is readily assimilable by plants and most microorganisms, being directly incorporated back into organic compounds. However, under oxic conditions a widespread group of prokaryotes, the chemolithotrophic nitrifying bacteria, obtain energy by oxidizing NH_4^+ via several intermediates to NO_3^-. This process, which goes on in any oxic terrestrial or aquatic environment, is known as *nitrification* (6.3) and is an inevitable sequel to ammonification under such conditions. NO_3^- is also readily assimilable by plants, which reduce N back to the appropriate -3 valence commensurate with tissue requirements by a process known as *assimilatory nitrate reduction* (6.4).

NO_3^- has been considered to be the most appropriate form of inorganic N for plants largely because, excepting gaseous N_2, it is the predominant inorganic N compound in oxic environments like good agricultural soils. However, plants could almost certainly cope with NH_4^+ as their major N

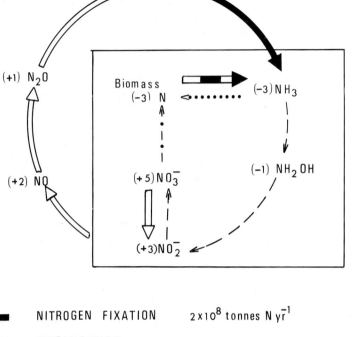

NITROGEN FIXATION 2×10^8 tonnes N yr^{-1}

NITRIFICATION

ASSIMILATORY NITRATE REDUCTION

DISSIMILATORY NITRATE REDUCTION 2×10^8 tonnes N yr^{-1}

AMMONIA ASSIMILATION

AMMONIFICATION 3×10^{10} tonnes N yr^{-1}

Figure 6.1 The nitrogen cycle. The transformations within the box are quantitatively the most significant.

source were nitrification to cease. Current opinion holds that nitrification may be positively disadvantageous under some circumstances, and so NH_4^+- rather than NO_3^--based fertilizers are increasingly used, sometimes in association with an inhibitor of nitrification such as N-SERVE (2-chloro-6-(trichloromethyl)-pyridine). Features of high NO_3^- levels which are considered undesirable include its ready leaching and consequent loss compared with NH_4^+, its capacity to promote eutrophication when leached into waterways (8.4) and its potential indirect toxicity in humans (6.4). Plants have also to expend energy and reducing power in incorporating NO_3^- into biomass, whereas NH_4^+ is already at the appropriate level of reduction.

A further indirect effect of nitrification is seen under anoxic conditions, when NO_3^- can act as an electron acceptor in place of O_2 for a variety of soil bacteria in a respiratory process known as *dissimilatory nitrate reduction* (6.4). Certain of the more reduced forms of N so produced are gaseous and the consequent loss of gaseous N from the system is known as *denitrification* (6.4). This process could constitute a major leak from the cycle, were it not for an approximately equal and opposing utilization of N_2 by certain prokaryotes that assimilate N_2 reductively into biomass by a process known as *nitrogen fixation* (6.5). Given the inevitability of nitrification followed by denitrification, it follows that N_2 fixation is vital to the continued maintenance of a balanced N cycle, and in agricultural areas where there is little or no input of nitrogenous fertilizer, N input via biological fixation limits productivity.

Quantitatively the most important transfers are between the major reservoir of biomass N (2×10^{12} tonnes) and that of inorganic N, mainly NH_4^+, NO_3^- and NO_2^- (2×10^{11} tonnes). There are, however, serious difficulties inherent in measuring products which may participate in several alternative pathways, and the figures are based on imprecise and incomplete information. Ammonification is believed to account for 3×10^{10} tonnes N yr^{-1}, and this is presumably roughly balanced by the sum of N uptake via NO_3^- and NH_4^+, although the relative contribution of each is not known in the absence of global nitrification figures. Denitrification balances N_2 fixation at about 2×10^8 tonnes yr^{-1}. The mass transfers between biomass N and the major inorganic forms of N are therefore larger by two orders of magnitude than those between gaseous N and inorganic N. The denitrification/N_2 fixation transfers can be considered to constitute a subsidiary loop outside a quantitatively much more important N cycle made up of nitrification/assimilation/ammonification transfers (figure 6.1).

6.2 Ammonification and ammonia assimilation

Most organic N remains in biomass until it is liberated following the death of the organism, although animals excrete significant quantities of NH_3 and simple organic N compounds like urea or uric acid. Tissue N is released from proteins and polynucleotides by a wide variety of micro-organisms by hydrolysis, first to amino acids and nitrogen bases, followed by fermentative or oxidative utilization releasing NH_3. Under anoxic conditions amines may be produced in large quantities, later to be assimilated releasing NH_3 under oxic conditions. At neutral pH, relatively little free NH_3 is present, since the equilibrium between NH_3 and NH_4^+ is such that NH_4^+ predominates.

There are three NH_4^+ assimilation reactions which operate at high NH_4^+ levels, one involving the condensation of NH_4^+ with α-ketoglutaric acid to give glutamic acid (glutamate dehydrogenase), and two others forming the amido groups of asparagine and glutamine (asparagine synthetase and glutamine synthetase). At low NH_4^+ levels another enzyme, glutamine-oxyglutarate amino transferase (GOGAT) is induced, catalysing the reaction

$$\text{glutamine} + α\text{-ketoglutaric acid} \xrightarrow[\text{GOGAT}]{} 2 \text{ glutamic acid}$$

Under such conditions the reaction catalysed by glutamine synthetase is the major route of NH_4^+ assimilation in association with the reaction catalysed by GOGAT; thus

$$\text{glutamic acid} + NH_4^+ \xrightarrow[\text{glutamine synthetase}]{} \text{glutamine}$$

$$\text{glutamine} + α\text{-ketoglutaric acid} \xrightarrow[\text{GOGAT}]{} 2 \text{ glutamic acid.}$$

Net reaction: α-ketoglutaric acid + $NH_4^+ \longrightarrow$ glutamic acid.

The glutamine synthetase/GOGAT pathway appears to operate as the major pathway in the assimilation of NH_4^+ produced as the result of N_2 fixation (6.5).

6.3 Nitrification

The importance of nitrification lies in producing an oxidized form of N which can participate in denitrification, permitting a potential loss of N from the system. The biological nature of nitrification was first realized over a hundred years ago when it was shown that the appearance of NO_3^- in soils and sewage was inhibited by antiseptics. Shortly after this, it was established that there were two distinct and separate groups of obligately aerobic bacteria involved, both capable of obtaining energy at the expense of different N compounds. Chemolithotrophic nitrifying bacteria are now grouped in the family Nitrobacteriaceae, and table 6.1 summarizes the currently recognized species and their habitats. All the examples, with the

Table 6.1 Nitrifying bacteria and their habitats

Substrate	Species	Habitat
NH_4^+ oxidized to NO_2^-	Nitrosomonas europaea	Soil, fresh water
	Nitrosospira briensis	Soil
	Nitrosolobus multiformis	Soil
	Nitrosovibrio tenuis	Soil
	Nitrosococcus nitrosus	Soil
	Nitrosococcus oceanus	Marine
	Nitrosococcus mobilis	Marine
NO_2^- oxidized to NO_3^-	Nitrobacter winogradskyi	Soil, fresh water
	Nitrospina gracilis	Marine
	Nitrococcus mobilis	Marine

exception of a few isolates of *Nitrobacter winogradskyi*, are obligate chemolithotrophs. Members of the group with the generic prefix "Nitroso" carry out a six-electron oxidation of NH_4^+ to NO_2^-, whereas the second group, all with the generic prefix "Nitro", oxidize NO_2^- to NO_3^-, a two-electron oxidation.

NH_4^+ oxidizers are usually enumerated and isolated in liquid inorganic media by MPN techniques (1.3) but can also be recognized on solid chalk-containing media as colonies producing acid (HNO_2) and therefore surrounded by clear zones. NO_2^- oxidizers are much more difficult to culture on solid media, and are almost exclusively isolated by MPN techniques in liquid media. *Nitrosomonas europeae* and *Nitrobacter winogradskyi* are the types most commonly isolated from soils, sewage, and the freshwater environment, and these organisms are accordingly often considered to be the most important nitrifiers, but their appearance may simply represent successful competition with other nitrifiers in isolation procedures. *Nitrosospira briensis* may have a special niche in weathered rocks, and is often isolated in large numbers along with other nitrifiers from the surface of both magmatic and sedimentary rocks, which may contain anything from 10–500 g NH_4^+ tonne^{-1}. Marine and fresh-water isolates appear to be virtually confined to sediments, which presumably reflects the dependence of the nitrifiers on NH_4^+ generation via ammonification, most of which occurs in sediments.

Viable counts of nitrifiers in soils and sediments range from 10^3–10^5 organisms g^{-1}, but much larger numbers (10^7–10^8 organisms g^{-1}) are generally described in high NH_4^+ environments such as activated sludge (9.3). Both groups are roughly equally represented. It may however be true that current estimates of numbers of some species are severe under-estimates, and are largely a reflection of the cultural conditions used in enumeration procedures. Independent estimates of nitrifier biomass may be made by relating rates of nitrification in pure culture experiments to those observed in soil or sediment samples. Estimates such as this confirm the view that conventional enumeration procedures considerably under-estimate the number of nitrifiers present. An alternative explanation, however, is that considerable non-lithotrophic nitrification occurs in some environments. Observations of N-SERVE-inhibited soils support the view that non-lithotrophic nitrification may be significant in some soils, particularly under extreme conditions. A number of soil microorganisms could be organotrophic nitrifiers, including soil fungi such as *Aspergillus* spp., and certain soil bacteria like *Arthrobacter* spp. Both of these will produce significant amounts of NO_2^-, NO_3^- and other oxidized N compounds when grown under conditions of high NH_4^+.

Considerable overall free energy change is available in the oxidation of NH_4^+ to NO_2^- ($-276\,kJ$ per mol NH_4^+ oxidized) and in the oxidation of NO_2^- to NO_3^- ($-73\,kJ$ per mol NO_2^- oxidized.) Chemolithotrophic bacteria, however, have to expend reducing power and therefore ATP in the reduction of CO_2. Also, NAD cannot be reduced directly by the oxidation of inorganic compounds such as NO_2^- because of the in-appropriate redox potential of the NO_2^-/NO_3^- couple, and cytochromes are the electron acceptors for many N and S (7.1) oxidations. NAD reduction therefore requires energy-dependent flow against the usual electrode-potential gradient. An inevitable consequence of growth on inorganic compounds is a relatively low growth yield (per mole substrate). Generation times of nitrifiers are generally measured in hours even under ideal conditions, and are almost certainly of the order of days in most soils and sediments.

Important factors affecting nitrification include temperature and redox. Nitrifiers are obligately aerobic, and nitrification is considered not to occur in significant amount at redox values lower than $+200\,mV$, although NO_2^- oxidation is more sensitive than NH_4^+ oxidation. NO_2^- tends to accumulate at low temperature ($<6°$). Plant exudates have also been reported to have suppressive effects on nitrification, and there is some dispute as to whether nitrification is inhibited under climax vegetation. It is certainly true that the removal of climax vegetation results in a massive increase in NO_3^- levels in soils, but it is possible that the low level of NO_3^- under extensive plant cover is merely a consequence of plant demand.

Several mathematical models of nitrification have been proposed. Such models can be used to predict nitrifier biomass, growth rates, and concentrations of NH_4^+, NO_3^- and NO_2^- under different conditions of NH_4^+ loading, and at different temperatures and oxygen concentrations. This kind of modelling can be of great practical value in designing sewage treatment plants (9.3), and can also be useful in the prediction of nitrifier response to NH_4^+ fertilizer applications.

The biochemistry of nitrification in organotrophs and lithotrophs is probably very similar, but remains relatively obscure. During the six-electron oxidation catalysed by the "nitroso" group, hydroxylamine (NH_2OH) is almost certainly an intermediate and traces of nitric oxide (NO) and nitrous oxide (N_2O) are evolved. However, N_2O and NO do not seem to be utilized by NH_4^+ oxidizers, and are probably produced as a by-product of some as yet undescribed intermediate, perhaps nitroxyl (HNO, valence $+1$). Accordingly the process may proceed in the following manner

$$NH_4^+ \rightarrow NH_2OH \rightarrow HNO \rightarrow NO_2^-.$$

The process is poorly understood and the existence of HNO, which is very unstable, has never been proven. The first enzyme involved in the oxidation of NH_4^+ to NH_2OH is an oxygenase which has a requirement for reducing power. Oxygen is directly incorporated into the substrate, and the reaction may be analogous to the oxygenase-catalysed oxidation of CH_4 by methylotrophs (5.7). N-SERVE operates by inhibition of this particular enzymic step. A subsequent cytochrome-linked oxidation of NH_2OH to NO_2^- occurs without detectable intermediates. The oxidation of NO_2^- is much better understood and appears to be a cytochrome-linked, single-step hydrolytic oxidation.

6.4 Nitrate reduction

Many microorganisms have the capacity to reduce N oxides (NO_3^-, NO_2^-, NO, N_2O) under anoxic conditions, when such compounds replace O_2 as a terminal electron acceptor in respiration. When the reduction proceeds as far as the generation of the gaseous products N_2 and N_2O which are lost from the system, the process is known as denitrification. Respiratory nitrate reduction (dissimilatory nitrate reduction) should be distinguished from the quite different process known as assimilatory nitrate reduction, where in plants and microorganisms NO_3^- is reductively assimilated into tissues to fulfil an N requirement. In the latter case the quantity of N being transferred is relatively small and subsequently immobilized, whereas in the former case large amounts of N oxides are used as electron sinks, are reduced, and released to the environment.

The ability to reduce N oxides in a dissimilatory fashion is widespread amongst soil and aquatic microbes, including eukaryotes, although not all microorganisms can carry out all potential reductive steps. More than 40% of soil and marine genera contain isolates capable of reducing NO_3^- to NO_2^-, but the more significant further reductive steps leading to denitrification are restricted to bacteria of relatively few genera. Quantitatively, members of the chemoorganotrophic genera *Bacillus*, *Micrococcus* and *Pseudomonas* are probably the most important in soils; *Pseudomonas*, *Aeromonas* and *Vibrio* in the aquatic environment. It is not uncommon to isolate 10^6 denitrifiers per g of soil or sediment.

The key factor in determining whether or not denitrification will take place is the redox of the environment. At redox levels of $+200\,mV$, the normal utilization of O_2 as a terminal electron acceptor is inhibited and dissimilatory nitrate reduction is activated. Vegetation promotes denitrification by providing electron donors and reducing conditions in the rhizosphere. Redox levels in sediments at depth are frequently lower than $+200\,mV$, and denitrification is a constant feature of such environments, the source of oxidized N compounds being the top layer where nitrification occurs. In soils, the water regime largely determines redox levels, and substantial denitrification occurs in waterlogged soils, releasing as much as 15% of the inorganic N under certain conditions. Some denitrification also occurs in well-drained soils because these contain waterfilled anaerobic micro-environments where the diffusion of O_2 is inhibited (1.6). On average on a yearly basis, NO_3^- respiration in soils may account for 10% of the carbon oxidized. Soil NO_3^- also fulfils a useful function as a redox "buffer" in that during the development of anoxic conditions when carbon oxidation is coupled to NO_3^- reduction, the redox of the immediate environment is maintained at $+200\,mV$ until all the NO_3^- is used (8.3). Temperature also has a marked effect on denitrification; in temperate climates most denitrification takes place between $10°$ and $40°$, with very little at temperatures $<5°$. pH also affects denitrification and acid soils tend both to build up significant quantities of NO_2^-, and to evolve significant amounts of gaseous products other than N_2.

N_2 has generally been considered to be the major product of denitrification, and it is certainly true that in a closed environment, the less fully reduced N products disappear with time, and N_2 accumulates (figure 6.2). However, substantial amounts of N_2O must also be released to the atmosphere—atmospheric levels of N_2O (0.2–0.5 ppm) confirm this view.

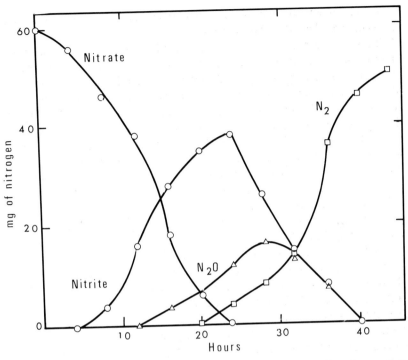

Figure 6.2 Products formed during denitrification in a loam (redrawn from Cooper, G. S. and Smith, R. L. (1963), *Soil Sci. Soc. Amer. Proc.* **27**, 659–662).

Significant quantities of N oxides are also produced by the internal combustion engine, and concern has been voiced over a possible build-up of these oxides in the upper atmosphere, which would contribute to the destruction of the earth's protective ozone (O_3) layer thus:

$$O_3 \xrightarrow{\text{light}} O_2 + [O]$$
$$N_2O + [O] \rightarrow 2NO$$
$$NO + O_3 \rightarrow NO_2 + O_2$$
$$NO_2 + [O] \rightarrow NO + O_2.$$

However, the oxides produced by denitrification and nitrification (6.3) probably greatly exceed in amount those resulting from human actions, and there is no evidence to suggest that this is increasing. Further public interest in N oxides arises from the toxic effects of NO_2^-. The disease known as methaemoglobinaemia arises when NO_2^- enters the bloodstream and reacts with haemoglobin, leading to an impairment of O_2 transport, particularly in infants. The disease is almost always attributable to high NO_3^- levels in drinking water supplies, and the subsequent reduction of NO_3^- to NO_2^- in the gastrointestinal tract by facultative anaerobes like *Escherichia coli*. There has also been concern over the possibility of the formation of nitrosamines in the environment by the chemical condensation of secondary amines with NO_2^-

$$\begin{array}{ccc} \underset{R}{\overset{R}{>}}NH + NO_2^- & \longrightarrow & \underset{R}{\overset{R}{>}}N-N{=}O + OH^- \\[4pt] \text{secondary amine} & & \text{nitrosamine} \end{array}$$

There is evidence that nitrosamines are teratogenic and carcinogenic, although whether toxicologically significant quantities of these compounds are produced via reactions as these is not known at present.

The production of NO_2^-, NO and N_2O by most denitrifiers suggests that the dissimilatory nitrate reduction pathway is as follows:

$$NO_3^- \to NO_2^- \to NO \to N_2O \to N_2.$$

The first enzyme in the sequence, nitrate reductase, is a membrane-bound iron and molybdenum-containing protein whose synthesis is repressed in the presence of O_2. Further reductions are carried out in a stepwise fashion by the other enzymes in the sequence, with cytochromes as electron donors, except in the case of nitrite reductase where a flavoprotein is involved. Assimilatory nitrate reduction is quite a different process, both in terms of the enzymology and the products evolved. The electron donors in this case are reduced coenzymes, and assimilatory nitrate reductase is not inhibited by O_2. The final product of assimilatory nitrate reduction is not N_2 but NH_4^+, and certain assimilatory nitrite reductases have been shown to contain the unusual sirohydrochlorin groups associated with multielectron transfers, thus resembling sulphite reductases (7.1). It has been suggested that assimilatory NO_3^- reduction pathways may be the reverse of nitrification, and that NH_2OH is therefore a likely contender for a transient intermediate

$$NO_3^- \to NO_2^- \to NH_2OH \to NH_4^+.$$

Evidence is now beginning to accumulate which suggests that under certain conditions microorganisms may be able to use NO_3^- as an electron sink in a fermentative fashion, producing NH_4^+ as an end product rather than reduced organic compounds. This special kind of dissimilatory nitrate reduction may be biochemically similar to the assimilatory process, and is sometimes called *fermentative nitrate reduction* to distinguish it from respiratory dissimilatory nitrate reduction.

6.5 Nitrogen fixation

Biological N_2 fixation transforms considerably smaller amounts of N than do ammonification and assimilation in the N cycle, although it necessarily plays a key role in offsetting denitrification. In balanced terrestrial ecosystems such as forests or permanent grasslands, productivity is generally limited by deficiencies of sulphur, potassium or phosphorus rather than nitrogen. However, the impact of man in perturbing the N cycle in such areas, largely by persistent cultivation, has ensured that on a global basis productivity is limited by the input of fixed N. Chemical fixation accounts for some 25% of the total global N_2 fixation, and is largely of consequence in the developed countries of the world, whereas in under-developed or developing countries the only input may be via biological fixation. The remarkable inertness of N_2, combined with the present cost of energy, have combined to make chemically fixed N_2 a very expensive commodity. As the world's demand for chemically fixed N_2 continues to grow (the total world demand in the year 2000 is estimated at 140×10^6 tonnes N compared with 1980 demand of 56×10^6 tonnes N), many developing countries find they have a considerable and increasing N deficit, largely because of the cost of N fertilizers. The key to maximizing food production in the future lies in increasing yields per unit of land, which can only be achieved by cultivating high-yield crops. N input has a major role to play in maximizing yields, and therefore much thought and effort has been and is being applied to exploring ways of exploiting biological N_2 fixation as a much cheaper, efficient and environmentally desirable way of maximizing crop yields.

The capacity to assimilate N_2 and reduce it to NH_4^+ has not been shown by any eukaryote so far investigated, and appears to be entirely restricted to prokaryotes. Many different types of prokaryotes possess this facility, and fossil heterocystous (and therefore presumably N_2-fixing) blue-green algae date from the time that the first eukaryotes appeared on earth (1.5×10^9 years ago). If one accepts the endosymbiont theory of the origins of the eukaryote (4.9), there is no really convincing explanation as to why all eukaryotes appear to be devoid of such a useful facility.

The enzyme responsible for N_2 fixation is called nitrogenase, and this enzyme quite fortuitously has the property of reducing a variety of triple-bonded compounds in addition to N_2 ($N{\equiv}N$), including hydrogen cyanide ($H{-}C{\equiv}N$), nitrous oxide ($N{\equiv}N^+{-}O^-$) and acetylene ($HC{\equiv}CH$). The ability of nitrogenase to quantitatively reduce C_2H_2 to ethylene (C_2H_4) is the basis of a rapid and sensitive assay procedure. Before the advent of the C_2H_2 technique, the detection of N_2 fixation involved laborious determinations of total N balances, or the use of the stable mass isotope $^{15}N_2$, which is expensive and can only be detected by a mass spectrometer, whereas C_2H_4 can easily be assayed by the relatively simple technique of gas–liquid chromatography.

Nitrogenase is composed of an association between two components, a non-haem iron/sulphur protein, and a non-haem iron, molybdenum and sulphur-containing protein. Active nitrogenase preparations can often be reconstituted in cell-free systems from a heterologous mixture of these proteins from different prokaryotes. The relatively small differences in structure and molecular weight between nitrogenase proteins from different prokaryotes may be largely attributable to peripheral modifications relating to oxygen protection mechanisms. Protein 1, the larger of the two proteins, contains 20–38 Fe atoms depending on organism, and 20–24 acid-labile S atoms in a molecule of molecular weight 200 000–230 000 daltons. Protein 1 also contains 1–2 atoms of molybdenum per molecule. Protein 2 contains 4 Fe atoms and 4 acid labile S atoms in a molecule of molecular weight of 55 000–72 000 daltons. Nitrogenase activity *in vitro* requires a source of reducing power, ATP, Mg(II) and strictly anoxic conditions; indeed, both proteins are irreversibly inactivated in the presence of O_2.

The precise mechanism by which triple-bonded compounds are reduced is not fully understood, but studies of nitrogenase complexes by electron paramagnetic resonance, Mössbauer spectroscopy and optical spectroscopy indicate that oxidation/reduction reactions occur within iron–sulphur clusters in proteins 1 and 2. It is believed that protein 2 is reduced via an electron donor of appropriate redox potential, probably ferredoxin (in cell-free systems the non-physiological donor $Na_2S_2O_3$ is often used). An electron transfer to protein 1 is induced by an ATP-Mg complex (figure 6.3) and triple-bonded compounds (which presumably bind at the molybdenum site) are reduced in a stepwise fashion. No intermediates have been detected, and in the case of N_2 reduction, NH_4^+ is the first detectable product. In cell-free systems, 15 molecules of ATP are required for each molecule of N_2 reduced, and presumably the six-electron reduction of N_2 requires six complete cycles of the system (figure 6.3).

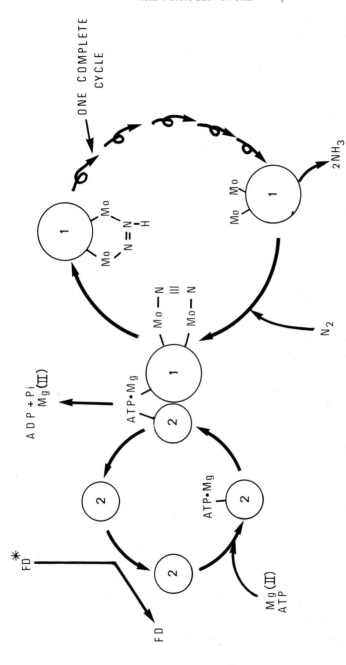

Figure 6.3 The mechanism of nitrogenase. The small subunit (2) is reduced by ferredoxin (FD*) and forms an ATP-Mg complex. This shuttles reductant to the large subunit (1), which in turn binds N_2 (modified from Postgate, J. R. (1976), *La Recherche* **66**, 335–347).

Table 6.2 N$_2$-fixing systems

A. Free-living genera and groups

Aerobes	Microaerophilic	Facultative anaerobes	Anaerobes
Azotobacter	*Corynebacterium*	*Klebsiella*	*Clostridium*
Beijerinckia	*Azospirillum*	*Bacillus*	Phototrophic bacteria
Azomonas	Blue-green algae	*Citrobacter*	*Desulfovibrio*
Azotococcus	*Rhizobium*	*Erwinia*	*Desulfotomaculum*
Methane oxidizers		*Enterobacter*	
Heterocystous blue-green algae			
Thiobacillus			

B. Symbiotic associations

Nodule	Rhizosphere Temperate	Rhizosphere Tropical	Phyllosphere	Blue-green algae	Others
Legume + *Rhizobium*	*Bacillus* (non-specific)	*Azospirillum* (non-specific)	*Beijerinckia*	Lichens	Termites + Enterobacteria
Alder etc. + *Frankia*	*Klebsiella* (non-specific)	*Beijerinckia* (non-specific)	*Azotobacter*	*Azolla* + *Anabaena azollae*	Other animals + Enterobacteria
		Azotobacter paspali + *Paspalum notatum*		Cycads + *Anabaena* or *Nostoc*	
				Gunnera + *Nostoc*	
				Protozoa? Sponges? Corals?	

Nitrogenase systems also catalyse the ATP-dependent reduction of protons to H_2 at a different site on the molecule. Precisely why this should be so is not clear, but there are practical consequences in that substantial amounts (up to 50%) of reducing power and energy are lost in H_2 generation. Some aerobic N_2 fixers appear to minimize this loss to some extent by the possession of a unidirectional hydrogenase which catalyses the O_2-dependent oxidation of H_2, regenerating reducing equivalents and energy.

NH_4^+ is directly assimilated via glutamine synthetase and GOGAT (6.2). High levels of NH_4^+ repress N_2 fixation, and the regulation of N_2 fixation by NH_4^+ operates through the enzyme glutamine synthetase. A complex enzyme cascade controlled by NH_4^+ levels in the cell promotes the adenylation of tyrosine residues on the enzyme, and adenylated enzyme is both inactive and inhibits the transcription of nitrogenase.

Since the advent of the C_2H_2 reduction test, the list of prokaryotes designated as N_2 fixers has expanded enormously. The requirement for anaerobic conditions during N_2 fixation is reflected in the kinds of organisms listed in table 6.2. Anaerobes, microaerophiles, and facultative anaerobes are clearly not exposed to the danger of oxygen damage to the N_2 fixation system, unlike the free-living aerobes, particularly blue-green algae that evolve O_2. Several of the mechanisms which have evolved to minimize O_2 damage are shown by the most common of the aerobic soil N_2-fixers, *Azotobacter vinelandii*. These mechanisms include the production of copious amounts of extracellular polysaccharide which inhibits O_2 diffusion to the cell surface, the possession of an additional low-affinity terminal oxidase, only partially coupled to ATP generation, which functions as an O_2 scavenger, and the conformational conversion of nitrogenase to a protected form. Heterocystous blue-green algae have solved the problem of O_2 repression by packaging nitrogenase in hetero-cysts to which access of O_2 is regulated by a thick, relatively impermeable cell wall, while a very active respiratory chain scavenges trace amounts of O_2. Heterocysts also lack photosystem II and ancillary light-harvesting pigments and therefore do not evolve O_2 during photosynthesis, although photophosphorylation does occur. Non-heterocystous blue-green algae normally fix N_2 under microaerophilic conditions only, but there is some evidence for repression of photosystem II in colonies of *Trichodesmium* spp. Root nodule systems such as the *Rhizobium* association have some requirement for O_2, and bacteroids have, like *Azotobacter* cells, an alternative low-affinity oxidase, largely independent of ATP generation, that functions as an O_2 scavenger. Effective N_2-fixing nodules also contain

Table 6.3   Relative agronomic efficiencies of some N_2-fixing systems (modified from Postgate and Hill, 1979)

Organism or system			N fixed (kg ha^{-1} yr^{-1})
Nodules	Legumes:	tick clover (tropical)	897
		lucerne (temperate)	45–673
	Non legumes:	*Alnus* (temperate)	139
		Alnus (arctic)	62
		Casuarina (tropical)	52
Rhizosphere associations		rye grass (temperate)	61
		Paspalum (tropical)	15–93
		grassland (temperate)	39
Blue-green associations		lichens (tropical)	10–100
		Azolla (tropical)	83–125
		lichens (arctic)	1–2
Free-living		blue-green crusts (temperate)	15–50
		blue-green in rice paddies (tropical)	10–80
		Azotobacter	<1
		Clostridium	<1

leghaemoglobin (4.6), an oxygen-carrying haemoprotein similar to haemoglobin, which facilitates transfer of O_2 at a concentration appropriate for nitrogenase activity but adequate for bacteroid respiration.

The relative inefficiency of free-living N_2 fixers, excluding phototrophic organisms, has been known for many years, and this is illustrated by the comparison with the efficiency of symbiotic associations shown in table 6.3. Non-phototrophic free-living N_2 fixers are unable to obtain the large amounts of reducing power and energy necessary for N_2 fixation when growing under normal conditions, whereas a consideration of table 6.3 indicates the agronomic importance of blue-green algae, which have almost unlimited access to energy and reducing power. This is best illustrated by rice culture, where up to 50 % of the N demand of the crop is met by N_2-fixing blue-green algae such as *Anabaena* spp., *Tolypothrix* spp. and *Calothrix* spp. There are, however, less dramatic examples where blue-green algae contribute to steady N gain in fields of temperate wheat, by growing in and around the base of stems of both the growing crop and the stubble left after harvesting. Blue-green algae are presumably almost entirely responsible for marine fixation on the global scale, although significant blooms of blue-green algae in the oceans are rare. A substantial amount of marine fixation may occur in coral reefs and in littoral areas in

Table 6.4 Global N_2 fixation rates (tonnes yr^{-1}) (compiled from Quispell, 1974)

			Area under cultivation (ha $\times 10^6$)
Agriculture	Legumes	35×10^6	250
	Rice	4×10^6	135
	Remaining terrestrial	100×10^6	12 000
Marine		60×10^6	36 000
Industrial		30×10^6	

symbiotic associations with marine plants and animals, although it is not known for certain if these associations fix free N_2.

Agronomically, by far the most significant N_2 fixation occurs in various symbiotic associations between prokaryotes and plants, particularly the legume–*Rhizobium* symbiosis, whose characteristics have already been discussed (4.6). A significant part of the large increase in the world's primary productivity since the beginning of this century has been brought about by the spread of legume crops to areas where legumes were previously lacking. New forage and pulse crops are constantly under test under a variety of conditions, and one of the greatest challenges to agriculture is to develop more efficient strains of *Rhizobium* capable of infecting tropical and subtropical legumes, which are poor N_2-fixers due to existing infection by members of the ineffective promiscuous "cowpea" miscellany. Legumes currently account for more N_2 fixation than any other single defined source (table 6.4). Other terrestrial N_2 fixation considerably exceeds that calculated for the marine environment, and C_2H_2 reduction assays indicate that the majority of this fixation goes on in the rhizosphere of plants where large amounts of substrate are present.

The importance of the *Frankia* root nodule association between actinomycete-like organisms and the roots of a variety of woody perennial plants including the alder, is now beginning to be recognized. Some 13 genera in 8 families of woody dicotyledonous plants are known to include species that have root nodules and show significant N_2 fixation rates. The significance of these plants in land reclamation is considerable, and they have other uses, such as forage potential (table 6.5). Until recently the actinomycete(s) seen in such root nodules had not convincingly been grown in pure culture, although several cross-infection groups based on crushed nodule inoculates had been described. However, the endophytes

Table 6.5 Examples of plants possessing nodules with actinomycete endosymbiont (abbreviated from Postgate and Hill, 1979)

Plant	Uses
Casuarina	Timber
Hippophae	Reclamation of sand dunes
Purshia	Forage
Myrica	Wax
Alnus	Timber and reclamation
Dryas	Reclamation
Ceanothus	Forage

from several different plants have recently been cultured and shown to produce effective N_2-fixing nodules in their host plants (4.6). This line of work opens the way to understanding the nature of the specificity of the endophytes, in order to explore the possibility of using them as endosymbionts of more useful food crops.

Blue-green algae can also form associations with higher plants (tables 6.2 and 6.3) and some of these almost rival the root nodule associations in agronomic significance. An example of this is the association between the heterocystous N_2 fixer *Anabaena azollae* and the small aquatic fern *Azolla*, which is used extensively as a "green manure" in rice culture in tropical and subtropical areas. Another example of an agronomically important blue-green association is the group of lichens collectively known as reindeer moss and which forms the main part of the diet of tundra ruminants.

Several other associations have received attention over the years, but by far the most interest has been generated by observations of agronomically significant N_2 fixation in the rhizosphere of certain tropical and semi-tropical grain crops and forage grasses. Genera which show significant C_2H_2 reduction rates include *Brachiaris*, *Hyparrhenia*, *Digitaria*, *Andropogon* and *Paspalum*. The rhizosphere organisms concerned are not true root inhabitants, although tending to concentrate on plant roots. Systems which have been studied include the *Azospirillum lipoferum* and *A. braziliense* association with the roots of maize and with a number of tropical grasses including *Digitaria decumbens*, and the association of *Beijerincka indica* with the roots of sugar cane. *Azotobacter paspali* is characteristically associated with the roots of the forage grass *Paspalum notatum*. Nitrogenase activity shows considerable seasonal variation and is insignificant below 25°C, and this has raised doubts as to the importance of temperate associations. However, they are rather more active than the equivalent temperate associations now known to exist between *Bacillus* and *Enterobacter* spp. and cereal crops and *Festuca* sward. The *A. paspáli–Paspalum* association is unusual and distinct in that *A. paspali* apparently has a very specific association with the roots of certain tetraploid *Paspalum* cultivars, whereas the other systems do not show such specificity. The *Paspalum* system can be considered to be intermediate between these loose N_2-fixing rhizosphere associations and the true nodule symbioses. Rhizosphere N_2 fixation is often a feature of tropical and subtropical plants which have anaplerotic CO_2 fixation mechanisms and which therefore excrete significant quantities of C_4 organic acids (C_4 plants). *Azospirillum* spp. are specifically stimulated by C_4 acids, and this may account for the common occurrence of these bacteria in the rhizosphere. Some reports suggest that tropical rhizosphere N_2 fixation is comparable in scale to that observed in leguminous crops (table 6.3), but we still do not know how agronomically significant these associations are, because current estimates of how much N transfer actually occurs are contradictory.

It is not surprising that the rhizosphere should be a site of active N_2 fixation, since the root provides substantial amounts of substrate, and roots also deplete the surrounding soil of fixed N, producing selective enrichment conditions for N_2 fixers. The organisms most frequently implicated have also been shown to produce antibiotics and plant growth regulating substances; indeed, there are those who believe that any improvement in plant yield can be exclusively attributed to such substances rather than to N_2 fixation. Rhizosphere N_2 fixation is clearly important in the general sense as the site of much of terrestrial N_2 fixation, but whether significantly more N transfer to plants can be achieved by encouraging particular rhizosphere bacteria remains to be established.

REFERENCES

Books

Fenchel, T. and Blackburn, T. H. (1979) *Bacterial and Mineral Cycling*, Academic Press.
Quispell, A. (1974) *The Biology of Nitrogen Fixation*, North Holland Publishing Company.
Stewart, W. D. P. (1975) *Nitrogen Fixation by Free-living Microorganisms*, Cambridge University Press.
Subba Rao, N. S. (1980) *Recent Advances in Biological Nitrogen Fixation*, Edward Arnold.

Articles

Bazin, M. J., Saunders, P. T. and Prosser, J. I. (1976) Models of microbial interactions in soil. *CRC Critical Reviews in Microbiology*, **4**, 463–498.
Belser, L. W. (1979) Population ecology of nitrifying bacteria. *Ann. Rev. Microbiol.*, **33**, 309–333.

Brown, C. M., McDonald-Brown, D. S. and Meers, J. L. (1974) Physiological aspects of inorganic nitrogen metabolism. *Adv. Microbial Physiol.*, **11**, 1–52.

Brown, M. E. (1974) Seed and root bacterization. *Ann. Rev. Phytopathol.*, **12**, 181–197.

Delwiche, C. C. and Bryan, B. A. (1976). Denitrification. *Ann. Rev. Microbiol.*, **30**, 241–262.

Fochte, D. D. and Chang, A. C. (1975) Nitrification and denitrification processes related to waste water treatment. *Adv. Appl. Microbiol.*, **19**, 153–186.

Fochte, D. D. and Verstraete, W. (1977) Biochemical ecology of nitrification and denitrification. *Adv. Microbial Ecol.*, **1**, 135–214.

Postgate, J. R. and Hill, S. (1979) Nitrogen fixation, in *Microbial Ecology: a Conceptual Approach*, editors J. M. Lynch and N. J. Poole, Blackwell Scientific, 191–213.

Robson, R. L. and Postgate, J. R. (1980) Oxygen and hydrogen in biological nitrogen fixation. *Ann. Rev. Microbiol.*, **34**, 183–208.

Soderlund, R. and Svennson, B. H. (1976) The global nitrogen cycle, in *Nitrogen, Phosphorus and Sulphur–Global Cycles*, Scope Report 7, Ecological Bulletins (Stockholm), 23–74.

Stouthamer, A. H. (1976) Biochemistry and genetics of nitrate reductase in bacteria. *Adv. Microbial Physiol.*, **14**, 315–375.

Suzuki, E. (1974) Mechanisms of inorganic oxidation and energy coupling. *Ann. Rev. Microbiol.*, **28**, 85–102.

Yoch, D. C. and Carruthers, R. P. (1979) Bacterial iron sulphur proteins. *Microbiological Rev.*, **43**, 384–421.

CHAPTER SEVEN

MICROBIAL TRANSFORMATIONS
OF OTHER ELEMENTS

7.1 The sulphur cycle

Microbial sulphur metabolism has a considerable impact on the biosphere by converting S to forms appropriate for the growth of cells, producing significant quantities of an electron acceptor (SO_4^{2-}) that can be used as an important electron sink under anoxic conditions, and by contributing to certain geochemical processes (7.7). S metabolism involves both oxidative and reductive processes, and the co-operative action of these gives rise to the S cycle shown in figure 7.1. The S cycle bears some similarity to the N cycle: it is essentially an eight-electron shuttle between the most oxidized (valence $+6$) form of S in the environment, SO_4^{2-}, and the most reduced (valence -2) form, S^{2-}. The S cycle also resembles the N cycle in that certain of the processes are accomplished exclusively by prokaryotes and it is these processes that will be dealt with in most detail.

The most conspicuous sulphur-containing compounds in biomass are the amino acids cysteine, cystine and methionine, which have thiol groups with valence -2, but sulphate esters, such as in polysaccharide sulphates and aromatic sulphates, also occur. Sulphate esters are readily hydrolysed by many different eukaryotic and prokaryotic microorganisms, releasing SO_4^{2-} to the environment. How much S is released by this means is not easy to calculate in the absence of global estimates for SO_4^{2-} production by other processes, but it is probably small compared with the other processes. Under oxic conditions, thiol groups are oxidized to SO_3^{2-} or SO_4^{2-}, or they may be desulphydrated to yield S^{2-}. Under anoxic conditions, desulphydration predominates and S^{2-} as H_2S may be released to the atmosphere. The capacity to oxidize or desulphydrate reduced S components is possessed by many eukaryotic and prokaryotic microorganisms. The global mineralization by these pathways is probably

147

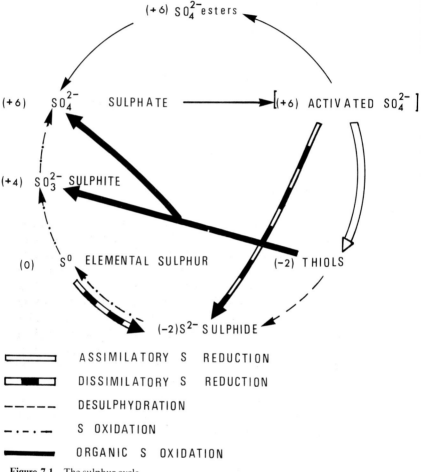

Figure 7.1 The sulphur cycle.

10^9–10^{10} tonnes S yr^{-1}, although the relative contribution of the alternative pathways is not known. The oxidation of methionine may also produce volatile S compounds like methane thiol (CH_3SH), and dimethyl-sulphide (CH_3SSCH_3).

Green plants and many microorganisms assimilate SO_4^{2-} as their sole source of S, and consequently there is a requirement for the reduction of this S to a level appropriate for incorporation into thiol groups. This reductive process is known as *assimilatory sulphate reduction*, and it is

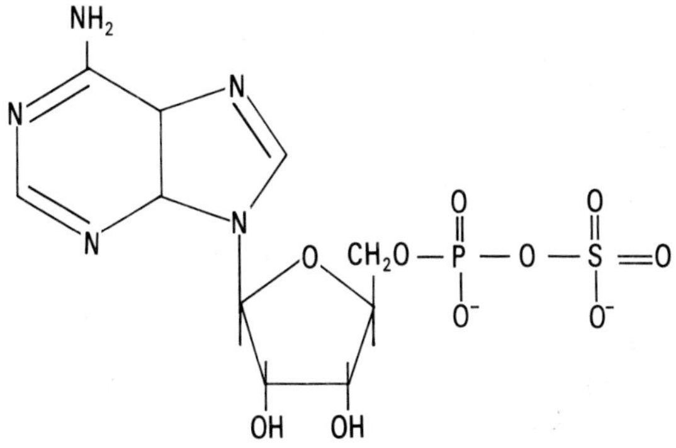

Figure 7.2 Adenosine-5'-phosphosulphate (APS).

analogous to assimilatory nitrate reduction (6.4), except that before reduction occurs there is a requirement for SO_4^{2-} to be "activated" as a high energy carrier form. Two activated forms of SO_4^{2-} exist, adenosine-5'-phosphosulphate (APS) (figure 7.2), which is formed by an adenylation reaction with ATP, and 3'-phosphoadenosine-5'-phosphosulphate (PAPS) which is formed by a further phosphorylation of APS at the 3' position. PAPS acts as a high-energy SO_4^{2-} donor in a variety of esterification reactions, and is usually the substrate participating in assimilatory sulphate reduction, although APS is sometimes implicated. Assimilatory sulphate reduction involves the NADPH-linked 2-electron reduction of PAPS to give SO_3^{2-} and 3-phosphoadenosine monophosphate, followed by an NADPH-linked 6-electron reduction of SO_3^{2-} to S^{2-} catalysed by sulphite reductase. S^{2-} is incorporated into biomass via a condensation with O-acetyl serine, generating cysteine (figure 7.3). Neither SO_3^{2-} nor S^{2-} is

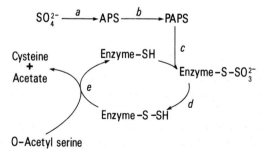

Figure 7.3 Assimilatory sulphate reduction. a, ATP sulphurylase; b, APS kinase; c, PAPS sulphotransferase; d, sulphite reductase; e, O-acetylserine sulphydrylase.

normally released from the enzyme complex during the entire process, although some eukaryotes produce H_2S presumably from "excess" assimilatory SO_4^{2-} reduction.

One of the most important features of the S cycle is the generation of vast amounts of S^{2-} through the SO_4^{2-}-linked oxidation of carbon compounds. In the marine environment, SO_4^{2-} at 28 mM (2.1) constitutes an enormous reservoir of S—about 3.6×10^{15} tonnes, and oceanic water contains more than 500 times more oxidation equivalents in the form of SO_4^{2-} than in the form of O_2, since O_2 has a relatively low solubility. Under anoxic conditions, certain obligately anaerobic bacteria carry out an anaerobic respiratory process known as *dissimilatory sulphate reduction*, where SO_4^{2-} or other oxidized S compounds are used as electron acceptors and reduced to S^{2-}. It is now believed that this process accounts for up to 50% of the carbon mineralized in marine sediments, and this kind of SO_4^{2-} reduction probably constitutes the greatest single flux in the S cycle. There are no global figures available for annual S^{2-} production, but it has been calculated that terrestrial coastal and swampy areas alone account for the transformation of 10^9 tonnes S, an amount comparable to the global total of S mineralized. Dissimilatory sulphate reduction is also important in that energy is transferred from carbon to S^{2-}, to be released later when S^{2-} participates in oxidative reactions in other food chains.

There are presently only three genera of SO_4^{2-}-reducing bacteria described: the motile vibroid genus *Desulfovibrio*, the thermophilic spore-forming genus *Desulfotomaculum*, and the non-motile genus *Desulfomonas*. The distribution of these bacteria is ubiquitous, representatives being found over a wide range of pH, temperature and salinity in soils and sediments. The organisms however constitute a physiologically distinct group, their oxidative metabolism being entirely based on the reduction of oxidized S compounds. *Desulfovibrio* spp. are mixotrophic, H_2 being oxidized as well as a variety of organic compounds, and such utilization of H_2 has important implications for methanogenesis in freshwater sediments (5.6, 8.3). Although SO_4^{2-} reduction has been investigated for many years, no other SO_4^{2-} reducing genera have been discovered. This may however simply reflect the capacity of these types to proliferate under the enrichment conditions in use to date, and a more determined attempt to develop other media might well yield a variety of types.

If electron donors and SO_4^{2-} are in sufficient quantity, the critical factor in SO_4^{2-} reduction is the redox potential of the environment. Redox values of 0 mV or below (dependent on pH) are necessary to allow the activity and proliferation of these bacteria, and consequently their culture and enumeration is not easy. In anoxic sediments, *Desulfovibrio* spp. may number 10^6–10^7 organisms gm^{-1}; in soils, SO_4^{2-} reduction is significant only when waterlogged conditions prevail, and normally relatively small numbers (10^2–10^3 gm^{-1}) of SO_4^{2-} reducers are to be found; a small but detectable amount of SO_4^{2-} reduction does go on in oxic soils, supporting the view that water-filled anoxic microenvironments exist even in well-drained soils. However, in terrestrial environments most SO_4^{2-} reduction occurs in waterlogged swampy areas (both marine and freshwater), and presumably the major emission of H_2S to the atmosphere occurs from these areas, since S^{2-} (as HS^-) from the deep-sea environment would be oxidized before reaching the surface.

High levels of S^{2-} are toxic to plants, and can have significant economic consequences (as in the wilting disease achi-ochi seen in paddy fields). Animals are also affected, and there have been human fatalities amongst sewage workers working in enclosed areas close to anoxic sewage. Other significant aspects of SO_4^{2-} reduction are considered in 7.7 and 7.8.

The mechanism of dissimilatory sulphate reduction is analogous to that of dissimilatory nitrate reduction (6.4) and is distinct from assimilatory sulphate reduction. "Activated SO_4^{2-}" (as APS) participates in the process, and APS reduction, sulphite reduction, trithionate reduction and thio-sulphate reduction are probably involved in a cyclical fashion as indicated in figure 7.4. The reduction of SO_3^{2-} generates $S_3O_6^{2-}$ and $S_2O_3^{2-}$, composite molecules containing S atoms of different valence, sulphane atoms at valence -1, and sulphone atoms at valence $+5$. Although SO_3^{2-} reduction differs in mechanism in the assimilatory and dissimilatory processes, the sulphite reductases in both pathways are very similar

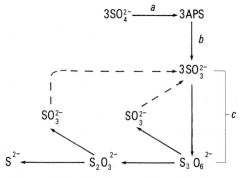

Figure 7.4 Dissimilatory sulphate reduction. a, ATP sulphurylase; b, APS sulphotrans-ferase; c, sulphite reductase.

enzymes, being very large iron- and flavin-containing proteins with characteristic reduced porphyrin groups known as sirohydrochlorins. In the dissimilatory process, specific cytochromes (including cytochrome C_3) donate electrons at the various reductive steps, rather than NADPH, and ATP is generated by these electron transfer reactions. The redox potentials of the S_{oxid}/S_{red} couples are considerably less positive than that of $\frac{1}{2}O_2/H_2O$, and as a consequence, large amounts of substrate are consumed, sustaining a relatively long microbial generation time.

There is evidence that a variety of eukaryotic and prokaryotic microorganisms may use S compounds fermentatively as electron sinks under certain conditions, e.g. elemental S (S^0) is reduced by phototrophic bacteria to H_2S during dark metabolism, but how this reduction is carried out is not clear. A few isolates of *Desulfovibrio* spp., and one aquatic organism, *Desulphuromonas acetoxidans*, do seem to reduce S^0 in a dissimilatory fashion through a cytochrome-linked reductase. These particular organisms are often to be found in consortial relationships with green phototrophic bacteria, oxidizing a restricted range of organic compounds at the expense of the reduction of S^0 to S^{2-}. The phototrophic bacteria oxidize S^{2-} to S^0, and thus an associative symbiosis is established where the tight coupling of S oxidation and reduction minimizes S leakage from the immediate environment. S^0 reduction is essentially restricted to areas where active S^0 deposition is taking place, and is insignificant on a global scale compared with dissimilatory SO_4^{2-} reduction.

S^{2-} is oxidized back to SO_4^{2-} partly chemically and partly through the activities of certain microorganisms. Quantitatively, the amount of S oxidized must roughly balance the total amount of S reduced by all reactions. The problem of differentiating enzymic and chemical oxidations has prevented a full understanding of the mechanisms of biological S oxidation to date, and indeed made it difficult to assess the importance of microbial activity during some of the transformations of S compounds. Certain specific prokaryotes have traditionally been considered to have a major role in S oxidation, and these can be divided into two main groups (table 7.1), the aerobic and microaerophilic chemotrophic S oxidizers (sometimes called the colourless S bacteria), and the anaerobic phototrophic S oxidizers (sometimes called the purple and green bacteria). The chemotrophic S oxidizers are a heterogeneous assortment of bacteria (table 7.1) including chemolithotrophs, best exemplified by the ubiquitous genus *Thiobacillus*, and a variety of bacteria of doubtful taxonomic status including gliding bacteria such as *Beggiatoa* and *Achromatium*. The chemotrophic S oxidizers also include the thermophilic archaebacterium

Table 7.1 Sulphur-oxidizing bacteria

	Genus or group	Habitat	Comments
Chemotrophs	Sulfobacillus	Mine tips	Lithotroph, sporer, Fe(II) oxidizer, thermophilic
	Thiobacillus	Soil, water, marine	Mostly lithotrophs, one Fe(II) oxidizer, some denitrifiers, some thermophiles: deposit S⁰ outside cells
	Thiomicrospira	Marine	Lithotroph
	Sulfolobus	Geothermal springs	Lithotroph, thermophile, archaebacterium, Fe(II) oxidizer ("Ferrolobus" type)
	Thiobacterium	Water	Not grown in pure culture, deposit S⁰ inside cell, energy status not known
	Macromonas	Water	
	Thiovulum	Water	
	Thiospira	Water	
	Beggiatoa	Water, soil, marine	Gliding bacteria; deposit S⁰ inside cells, difficult to isolate and energy metabolism unknown
	Thioploca	Water, soil	
	Thiothrix	Water, soil, marine	
	Achromatium	Water	
	Thiodendron	Water, soil	Appendaged, energy status unknown
Phototrophs	Chromatiaceae (purple S bacteria)	Water, marine	Mixotrophs, deposit S⁰ inside cell except for Ectothiorhodospira spp. which deposit S⁰ outside cell
	Chlorobiaceae (green S bacteria)	Water, marine	Lithotrophs, S⁰ deposited outside cell
	Chloroflexaceae	Geothermal springs	Mixotrophs, S⁰ deposited outside cell; thermophiles
	Oscillatoria (blue-green alga)	Water	S⁰ deposited outside cell under anoxic conditions

Sulfolobus acidocaldarius, which occupies a characteristic geothermal niche (3.1, 3.3, 3.5). The phototrophic bacteria comprise the *Chromatiaceae* (purple S bacteria), the *Chlorobiaceae* (green S bacteria) and the newly described filamentous thermophilic flexibacteria exemplified by *Chloroflexus aurantiacus* (3.1). It is now known that at least one blue-green alga, *Oscillatoria limnetica*, is also capable of anaerobically oxidizing H_2S under certain conditions.

The main contributors to S oxidation in terrestrial environments are certainly the chemolithotrophic bacteria, which are widely distributed in soils and water, and indeed since many marine isolates are also known on a global basis they probably make the most important contribution. The phototrophic bacteria, some of which use reduced S compounds as electron donors in photosynthesis, are dependent on both light and anoxic conditions, and characteristically they predominantly occupy the upper layers of S^{2-}-rich sediments in fresh water and estuarine environments, occasionally producing blooms in the upper layers of stratified lakes and estuaries. The contribution of certain phototrophic bacteria to both the S cycle and primary productivity in certain shallow aquatic environments is not in doubt, but cannot be significant in mid-ocean since they are limited by light availability to depths where S^{2-} would not be present in

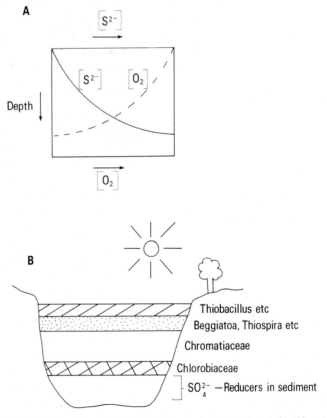

Figure 7.5 The distribution of sulphur-oxidizing bacteria and the relationship to sulphide and oxygen concentration. A, concentration of oxygen and sulphide in the lake according to depth; B, distribution of sulphur-oxidizing bacteria in an unmixed lake.

significant amounts. The niches which S-oxidizing bacteria occupy are principally determined by light, O_2 concentration and S^{2-} concentration (figure 7.5A). Figure 7.5B illustrates the likely distribution of various types of S oxidizers in a stratified lake, but it could equally well represent the distribution of types down the profile of a waterlogged soil, although clearly phototrophic bacteria are unlikely to contribute significantly in such an environment unless the top layers are translucent (as in certain estuarine sands).

The unusual prokaryotes listed in table 7.1 are generally considered to be the main contributors to S oxidation in the S cycle, but a considerable number of common fungi and bacteria including *Aspergillus* spp., *Bacillus* spp. and *Arthrobacter* spp. have also been shown to oxidize significant amounts of reduced S compounds when grown in pure culture. Even if such transformations are incidental, these organisms are present in large numbers in soils and the aquatic environment compared with *Thiobacillus* spp., suggesting that non-lithotrophic S oxidation may be quantitatively important. Unfortunately, no specific inhibitor of lithotrophic S oxidation is available to test the hypothesis.

The enzymic mechanisms involved in S oxidation are not fully understood, and what is known has been gleaned from the study of lithotrophic S oxidation by thiobacilli and phototrophic bacteria. Considerable variations in the types of enzymic interconversions are found from species to species, and it is unwise to generalize about the mechanisms involved; nevertheless, some general trends emerge. S^0 is deposited by cells growing in the presence of S^{2-} under both oxic and anoxic conditions (table 7.1). Despite the ready chemical oxidation of S^{2-} under oxic conditions, there is no doubt that both aerobes and anaerobes possess a cytochrome-linked oxidase which is responsible for the deposition of S^0. Many cells are also capable of oxidizing S^{2-}, producing a mixture of S^0, SO_3^{2-}, $S_2O_3^{2-}$ and various polythionates. The current view is that SO_3^{2-} is the first product of S^{2-} oxidation (at least one type of enzyme may be a kind of reverse sirohydrochlorin SO_4^{2-} reductase), and that the other compounds are normally produced by chemical condensations (although there are examples of S oxidizers that enzymically interconvert some of these compounds). Aerobic S oxidizers contain a specific oxygenase which catalyses the insertion of two of the three oxygen atoms in SO_3^{2-} from atmospheric O_2, whereas in the anaerobes, O_2 is not involved, and the oxygen atoms in SO_3^{2-} are derived from water. Specific cytochromes are involved in these oxidations. $S_2O_3^{2-}$ is usually one of the main products due to the chemical condensation of S^{2-} or S^0 with SO_3^{2-}, and many S oxidizers carry out a cleavage of this molecule, either in a reductive fashion or by an oxidation-reduction disproportion reaction:

$$^-S-\overset{\overset{\displaystyle O}{\|}}{\underset{\underset{\displaystyle O}{\|}}{S}}-O^- \xrightarrow{2e} SO_3^{2-} + S^{2-}$$

or

$$^-S-\overset{\overset{\displaystyle O}{\|}}{\underset{\underset{\displaystyle O}{\|}}{S}}-O^- \longrightarrow SO_3^{2-} + S^0$$

SO_3^{2-} oxidation is well understood, and in some organisms is essentially the reverse of part of the dissimilatory SO_4^{2-} reduction pathway:

$$SO_3^{2-} + AMP \rightarrow APS$$
$$APS + P_i \rightarrow ADP + SO_4^{2-}$$
$$2ADP \rightarrow AMP + ATP$$

A phosphate bond is generated by these reactions, and this is the only known example of a substrate level phosphorylation involving the metabolism of an inorganic compound. Other organisms appear to have a quite different non-APS-linked SO_3^{2-} oxidase operating through a specific cytochrome. S^0 is also oxidized both aerobically and anaerobically, and the mechanism of activation of such a poorly soluble compound is something of a mystery (although it is somewhat easier to imagine how internally-deposited sulphur is utilized). There is some evidence which suggests that the "active" form of S^0 is not the usual crystalline ring molecule made up of 8S atoms, but a reactive polysulphide sulphane sulphur, thus:

$$nS^0 \rightleftharpoons R-SS_{n-1}^-$$

This transition could explain the observation that S^{2-}-oxidizing enzyme preparations often show activity toward S^0 also, since sulphane sulphur is not very different chemically from S^{2-}. The deposition of very large S^0 granules outside certain cells also becomes easier to understand if a soluble sulphane sulphur undergoes such a transition.

Some of the postulated transformations during S oxidation are shown in figure 7.6. The free energy available from the oxidation of S compounds is high ($S^0 - 489.5 \, kJ \, mol^{-1}$), but the redox of the various S_{oxid}/S_{red} couples is such that for chemolithotrophic S oxidizers the direct reduction of NAD is not possible, reduction necessitating energy-dependent flow against the electrode potential gradient. Thus, like the nitrifiers, chemolithotrophic S oxidizers show low growth yields, although capable of

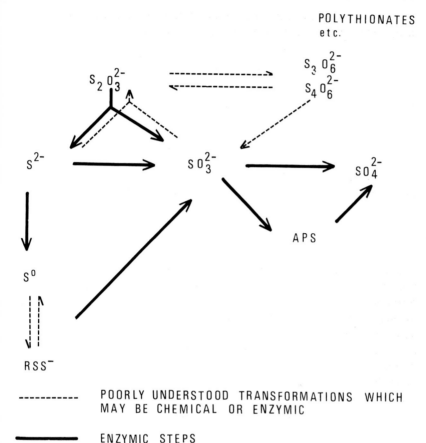

Figure 7.6 Oxidative transformations of sulphur compounds.

relatively rapid growth under certain conditions (*Thiobacillus neapolitanus* for example shows a doubling time of < 2 h when grown on $S_2O_3^{2-}$).

7.2 The S cycle and biodeterioration

In areas where large quantities of metal sulphides are exposed to the air, the production of H_2SO_4 by S-oxidizing bacteria (normally thiobacilli) can be a problem of major consequence. Run-off waters from such areas often have pH values as low as 2–3; for instance considerable areas of the

Appalachian coal fields that are largely worked by open-cast mining are affected by this problem. Acid conditions cause deterioration of stone, concrete, and metals, and are inimical to plant life, and may solubilize substantial amounts of toxic metals (7.8). More localized acid-induced deterioration may occur in any environment where air and reduced sulphur compounds occur—there have been instances of the total collapse of concrete cooling towers and sewage pipes. Concretes containing high concentrations of S^{2-} are particularly at risk and certain isolates of *Th. thiooxidans* (originally named *Th. concretivorus*!) are often implicated in this kind of deterioration. The sulphur compounds present in calcareous rocks and limestone ores are also oxidized under humid conditions, leading to the gradual decay of limestone monuments and sculptures. In tropical climates where buildings are erected on S^{2-}-containing laterite (1.1) sorption of S^{2-} by porous stone may result in catastrophic deterioration, exemplified by certain of the Kampuchean monuments at Angkor.

Organisms of the sulphur cycle, amongst others, are also involved in metal corrosion by amplifying the essentially electrochemical process. When ferrous metals are immersed in a solution, metal passes into solution as cations, producing an anode, thus:

$$Fe \rightleftharpoons Fe(II) + 2e$$

If electrons are removed by flowing to another less negatively charged area in the metal, or by transfer to a more noble metal in contact, the corrosive process at the anode continues. Iron bacteria may produce the same effect by the constant oxidation and removal of Fe(II). The site which accumulates electrons constitutes a cathode, and there are two possible fates for these electrons depending on whether oxic or anoxic conditions prevail:

(1) $O_2 + 2e + 2H^+ \rightleftharpoons 2OH^-$ (under oxic conditions), or
(2) $2H^+ + 2e \rightleftharpoons H_2$ (under anoxic conditions).

Under oxic conditions OH^- continually reacts with metal cations originally generated at the anode, producing characteristic rusty deposits. Under sterile anoxic conditions H_2 eventually blankets the cathode and inhibits reaction (2), stifling the corrosive process at the anode. However, these electrochemical processes are augmented by microbial activity in the following ways:

(a) Microbial surface growths change the concentration of compounds (including O_2) at the surface of metals, effectively increasing the number of charge irregularities in the metal, promoting the formation of anodes and cathodes.

(b) Microorganisms produce acids and chelating substances which attack the lattice structure of the metals in much the same way that aluminosilicates are attacked (1.1). Non-ferrous metals are particularly vulnerable and the best-known example of this kind of attack is the corrosion of the aluminium alloy of aircraft fuel tanks by the fungus *Amorphotheca (Cladosporium) resinae*. Many organotrophic bacteria and fungi are however implicated in the corrosion of metal parts in a variety of fuel storage tanks and cold-running diesel engines. Chemolithotrophic S-oxidizing bacteria are particularly active under certain circumstances since they produce large quantities of H_2SO_4.

(c) Certain chemomixotrophic bacteria, particularly SO_4^{2-}-reducing bacteria of the genus *Desulfovibrio*, oxidize H_2 under anoxic conditions coupled to SO_4^{2-} reduction, allowing reaction (2) to continue. This kind of corrosion is most significant with mild steel and the resultant chemical precipitation of FeS also has a corrosive effect since FeS is cathodic to Fe.

Anaerobic corrosion is a particularly insidious process since there are no tell-tale signs of rust formation. Mild steel installations buried in anoxic marine sediments are constantly at risk. The offshore oil industry has particular problems since sea water under anoxic conditions is invariably used as ballast in partly filled storage tanks, and is constantly present in the plant in pipes and storage tanks from source, or because leaks develop. Prevention is costly and includes the use of resistant coatings, the insertion of sacrificial anodes of less noble metals, and the electrical charging of metal surfaces to prevent metal cations leaving the surface, while in restricted environments biocides may be useful.

7.3 Iron and manganese

Fe and Mn can be conveniently considered together since they have many properties in common and are often found in association. The transformations of Fe and Mn in the environment essentially consist of a simple shuttle between the most reduced forms Fe(II), Mn(II) and the most oxidized forms Fe(III), Mn(IV).

Many microorganisms are known to deposit insoluble Fe(III) or Mn(IV) oxides or hydroxides under certain conditions, and they are therefore by implication considered to be involved in Fe(II) and Mn(II) oxidation. Bacteria are traditionally supposed to be the most significant

Table 7.2 Organisms involved in Fe and Mn transformation

Genus, species or group	Habitat	Comments
Thiobacillus ferrooxidans Leptospirillum ferrooxidans *Sulfolobus ("Ferrolobus" type) *Sulfobacillus thermosulfoxidans	Mine waste minerals	Lithotrophs, Fe(II) only. S oxidizers and acidophiles
Sheathed bacteria including Leptothrix, Sphaerotilus, etc.	Water	Fe(II) and Mn(II) oxidizers, some not grown in pure culture, probably organotrophs
Appendaged bacteria including Pedomicrobium, Metallogenium Gallionella	Soil, water	Fe(II) and Mn(II) oxidation; probably organotrophic Gallionella and some Metallogenium spp. may be lithotrophic
Siderocapsa, etc.	Soil, water, marine	Taxonomy dubious; Fe(II) and Mn(II) oxidizers probably common soil microorganisms

* Thermophiles

microorganisms concerned, and table 7.2 lists the main groups and habitats. The deposition of Mn(IV) and Fe(III) is not however in itself an indication of the enzymically mediated oxidation of Fe(II) and Mn(II), since both Fe(II) and Mn(II) are readily chemically oxidized. Fe(II) in particular is unstable above pH 5 and at redox potentials of above $+200$ mV. However, there is no doubt that some of the bacteria listed in table 7.2 do carry out enzymic oxidations of Fe(II) and Mn(II). The most widely studied example is the acidophilic S-oxidizing organism *Thiobacillus ferrooxidans* which, in addition to chemolithotrophically oxidizing S compounds, lithotrophically oxidizes Fe(II) to Fe(III) under acid conditions where one can be certain that Fe(II) does not oxidize chemically. This remarkable organism is characteristically associated with environments such as mine waste tips where large amounts of metal sulphides, including Fe sulphides, are exposed to air. The organism attacks pyrite (FeS_2) via S oxidation thus:

(1) $FeS_2 + 2H_2O + 7O_2 \rightarrow 2Fe(II) + 4SO_4^{2-} + 4H^+$

then oxidizing Fe(II),

(2) $4Fe(II) + O_2 + 4H^+ \rightarrow 4Fe(III) + 2H_2O.$

There is also some evidence that the organism oxidizes Cu(I), probably in a lithotrophic fashion. Lithotrophic oxidation of Fe(II) is thoroughly authenticated only in this organism, although some Fe(II)-oxidizing isolates of the thermophilic and acidophilic *Sulfolobus acidocaldarius* ("*Ferrolobus*" type), the recently described sporing thermophile *Sulfobacillus thermosulfoxidans*, and certain *Metallogenium* spp. may also have a lithotrophic mode of growth. A spiral bacterium, *Leptospirillum ferrooxidans*, found in mine waste tips, may also be an Fe(II)-oxidizing lithotroph. H_2SO_4 generated by S oxidation (equation 1) creates problems of acid pollution in the surroundings of these waste tips (7.2), and although Fe(II) remains soluble as long as conditions are acid, eventual unsightly precipitation of $Fe(OH)_3$ occurs when neutral sites are reached. The curious appendaged bacteria of the genus *Gallionella*, which deposit $Fe(OH)_3$ under microaerophilic conditions in waterlogged soils and sediments, also oxidize Fe(II), which is stable under these conditions, but whether this oxidation is lithotrophic remains to be confirmed. None of these bacteria oxidizes Mn(II), and no convincing lithotrophic Mn(II) oxidizers have yet been described although some mixotrophic utilization may occur. There are many bacteria which enzymically oxidize Mn(II), presumably without benefit, including sheathed bacteria in the *Sphaerotilus/Leptothrix* group, and several poorly characterized marine isolates.

Cationic metals form stable complexes with both simple and complex organic molecules, including some of the components found in humic materials, and both Fe(II) and Fe(III) are stable and soluble in this form even under neutral oxic conditions. Many of the bacteria listed in table 7.2 are capable of breaking down such complexes, releasing Fe(III) directly, or Fe(II) which chemically oxidizes. Such organometal complexes must be the source of soluble Fe for all iron-precipitating bacteria that grow in neutral oxic conditions. Organometal complexes containing Mn are presumably less important as a source of soluble Mn since Mn(II) is more stable under neutral oxic conditions (sea water contains $2 \mu g l^{-1}$).

Considerable developments of sheathed bacteria (table 7.2) may occur at soluble Mn and Fe concentrations above $0.5 \mu g l^{-1}$, producing unsightly slimes, and these bacteria may constitute part of the "sewage fungus" complex found in polluted water courses (8.3). Undesirable effects on drinking water supplies include taste, smells, clogging of pipes, and the contribution of these bacteria to metallic Fe corrosion (7.2). Fe-containing organometal complexes are attacked by appendaged bacteria (table 7.2) in the Fe-rich B_2 horizon of podzols (1.1), contributing to the formation of this horizon by the precipitation of Fe(III) at a particular site in the soil profile determined by redox and pH. Mn(IV) and Fe(III) precipitation in the biosphere has at least one short-term consequence in that Mn-deficiency in plants is correlated with high numbers of Mn(II) oxidizers in soils, but the main importance of Mn(IV) and Fe(III) precipitation is in long term geochemical effects (7.7).

A group of aquatic bacteria including the genus *Siderocapsa* were once thought to constitute a taxonomically distinct group of Fe(III)- and Mn(IV)-depositing bacteria. However, *Siderocapsa* spp. have now been shown to be indistinguishable from *Arthrobacter* spp., and it is likely that this whole group is comprised of common soil and aquatic micro-organisms (both eukaryotic and prokaryotic). It is now known that the ability to precipitate oxides and hydroxides of Fe and Mn from organometal complexes is widely distributed amongst organotrophic soil, freshwater, and marine microorganisms, including *Bacillus* spp., *Arthrobacter* spp., *Pseudomonas* spp., *Aspergillus* spp., *Cephalosporium* spp., and *Fusarium* spp. Organisms such as these occur in high numbers ($10^7 \, g^{-1}$ soil or sediments) and can be readily detected by the development of metal-encrusted colonies on solid culture media containing metal oxalates and citrates. This ability of these common organisms has been largely overlooked or underestimated, and as their numbers in the most common environments are enormous compared with the more exotic bacteria listed in table 7.2, it is likely that the major part of Fe(III) and Mn(IV) precipitation is due to these microorganisms.

The biochemistry of Fe(II) oxidation has been more or less exclusively studied with *Th. ferrooxidans*. The Fe(II)-oxidizing enzyme system is membrane-bound and includes cytochromes and a unique blue copper-containing electron transport protein. In view of the very high redox potential of the Fe(II)/Fe(III) couple, O_2 is the obligate electron acceptor. The free energy available from the oxidation of Fe(II) is extremely small ($-46 \, kJ \, mol^{-1}$), the lowest available from any lithotrophic oxidation, and accordingly very large quantities of substrate are consumed. Mn(II) oxidation has mainly been studied in *Sphaerotilus* spp., and in certain marine *Bacillus* spp. A membrane-bond oxidase is linked to O_2 via flavoproteins and cytochromes, but the system differs from Fe(II) oxidation, as the oxidase is not thought to be coupled to ATP formation.

There is some evidence that Fe(III) and Mn(IV) function as electron sinks for microorganisms under certain conditions. *Th. ferrooxidans* and "*Ferrolobus*" produce an acidic environment where Fe(III) and Mn(IV) remain soluble, and under microaerophilic conditions they appear to reduce the metals while oxidizing S. A number of common soil bacteria and fungi, including *Bacillus* spp. and *Cephalosporium* spp., reduce Fe(III) and Mn(IV) under anoxic or microaerophilic conditions. The enzymology of these reductions is obscure, but some of the soil bacteria involved are denitrifiers, suggesting that nitrate reductase may be of low specificity and capable of reacting with oxidized metals in place of NO_3^-. Specific Mn(IV)-reducers are found in marine sediments and manganese nodules (7.7). These bacteria, generally of the genera *Bacillus* and *Arthrobacter*, reduce Mn(IV) even under oxic conditions, utilizing a metalloprotein Mn(IV)-inducible reductase.

7.4 Phosphorus and calcium

These elements occur together in nature in the apatite series of minerals $(Ca_5 (PO_4)_3 Cl, Ca_{10} (PO_4) F_2,$ etc.) and neither element undergoes any significant change in valence state during transformation in the environment. They may therefore conveniently be considered together.

Phosphorus occurs almost exclusively as orthophosphate (PO_4^{3-}) in which P has a valence of $+5$. Tissue P, largely in the form of PO_4^{3-} esters and anhydrides is released as PO_4^{3-}, and taken up in this form by plants and microorganisms. In theory, P has several possible oxidation states ranging from PO_4^{3-} to the most reduced form phosphine $(PH_3,$ valence -3). A number of soil bacteria including members of the genera *Bacillus*, *Pseudomonas* and *Clostridium* have been shown to reduce PO_4^{3-} to hypophosphite $(PO_2^-,$ valence $+3)$ and phosphite $(PO_3^{3-},$ valence $+1)$ under anoxic conditions. The enzymology of these reductive processes is obscure, but it is probably comparable to dissimilatory nitrate and sulphate reduction. PO_3^{3-} and PO_2^{3-} are also used as P sources by several soil fungi and bacteria implying an "assimilatory P oxidation". However, these transformations of valence state are thought to be limited and quantitatively insignificant compared to the mobilization and transfer of PO_4^{3-} between lithosphere and biosphere.

The main features of P transfer are outlined in figure 7.7. P is solubilized from rocks partly by microbial activity, and it is not uncommon to isolate from soils up to 10^5–10^7 organisms per g capable of utilizing crushed apatite as a sole P source. Chelation and acid production have been shown to be the main factors promoting P solubilization (1.1, 7.2), and there have been attempts to increase the solubilization of P from soils by adding sulphur to promote the growth of *Thiobacillus* spp. (the Lipman process), or by inoculating soils with very active apatite-solubilizing bacteria such

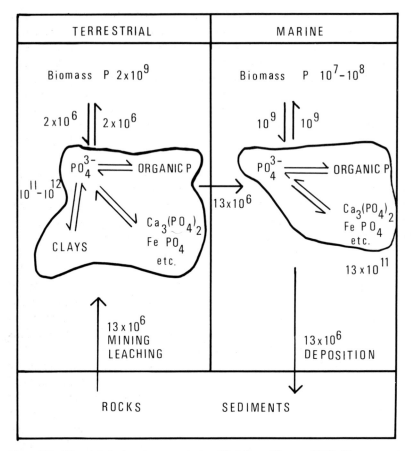

Figure 7.7 The global phosphorus cycle (modified from Pierron, 1976). Figures are in metric tonnes.

as *Bacillus* spp. ("phosphobakterin"). Most soils contain large amounts of P, but nevertheless P is commonly a limiting nutrient because most of it is unavailable to plants. The major part of P in soils is in the organic fraction (up to 80% in some cases), largely as inositol phosphates (1.2) which are probably not utilized by plants. Inorganic P availability depends mainly on the pH of the soil. At acid pH, binding to clays via cationic bridges occurs, and the precipitation of $AlPO_4$ and $FePO_4$ occurs, whereas at alkaline pH $Ca_3(PO_4)_2$ precipitates. The redox potential of the environment also plays a role to some extent, since at low redox potentials Fe(III) is reduced to Fe(II) releasing PO_4^{3-} (8.3). Soluble PO_4^{3-} is therefore seldom present in high concentrations in most soils, and has a low diffusion coefficient, hence the importance of endomycorrhiza in extending the "catchment area" for P uptake (4.5). Microbial activity clearly plays an important role in solubilizing PO_4^{3-} from inappropriate organic and inorganic forms, although our knowledge of how this is brought about in the environment is largely deductive and incomplete. However, it is known that large numbers of common soil and marine microorganisms solubilize apatites and other forms of insoluble inorganic P, and possess phosphatases which will release PO_4^{3-} from organic forms of P including inositol phosphates.

Very little P is deposited in oceanic sediments in comparison to the total biomass P (figure 7.7), but the amount deposited roughly balances the run-off from the terrestrial environment which in turn equals the global input from rock P via leaching and mining. In the slightly alkaline oceanic environment co-precipitation with Ca(II) often occurs and eventually (10^8–10^9 years) geochemical conversion to minerals of the apatite series occurs. The marine environment has an almost unlimited capacity for immobilization of P via sediments, combined with an enormous pool of soluble P (figure 7.7), and consequently there is no evidence for an increase in marine P concentration with consequential eutrophication problems (8.4), despite the increasing input of P through man's activities. This situation differs considerably from that in inland waterways.

Ca is found in the environment largely as Ca(II), both in the biosphere and the lithosphere. In the lithosphere Ca occurs in the apatite series of minerals, and also in extensive sedimentary deposits of $CaCO_3$ in the different crystalline forms, calcite and aragonite. Transfers of Ca occur mainly in the marine environment where Ca(II) is precipitated and solubilized. The surface waters of many parts of the world's oceans are supersaturated with $CaCO_3$, and the equilibrium between $CaCO_3$, $Ca(HCO_3)_2$ and CO_2 constitutes the main pH buffer in the marine environment (2.1):

$$Ca(HCO_3)_2 \rightleftharpoons CaCO_3 + H_2O + CO_2$$

The large-scale withdrawal of CO_2 by any biological CO_2 fixation process accordingly results in the generation of $CaCO_3$, which is poorly soluble. Clearly lithotrophic growth, particularly photolithotrophic growth, is most significant in this respect and presumably enormous amounts of $CaCO_3$ are deposited by marine phytoplankton by this means. Ca(II) also binds to negatively charged structures such as microbial exopolysaccharides and microbial cell walls, producing a nucleus for further

Ca(II) precipitation. A large number of marine organisms including echinoderms, molluscs and corals have calcareous skeletons which are probably generated by mechanisms similar to this.

A further notable example of $CaCO_3$ deposition occurs in certain extreme environments colonized by gliding prokaryotic phototrophs, including a variety of blue-green algae and the phototrophic bacterium *Chloroflexus aurantiacus*. Under conditions where metazoan predation is excluded, mats or pillars of microbial biomass are generated as phototroph filaments glide upwards towards the light over older moribund filaments, to create a characteristic calcareous laminated structure known as a *stromatolite*. Stromatolites are now rare and confined either to geothermal springs or to highly saline environments. Permineralization can occur by the reaction

$$CaCO_3 + SiO_2 \rightarrow CaSiO_3 + CO_2$$

and the characteristic laminated structure can be preserved in rocks. Some years ago it was realized that Pre-Cambrian sedimentary rocks, which had previously been thought to be devoid of fossil organisms, contained structures which were indistinguishable from present day stromatolites. It is now known that stromatolithic structures (and therefore presumably biological activity) date back as far as 3.4×10^9 years, and stromatolithic strata have proved invaluable macroscopic markers in the current search for older and older microfossils. Most authenticated Pre-Cambrian micro-fossils found to date originate from stromatolithic cherts like the Gunflint formation in Canada and the Bitter Springs formation in Western Australia.

7.5 Silicon

Silicon is the most abundant crustal element after oxygen, and insoluble silicates account for 95% of the earth's crust. $Si(OH)_4$ is the main soluble form of silica in both the marine and terrestrial environments, and the cyclic interconversions of soluble and insoluble forms of silicon are largely a consequence of biological activity. Microorganisms contribute to the solubilization of crystalline silicate, equations (1) and (2), by chelation and acid production (see 1.1).

$$SiO_2 \underset{-H_2O}{\overset{+H_2O}{\rightleftharpoons}} O = Si \begin{matrix} OH \\ \diagup \\ \diagdown \\ OH \end{matrix} \underset{-H_2O}{\overset{+H_2O}{\rightleftharpoons}} Si(OH)_4 \qquad (1)$$

or for metal substituted silicates:

$$-M(II)-O-\overset{\overset{|}{O}}{\underset{\underset{|}{O}}{Si}}-O^- + H^+ + H_2O \rightarrow M(I) + OH^- + O=Si\overset{OH}{\underset{OH}{\diagdown}} \qquad (2)$$

The biogenic deposition of insoluble silica (SiO_2) occurs according to the reactions indicated in equation (1), although it is likely that organo-silicate intermediates ($R-Si(OH)_3$) are involved in the deposition of silica within cells and tissues. Silicon readily replaces carbon in certain organic compounds, particularly in ester and ether linkage, and a number of silicon analogues of particular carbon compounds have been described.

The effect of biological activity is most pronounced in the marine environment, where the cycling of soluble and insoluble forms is due largely to diatoms. Diatoms account for 70–90% of suspended silica in the oceanic environment, and it is believed that 2.5×10^{10} tonnes of silica are solubilized annually from marine waters, mostly from diatom frustules. The annual deposition of 1×10^9 tonnes to marine sediments is roughly balanced by the input of silica from the terrestrial environment. The geological record indicates that following the appearance of silica-utilizing microorganisms, the dissolved silica concentration of the world's oceans decreased to a tenth of its former level. This permanent change in the geochemistry of the earth is a particularly compelling illustration of the profound effects of biological processes in element cycling.

7.6 Microbial transformations of other metals and metalloids

A number of specific enzymic transformations of toxic metals and metalloid elements occur in the environment. These are carried out by a hetero-geneous group of unrelated organisms, and are of two types:

(1) changes in the oxidation state of inorganic forms of the element
(2) methylations of the element which may or may not involve a change in the oxidation state.

Table 7.3 lists some of the elements known to undergo such transfor-mations. The transformations appear to be detoxification mechanisms and therefore involve expenditure of energy. The capacity to perform these transformations is fairly widespread amongst microorganisms and may

Table 7.3 Microbial transformations of metals and metalloids excluding Fe and Mn (after Summers and Silver, 1978)

Transformation	Metal	Microorganisms
Oxidation	As(III)	Pseudomonas, Actinobacter, Alcaligenes
	Sb(III)	Stibiobacter (lithotrophic?)
	Cu(I)	Thiobacillus (ferrooxidans) (lithotrophic?)
Reduction	As(V)	Chlorella
	Hg(II)	Pseudomonas, Escherichia, Staphylococcus, Aspergillus
	Se(IV)	Corynebacterium, Streptococcus
	Te(IV)	Salmonella, Shigella, Pseudomonas
Methylation	As(V)	Aspergillus, Mucor, Fusarium, Paecilomyces, methanogens (reduction to As(III) also occurs)
	Cd(II)	Pseudomonas
	Te(IV)	Pseudomonas
	Se(IV)	Pseudomonas, Aspergillus, Candida, Cephalosporium, Penicillium
	Sn(II)	Pseudomonas
	Hg(II)	Bacillus, Clostridium, methanogens, Aspergillus, Neurospora
	Pb(IV)	Pseudomonas, Aeromonas

reflect the lack of the specific metal-binding and detoxifying sulphydryl-containing metallothionein proteins produced by animals.

The newly-described bacterium *Stibiobacter senarmontii* is exceptional in that it may lithotrophically oxidize non-toxic trivalent antimony Sb(III) to Sb(V). In addition, *Thiobacillus ferrooxidans* may oxidize Cu(I) in addition to Fe(II) under certain circumstances (7.3). The only other example of an oxidative transformation known is the oxidation of arsenite (AsO_2^-, valence $+3$) to arsenate ($AsO_3^{\,-}$, valence $+5$) by a variety of soil bacteria including members of the genera *Achromobacter* and *Pseudomonas*.

Reductive detoxification mechanisms are common however and a variety of soil fungi and bacteria are capable of reducing oxidized forms of mercury (Hg), tellurium (Te) and selenium (Se) to metallic forms of the elements which are either less soluble or volatile (table 7.3). Hg reduction is best understood and an inducible FAD-containing NADPH-linked reductase is known to be involved. The resistance of certain bacteria such as *Salmonella* spp. to high levels of oxidized Se and Te salts is a consequence of reductive capacity, and is the basis of certain selective and differential media. Resistance to Hg(II) has been shown to be plasmid-determined in bacteria and this may also be the case with resistance to the other metals mentioned.

The methylation of metals and metalloids is again best understood for Hg. Human concern over this reaction originates from the finding that methyl mercury (CH_3Hg^+) is some 50–100 times more toxic than Hg(II). The best-documented example of methyl mercury poisoning relates to an incident at Minimata Bay in Japan, where a large number of fishermen became severely ill (Minimata disease), some fatally, through eating fish contaminated with CH_3Hg^+. The source of the Hg in this case was a factory producing acetaldehyde using inorganic Hg(II) as a catalyst, and it was subsequently found that the microbiological transformations in marine sediments were responsible for the transformation of Hg(II) to CH_3Hg^+ and dimethylmercury $(CH_3)_2Hg$, which were accumulated in the food chain culminating in man. A considerable number of bacteria and fungi including *Bacillus* spp., *Pseudomonas* spp., *Aspergillus* spp. and *Neurospora* spp. produce significant amounts of CH_3Hg^+ aerobically when grown in the presence of Hg(II), and the methanogenic bacteria also generate CH_3Hg^+ anaerobically. Current opinion however holds that Hg(II) is chemically methylated by methyl donors, such as cyanocobalamin, and microbial responsibility is therefore indirect. Other metals (table 7.3) are methylated in soils and sediments, probably by the same mechanism. These methylated compounds are volatile and generally more toxic to man than the original inorganic salts. The toxicity of methylated arsenicals in particular has been known for many years following human poisoning by dimethyl arsine, $(CH_3)_2AsH$, and trimethyl arsine, $(CH_3)_3As$, produced by moulds growing in damp wallpaper containing arsenical pigments.

7.7 The role of microorganisms in the deposition of minerals

The observation that present-day microorganisms are capable of depositing a variety of minerals from solution has led to speculation as to whether many of our mineral ores are the consequence of microbial activity in the past. Early mineral formation and degradation must however have proceeded without biological intervention, and there are existing mineral deposits which are of magmatic origin (particularly metal sulphide ores). However, many mineral deposits are found in sedimentary strata which date from after the time when the first microorganisms were present on earth, and indeed, fossil microorganisms are characteristically associated with certain types of metal ore. Sedimentary deposits, which are of two main types, are classified in relation to the surrounding host rocks: syngenetic deposits are considered to have been laid down simultaneously with the surrounding rock strata, whereas epigenetic deposits are considered to have formed subsequent to the deposition of the host rock.

About 90 % of the world's elemental S (S^0) deposits are sedimentary in origin. Sedimentary S^0 deposits date back to the Cambrian/Pre-Cambian boundary, but the most important periods of deposition appear to have occurred in the Ordovician/Silurian and Jurassic/Cretaceous periods when warm, shallow seas covered much of the earth. There are a number of present-day deposition systems which are believed to be good models for the original syngenetic and epigenetic deposition.

Syngenetic S^0 deposition occurs in some lakes, notably Lake Sernoe in the U.S.S.R. and certain North African desert lakes such as Ain-ez-Zauni, and these habitats are essentially similar throughout the world. Such lakes produce enough S^0 to support local mining operations. The requirements for S^0 deposition include an abundant source of H_2S (either volcanic or produced from SO_4^{2-} deposits by dissimilatory reduction), strong illumination, and an active population of S-oxidizing bacteria. Those habitats with a complete S cycle are known as *sulphureta* (sing. sulphuretum). The lakes can be either totally anoxic, and populated exclusively by purple and green phototrophic bacteria, or stratified, supporting aerobic or microaerophilic colourless S oxidizers in the upper layers, and phototrophic bacteria beneath these in the anoxic depths (figure 7.8).

A possible present-day model for epigenetic S^0 deposition is seen in the

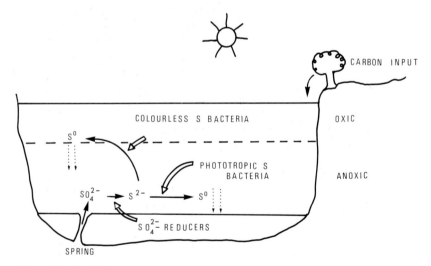

Figure 7.8 A sulphuretum.

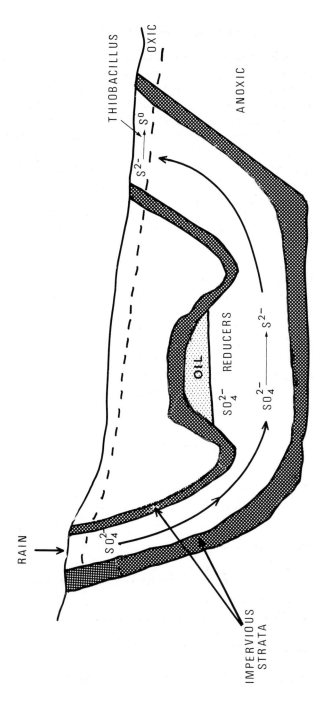

Figure 7.9 Possible mode of formation of epigenetic sulphur deposits (modified from Doetsch, R. N. and Cook, T. N. (1973), *An Introduction to Bacteria and their Ecobiology*, Medical and Technical Publishing Co. Ltd., Lancaster).

Shor-Su deposits in the U.S.S.R. where SO_4^{2-} reduction occurs in permeable gypsum-containing strata between impermeable strata (figure 7.9). Electron donors for SO_4^{2-} reduction are supplied partly by wash-in from vegetation, but perhaps also from subterranean oil deposits. Where H_2S-rich waters escape and mix with aerated surface water, S^0 deposition occurs, largely due to the growth of *Thiobacillus* spp.

The discovery that biological systems preferentially fractionate naturally-occurring S isotopes has provided further evidence for the biogenic origins of S^0 deposits. Particular attention has been paid to the ratio of ^{32}S to ^{34}S in various S compounds. Present-day SO_4^{2-} reducers such as *Desulfovibrio* spp. preferentially use the lighter isotope, whereas the oxidation of S^{2-} to S^0 results in much less striking enrichment of the lighter isotope. The S cycle involves many different S compounds with potential for considerable variations in the proportions of ^{32}S and ^{34}S at each step depending on which organisms are involved, but it would nevertheless be predicted that S^0 deposited from S^{2-} by biological activity would be enriched in ^{32}S, and any surrounding source SO_4^{2-} would be correspondingly depleted in ^{32}S. Observed S isotope ratios in many S^0 deposits support the view that such deposits are the result of biological activity. Often S^0 deposits are found associated with calcite ($CaCO_3$), NaCl, and oil deposits in the same or adjacent strata. It is probable that in ancient seas marine phytoplankton (which eventually becomes oil (5.6)) provided most of the electron donors for SO_4^{2-} reduction, and that lithotrophic growth resulted in the deposition of $CaCO_3$ (7.4). Biological systems also fractionate carbon isotopes, and the ratio of ^{12}C to ^{13}C found in such calcite deposits is commensurate with biological involvement.

Sedimentary sulphide ores are imagined to have arisen from the chemical precipitation of metal cations with S^{2-} (produced from SO_4^{2-} by dissimilatory reduction), followed by geochemical modification, exemplified by pyrite formation (figure 7.10). The other common sulphide ores such as galena (PbS), covellite (CuS) and sphalerite (ZnS) are invariably associated with pyrite. Other forms of metal ores containing relatively reduced metals, such as carbonates like rhodochrosite ($MnCO_3$), and siderite ($FeCO_3$), are supposed to have been deposited chemically under anoxic or microaerophilic conditions by equilibrium of metal bicarbonates with $CaCO_3$

$$Fe(HCO_3)_2 + CaCO_3 \rightleftharpoons Ca(HCO_3)_2 + FeCO_3$$

Oxidized Fe and Mn ores such as haematite ($Fe_2O_3 \cdot nH_2O$) and pyrolusite ($MnO_2 \cdot H_2O$) which are often associated, were deposited

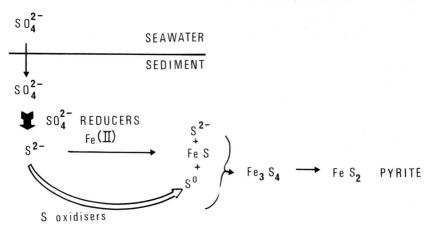

Figure 7.10   Possible mode of formation of sulphide ores. Greigite (Fe_3S_4) is formed under reducing conditions in sediments by chemical condensations of sulphide (or elemental sulphur) with FeS. Further geochemical change produces pyrite (FeS_2).

during much the same period as S^0, particularly the Silurian period. It is imagined that microbially-mediated Fe(II) and Mn(II) oxidation and precipitation occurred in the marine environment, followed by geochemical change. The Fe(II) must presumably have been in organometal complexes (7.3), or derived from an adjacent anoxic environment. Ores of this type often contain structures which have been interpreted as fossil bacteria similar to the *Sphaerotilus/Leptothrix* group. A comparison may be drawn with some present-day sites where co-precipitation of Mn and Fe produces ferromanganese concretions. These concretions, which are known as "bog ores", contain varying amounts of MnO_2, $Fe(OH)_3$, and organic material, and are found in bogs and lakes in acid waters, particularly in the Eurasian podzol belt. Bacteria of the *Sphaerotilus/Leptothrix* group and occasionally *Gallionella* spp. are commonly isolated from these concretions.

Similar, but much older ferromanganese concretions occur on the ocean floors throughout the world, and are particularly abundant in equatorial regions. These concretions or "manganese nodules" which were first described by the Challenger expedition in 1890, contain 20–40% Mn and 10–50% Fe, depending on location. The metals are often in the form of haematite and todokerite ($Mn_2Mn_5O_{12} \cdot 2H_2O$) and substantial amounts of Ni and Co (1–2%) may be associated. Some deposits of these nodules are potentially valuable sources of Ni and Co; the estimated reserves of these metals in this form exceed the projected world requirement for several hundred years. At present there is something of a race to develop the technology for scooping these off the sea bed, and to unravel the legal aspects of mid-ocean deep-sea mining. Bacteria isolated from these nodules oxidize Mn(II) to Mn(IV), and Mn(IV)-reducers are also present. Unlike the bacteria from bog ores, these bacteria are generally similar to common soil and aquatic genera like *Bacillus* and *Arthrobacter*, although they are capable of carrying out these enzyme reactions at low temperatures and very high pressure. Ni and Co uptake is probably chemical, following enzymic oxidation of Mn(II). A mineral such as todokerite which contains manganese in both the (II) and (IV) state is necessary for reactions such as

$$Mn(II) \cdot Mn(IV) \cdot O_3 + 2H_2O + \tfrac{1}{2}O_2 \rightarrow 2H_2 \cdot Mn(IV) \cdot O_3 \text{ (enzymic)}$$
$$H_2MnO_3 + Ni(II) \text{ etc.} \rightarrow NiMnO_3 + 2H^+ \text{ (chemical)}$$

Present-day manganese nodules are very old ($> 10^6$ years) and grow very slowly indeed, but concretions such as these, formed in earlier times, may have been the precursors for many modern Mn(IV) and Fe(III) ores.

7.8 The exploitation of biogeochemical activities

Hydrometallurgical processes play an important role in the extraction of metals from certain low-grade ores. Hydrometallurgy consists of the dissolution of metal from minerals, usually by the constant percolation of a leach solution through beds of ore. A number of different solubilizing agents may be added to leach liquors, but the basis of many mining operations of this kind is the exploitation of microbial activity. Microbial involvement in leaching was first identified some 30 years ago when examples of leach liquor were examined and shown to contain large numbers of bacteria. Leaching is still the main technique used to extract copper from low-grade ore ($< 1\%$ Cu by weight) and has recently been applied to the recovery of uranium, and laboratory studies have demonstrated the feasibility of extracting a wide variety of metals. The natural process is most effective in ores which contain substantial amounts of pyrite (FeS_2) and the process is based essentially on the rapid oxidation of S^{2-} and Fe(II) promoted by chemolithotrophic bacteria. The organism most commonly implicated is *Th. ferrooxidans* which oxidizes both Fe(II) and reduced S compounds (7.3), although the physiologically similar organisms of the genera *Sulfolobus* ("*Ferrolobus*") and *Sulfobacillus* are thought to function in high temperature leaching sites. *Leptospirillum ferrooxidans*, other *Thiobacillus* spp., and certain *Metallogenium* spp. are also associated.

The solubilization of copper (or other metals) from reduced sulphide ores is the consequence of several reactions:

(1) $Fe(II) \cdot S_2 + 3\frac{1}{2}O_2 + H_2O \rightarrow Fe(II) \cdot SO_4 + H_2SO_4$

(2) $4Fe(II) \cdot SO_4 + O_2 + 2H_2SO_4 \rightarrow 2Fe_2(III) \cdot (SO_4)_3 + 2H_2O$

(3) $CuFeS_2(chalcopyrite) + Fe_2(SO_4)_3 + H_2O + 3\frac{1}{2}O_2 \rightarrow CuSO_4 + 3FeSO_4 + H_2SO_4$

Reactions (1) and (2) occur chemically, but *Th. ferrooxidans* catalyses the generation of $Fe_2(SO_4)_3$ at a pH-dependent rate which may be up to 10^6 times as fast as the chemical rate. The generation of $Fe_2(SO_4)_3$ is the hub of the process since the compound is a powerful chemical oxidizing agent and reaction (3) catalyses the chemical oxidation of more sulphide minerals (FeS_2, $CuFeS_2$, etc.) releasing the desired metal as a soluble metal sulphate which can be recovered by cementation with iron or by other means. $FeSO_4$ generated by the oxidation of FeS_2 recycles to regenerate $Fe_2(SO_4)_3$—equation (2)—in a cyclical process. H_2SO_4 produced during the process is an additional powerful solubilizing agent. Direct bacterial oxidation of copper and other sulphide minerals occurs as well as their degradation by $Fe_2(SO_4)_3$. Biological leaching is a cheap and efficient process, requiring little attention—adequate amounts of N and P in the leach liquor should be ensured, and excess acid should be periodically neutralized. The principal methods employed are to sprinkle heaps of mine waste with leach liquor, or to pump the leach liquor into underground workings or caverns filled with rocks fractured by explosives, later collecting the "pregnant" leach liquor in run-off ponds or secondary shafts.

For some thirty years or so the oil and petrochemicals industry has flirted with the notion of utilizing microbial activity to enhance the recovery of oil from depleted reservoirs, and to modify certain products. Until the present time the cheapness of oil has relegated the use of micro-organisms as a method of uncertain potential, and largely restricted their use to the reduction of S^{2-} (by S oxidizers) in certain oil products, but now that the economic and supply positions have changed irrevocably there is considerable interest once more in appraising other microbiological applications. Certain organisms of the S cycle have traditionally been prime contenders in the field since they are lithotrophic or mixotrophic and therefore cheap to maintain in culture, and are compatible with the environment, often found in close proximity to oil deposits in nature.

However, one of the problems encountered in these studies is that any beneficial effect of a specific microorganism may be offset by the general undesirability of producing substantial microbial biomass that may cause plugging of the reservoirs. Microorganisms (particularly *Desulfovibrio* spp.) have been introduced into reservoirs to increase the mobility of the residual oil by the production of gas or surfactants, or by partial degradation. The generation of S^{2-} however "sours" the oil, and may contribute to the formation of asphalts and tars that may produce blockages. Sea water injections to force out residual oil from offshore wells raise serious difficulties in this respect. A current modification of this general theme is the projected use of microbial exopolysaccharides in order to displace and recover residual oil. An alternative approach concerns the surface oil shales that are found in great abundance in many parts of the world, and which are leachable since they contain significant amounts of FeS_2. Leaching increases the porosity of the rock and simplifies the extraction procedure, and an additional benefit accrues since the S^{2-} content of the oil is correspondingly reduced. These processes may all find an opportunity for testing on a large scale when the likely shortage of oil by the end of the century provides an incentive.

REFERENCES

Books

Fenchel, T. and Blackburn, T. H. (1979) *Bacteria and Mineral Cycling*, Academic Press.
Miller, J. D. A. (1971) (ed.) *Microbial Aspects of Metallurgy*, Medical and Technical Publishing Co., Aylesbury.
Murr, L. G., Torma, A. E. and Brierley, J. A. (1978) (eds.) *Metallurgical Applications of Bacterial Leaching and Related Microbiological Processes*, Academic Press.
Postgate, J. R. (1979) *The Sulphate-Reducing Bacteria*, Cambridge University Press.
Trudinger, P. A. and Swaine, D. J. (1979) *Biochemical Cycling of Mineral-forming Elements*, Elsevier.
Zajic, J. E. (1969) *Microbial Biogeochemistry*, Academic Press.

Articles

Aristovskaya, T. V. and Zavarsin, G. A. (1971) Biochemistry of iron in soil. In *Soil Biochemistry*, Vol. 2, eds. A. D. McLaren and J. Skujins, Marcel Dekker, pp. 385–408.
Brierley, C. L. (1978) Bacterial leaching. *CRC Critical Reviews in Microbiology*, 6, 207–262.
Convey, F. K. (1976) Enhanced recovery of petroleum using microorganisms—a literature review. *Institute of Petroleum Conference Proceedings*, 57–75.
Cosgrave, D. J. (1977) Microbial transformations in the phosphorus cycle. *Adv. Microbial Ecol.* 1, 95–134.
Cronan, D. S. (1978) Manganese nodules—controversy upon controversy. *Endeavour (New Series)* 2, 80–84.
Cullimore, D. R. and McCann, A. G. (1977) The identification, cultivation and control of iron bacteria in ground water. In *Aquatic Microbiology*, eds. J. A. Skinner and J. M. Shewan, Academic Press, pp. 219–262.
Ehrlich, H. L. (1975) The formation of ores in the sedimentary environment of the deep sea and microbial participation: the case for ferromanganese concretions. *Soil Sci.* 119, 36–41.
Ehrlich, H. L. (1979) Inorganic energy sources for chemolithotrophic and mixotrophic bacteria. *Geomicrobiol. J.* 1, 65–83.

Goldhaber, M. B. and Kaplan, I. R. (1974) The sulphur cycle. In *The Sea*, Vol. 5, ed. E. D. Goldberg, John Wiley & Son, pp. 569–656.

Granat, L. and Rodhe, H. (1976) The global sulphur cycle. In *Nitrogen, Phosphorus and Sulphur—Global Cycles*, Scope Report 7, *Ecol. Bull.* (Stockholm) 22, 89–134.

Halstead, R. L. and McKercher, R. B. (1975) Biochemistry and cycling of phosphorus. In *Soil Biochemistry*, Vol. 4, eds. E. A. Paul and A. D. McLaren, Marcel Dekker, pp. 31–64.

Iverson, W. P. and Brinkman, F. S. (1978) Microbial metabolism of heavy metals. In *Water Pollution Microbiology*, Vol. 2, ed. R. Mitchell, John Wiley & Son, pp. 201–232.

Kelly, D. P. (1978) Bioenergetics of chemolithotrophic bacteria. In *Companion to Microbiology*, eds. A. T. Bull and P. M. Meadow, Longmans, pp. 363–386.

Kuenen, J. G. (1975) Colourless sulphur bacteria and their role in the sulphur cycle. *Plant and Soil*, 43, 49–76.

Le Gall, J. and Postgate, J. R. (1973) The physiology of sulphate-reducing bacteria. *Adv. Microbial Physiol.* 10, 81–128.

Lundgen, D. G. and Silver, M. (1980) Ore leaching by bacteria. *Ann. Rev. Microbiol.* 34, 263–284.

Miller, J. D. A. and Kind, R. A. (1975) Biodeterioration of metal. In *Microbial Aspects of the Biodeterioration of Materials*, eds. D. W. Lovelock and R. J. Gilbert, Academic Press, pp. 83–104.

Pierron, U. (1976) The global phosphorus cycle. In *Nitrogen, Phosphorus and Sulphur—Global Cycles*, Scope Report 7, *Ecol. Bull.* (Stockholm) 22, 75–88.

Siegel, L. M. (1975) Biochemistry of the sulphur cycle. In *Metabolism of Sulphur Compounds*, (Metabolic Pathways Vol. VII), ed. D. M. Greenberg, Academic Press, pp. 217–286.

Silverman, M. P. and Ehrlich, H. L. (1964) Microbial formation and degradation of minerals. *Adv. Appl. Microbiol.* 6, 153–206.

Summers, A. C. and Silver, S. (1978) Microbial transformations of metals. *Ann. Rev. Microbiol.* 32, 637–672.

Trudinger, P. A. (1969) Assimilatory and dissimilatory metabolism of inorganic sulphur compounds. *Adv. Microbial Physiol.* 3, 111–158.

Trudinger, P. A. (1976) Microbiological processes in relation to ore genesis. In *Handbook of Strata-Bound and Stratiform Ore Deposits. Principles and General Studies*, Vol. 5, ed. K. H. Wolf, Elsevier, pp. 135–190.

Trüper, H. G. (1978) Sulphur metabolism. In *The Photosynthetic Bacteria*, eds. R. K. Clayton and W. R. Sistrom, Plenum Press, pp. 677–690.

Van Veen, W. L., Mulder, G. C. and Dienema, M. H. (1978) The *Sphaerotilus-Leptothrix* group of bacteria. *Microbiol. Rev.* 42, 328–356.

PART 3—MICROORGANISMS AND POLLUTION

CHAPTER EIGHT

THE MICROBIAL CONTRIBUTION TO POLLUTION

8.1 General aspects of pollution

Pollution occurs when undesirable compounds or microorganisms enter an environment and change the quality of this environment so that the balance of the community structure is endangered. A more cynical definition might include any factor which produced an impact on man's life style. In the past, too little attention has been focused on the microbiology concerned, although often the first indications of impending trouble are to be seen in changes in the microbial population of a particular environment, and the final results of pollution may be largely a consequence of microbial activity.

Microorganisms may contribute to pollution in a number of ways—they may themselves produce disease, they may create an aesthetically unpleasant biomass, or they may generate toxic metabolites. Microorganisms can contribute to atmospheric pollution by the production of volatile S (7.1) or N compounds (6.4) (which in turn may be removed by other microorganisms), or their activities may contaminate soil or water. The kind of pollution most commonly encountered and best recognized by the general public is that produced by the input of undesirable compounds or microorganisms into water courses, with consequent changes in amenity value. In truth, the pollution of most environments eventually manifests itself somewhere in the aquatic environment, and accordingly this chapter concentrates on this aspect of pollution.

8.2 Pollution by pathogenic microorganisms

Pathogenic microorganisms are found in all sewage effluents (9.1), and where the same watercourses are used for bathing, drinking, and sewage disposal, the population is at risk unless the drinking water supplies are

Table 8.1 Recognized pathogens which may be transmitted by water

Bacteria	Viruses	Protozoa and Metazoa
Escherichia (enteropathogenic)	Enteroviruses	Entamoeba
Salmonella	Hepatitis A	Acanthamoeba
Shigella	Adenoviruses	Naegleria
Vibrio	Coxsackie A and B	Hartmanella
Leptospira	Reoviruses	Giardia
Mycobacterium	Parvoviruses	Schistosoma
Francisella		Ascaris
		Trichuris
		Taenia

carefully processed and monitored. Obviously, the isolation of particular pathogens would constitute the most compelling proof of potential danger, but pathogens may be present in such small numbers that their isolation would be difficult, and unsuitable as an "early-warning" system. Instead, the rationale behind the present procedures for water testing is that the majority of water-borne pathogenic microorganisms (table 8.1) enter water supplies as a result of faecal contamination, and therefore the ability to detect faecal contamination at low level is the main safeguard in preserving the potability of water supplies.

Faecal contamination can be demonstrated in a very sensitive fashion by the detection in water of certain bacteria that are present in very large numbers in the intestinal content of man and other animals. The only statutory microbiological test in force in Britain and many other parts of the world is the "Presumptive Coliform Test". This is normally an MPN count using liquid medium (1.3). In essence, any *change* from the normal numbers of coliform organisms would be considered significant and worthy of further investigation. A coliform organism is defined as a Gram-negative, oxidase-negative, non-spore-forming rod which can grow aerobically in a medium containing bile salts, and which is able to ferment lactose within 48 h, producing acid and gas at 37°. This definition encompasses a number of intestinal bacteria, including *Escherichia coli*, *Citrobacter*, *Klebsiella* and *Enterobacter* spp., and although *E. coli* is probably confined to the intestinal tract, certain of the other coliforms are not uncommonly found growing in uncontaminated water supplies, so a confirmatory test specific for *E. coli* is usually carried out if a water sample has a suspiciously high Presumptive Coliform count.

Obviously, a strictly bacteriological standard does not completely guarantee that a water sample is necessarily free of other types of pathogen (table 8.1), since they may have different survival characteristics. There are no statutory virus standards in force, nor do many laboratories routinely screen water samples for viruses, largely because the techniques required are sophisticated, difficult and time-consuming. There have been cases where drinking waters which were "clean" bacteriologically produced outbreaks of viral diseases such as infectious hepatitis and non-bacterial gastroenteritis, but virus transmission (and the transmissions of other non-bacterial pathogens) is not considered to be a serious problem in the developed countries of the world. In the final analysis, the suitability of the bacteriological standard depends on the degree of freedom from other types of disease believed to be transmitted by water. A general increase in their rate of incidence would rapidly bring into force the more complicated facilities required for other types of microbiological testing.

8.3 Pollution with oxygen-demanding carbonaceous material

Biodegradable carbonaceous material derived from domestic, agricultural or industrial sources can often cause marked changes in the amenity value of a watercourse, largely as a consequence of alteration in the O_2 balance of the immediate environment. O_2 has a relatively low solubility in water (9.8 p.p.m. ($mg\,l^{-1}$) at 20°), and microbial activity may rapidly deplete dissolved O_2. The public is well aware of the sequence of events that occurs under these conditions, from the initial disappearance of fish at O_2 concentrations of about 4 p.p.m., to the terminal stages, where the watercourse characteristically turns into an evil-smelling black swamp devoid of any higher forms of life. It is possible to predict the loading of biodegradable carbonaceous material that a particular watercourse is capable of accommodating, if the flow rate, dilution factors, temperature etc., are known, and also the "strength" of the inflow of material. Mathematical modelling of estuaries and rivers with respect to the possible effect of sewage outfalls is extensively employed in determining whether or rot a particular discharge is allowable at a particular point.

There are a number of procedures available to calculate the "strength" or carbonaceous content of a particular effluent relative to its oxygen demand, including the dichromate Chemical Oxygen Demand (COD) test used in the U.S.A., and the roughly equivalent Permanganate Values used in Britain. Both of these assays estimate *all* the carbonaceous material, including poorly biodegradable or non-biodegradable material. Such estimations have their uses, particularly in the monitoring of trade effluents, but since the most important effects produced in a watercourse are often a consequence of biological activity, an estimation of the carbonaceous material in relation to its biological effect is often more appropriate. The 5-day Biological Oxygen Demand (BOD or BOD_5) test is widely used. The assay is carried out by completely filling standard bottles with water samples and incubating these at 20° for 5 days in the dark. Dissolved O_2 is measured at the beginning and at the end of the incubation period, and the change in dissolved O_2 concentration in p.p.m. over the intervening period (due to the aerobic transformation of the carbonaceous material by the indigenous microflora) is the BOD of that particular sample. Since fully aerated water has a dissolved O_2 concentration of only 9.8 p.p.m. at 20°, appropriate dilutions of the sample have to be made. A certain amount of lithotrophic O_2 demand, due to nitrifying bacteria, may also be encountered in waters with high concentrations of NH_4^+, but this can be allowed for by using an appropriate inhibitor of nitrification. In practice, BOD is particularly suitable for monitoring domestic effluents which are relatively constant in composition. It is not unusual to find when analysing trade wastes that abnormalities occur in the dissolved O_2 uptake course, so that the O_2 demand is not executed in 5 days, and the biological effects can then be underestimated. Chemical oxygen demand measurements are therefore particularly important for trade wastes.

The normal population of a "clean" low-nutrient (oligotrophic) watercourse consists of a large number of different species with a relatively small number of individuals within any one species. The most readily isolated bacteria are Gram-negative rods of the genera *Pseudomonas, Achromobacter,* and *Flavobacterium,* and these are present in numbers generally not exceeding 10^2–10^3 cells ml^{-1}. Following an input of carbonaceous material, the first detectable response in the microbial population is a rapid increase in Gram-negative rods and numbers sufficiently high to produce turbidity may occur ($\sim 10^6 ml^{-1}$). The consequent utilization of dissolved O_2 produces increasingly anoxic conditions, and results in the selection of a succession of microorganisms, each contributing in turn to the lowering of the redox potential of the environment. In most environments NO_3^-, SO_4^{2-} and CO_2 are in turn utilized as terminal electron acceptors when O_2 is depleted, culminating in methanogenesis. In the marine environment SO_4^{2-} is present in such large amounts that CO_2 reduction is less significant, probably as a consequence of competition for H_2 between methanogens and SO_4^{2-} reducers (5.6).

Table 8.2 Microbial events following O_2 depletion of a watercourse*

Redox	Microbial population	Comments
+600 mV	Gram-negative rods (*Pseudomonas, Alcaligenes, Achromobacter*, etc.). Aquatic phycomycetes, hyphomycetes, appendaged bacteria. Diatoms (*Pinnularia, Navicula*), non-motile Chlorophyceae (*Ankistrodesmus, Staurastrum*, etc.).	Normal redox potential for well aerated water. Large numbers of different species, relatively few individuals within species. Metabolism oxidative.
+600 mV $\downarrow$ +200 mV	Gram-negative rods, especially denitrifiers such as *Pseudomonas*. Diatoms (*Nitzschia, Synedra*). Filamentous Chlorophyceae (*Stigeoclonium*, etc.). Blue-green algae (*Calothrix*).	Dominance of facultatively anaerobic Gram-negative rods. NO_3^- reduction poises redox at +200 mV until NO_3^- exhausted. Mn(IV) reduction (+400 mV) and Fe(III) reduction (+300 mV) may release soluble P. Switch to different diatom and chlorophyceaen population.
+200 mV $\downarrow$ 0 mV	Blue-green algae (*Oscillatoria, Phormidium*), Gram-negative rods (*Pseudomonas*, etc.). Microaerophilic bacteria (*Spirillum*). Flagellates (*Chlamydomonas, Euglena*, etc.). "Sewage fungus" complex (*Sphaerotilus, Leptomitis*, etc.).	Dominance of blue-green algae, flagellates and microaerophilic bacteria. "Sewage fungus" complex often present. Nitrification beginning to be inhibited.
0 mV $\downarrow$ -150 mV	*Desulfovibrio*, strict anaerobes (*Clostridium*, etc.). Microaerophilic colourless S oxidizers (*Beggiatoa*) in upper layers initially. Phototrophic bacteria (*Chromatium*, etc.).	Nitrification ceases, build-up of H_2 and fermentation products. SO_4^{2-} reduced to S^{2-}. Blooms of phototrophic bacteria growing on H_2S. FeS produced from reduced Fe(III). Complete switch of population to anaerobic metabolism and disappearance of all microaerophiles and most facultative anaerobes.
-150 mV $\downarrow$ -350 mV	*Desulfovibrio*, methanogens, strict anaerobes.	CH_4 evolution, FeS. Terminal stage devoid of eukaryotes except anaerobic protozoa (*Bodo* spp.) and occasional metazoans like *Tubifex* spp. Very few species.

* Redox depends on pH — the sequence as described is for a water course at neutral pH.

This sequence of events is outlined in table 8.2, which summarizes some of the microbiological and chemical features of changes in redox potential in an aquatic environment. Common "early warning" symptoms include the appearance of blooms of blue-green algae, and the appearance of the "sewage fungus" complex attached to rocks (a matrix of the bacterium *Sphaerotilus natans*, the fungus *Leptomitus lacteus*, the protozoan *Cachesium polypirium* and other microorganisms). Major and obvious changes occur at redox potentials of 0 mV and below, when the population shifts from aerobic or microaerophilic to anaerobic. A comparable series of changes can be seen in the macroflora of a polluted water course, although higher organisms in a terminally polluted water course (redox potential < −150 mV) may be entirely absent or restricted to tubificid worms. A further deleterious effect may be the solubilization of metal phosphates as a consequence of redox-induced reductions, with consequent problems which are discussed below (8.4).

At first sight it would seem reasonable that the monitoring of a few selected bacterial groups would provide an "early warning" system useful in predicting the onset of pollution. However, in practice, the enumeration and identification of bacteria requires relatively sophisticated techniques, and bacterial changes may be so rapid as to reflect local rather than general trends. There are however a number of approaches to attempting to monitor water quality by identifying and enumerating small benthic invertebrates or different types of algae. This procedure depends on the analysis of community structure rather than individual marker species. Numerical scores can be given to sites depending on the numbers and types of different organisms ("biotic indices"), and these can be incorporated into sophisticated models of watercourses which take into account geographical, biological, and chemical parameters in predicting behaviour under various conditions.

8.4 Mineral pollutants

This category of pollution tends to be delineated according to the preferences and prejudices of the author(s); it is really a category of convenience where a number of unrelated types of pollution are grouped together for discussion. In this section, it is considered to include heavy metals (including radioisotopes), compounds that alter the pH of the environment, and the inorganic substances which promote algal and higher plant growth.

Low pH is usually a consequence of the production of H_2SO_4 by the growth of S-oxidizing bacteria in pyritic materials exposed to air. This aspect of S oxidation, and its environmental effects, is discussed in 7.2; control measures usually include liming. Certain trade wastes produce alkaline conditions in water courses, and the effects on the higher forms of life can be just as serious as those documented for highly acid conditions. The most common type of alkaline trade waste is that derived from cement factories where the source of the alkalinity is $Ca(OH)_2$ produced in the cement manufacturing process. Such environments which often have pH values in excess of 11 are devoid of higher forms of life, and the microbial population is restricted largely to bacteria of the genus *Bacillus* (3.3).

Considerable amounts of heavy metals are discharged by industry, and the solubilization of metals is also associated with S oxidation in pyritic minerals (7.8). The rapid metabolic rate of microorganisms predisposes towards the utilization and concentration of metals. Metal transformations are discussed in 7.3; the possibility of microbial transformation to alkyl metal derivatives is a significant factor to be taken into account. The maintenance of large mixed cultures of microorganisms in sewage treatment plants poses potential problems, in that infinite possibilities exist for microbial transformations and the transmission of plasmids coding for particular transformations. Careful monitoring of trade wastes appears to be the only practical preventive measure.

Radioactive isotopes present a special example of mineral pollutants. It is clear that microorganisms are relatively resistant to radioactive damage largely because of efficient DNA repair mechanisms; lichens and algae in polar regions for instance have in the past shown high concentrations of ^{90}Sr and ^{137}Cs as a consequence of the testing of atmospheric nuclear weapons. These organisms are a major source of food for tundra ruminants, and therefore indirectly man, and so their resistance to radiation damage allows radioactive elements to reach the top of the food chain.

The separation of pollution by inorganic plant and algal nutrients from pollution by oxygen-demanding waste is, to some extent, artificial, since the discharge of oxygen-demanding waste usually includes or produces substantial amounts of such nutrients. However, as these nutrients may also be independently released by agricultural drainage, it is convenient to discuss them separately. Algal growth is largely governed by the availability of N and P, although occasionally other nutrients may be limiting. An estimate of the possible effect of algal nutrients can be obtained from a consideration of the equation linking production (P) and respiration (R):

$$106\,CO_2 + 16\,NO_3^- + PO_4^{3-} + 122\,H_2O + 19\,H^+$$

$$P \downarrow\uparrow R$$

$$C_{106}H_{263}O_{110}N_{16}P_1 + 138\,O_2,$$

thus if phosphorus is limiting, the introduction of 1 mg P allows the synthesis of ca. 0.1 g algal biomass. This biomass will subsequently exert a BOD of ca. 138 when it is transformed. Consideration of the stoichiometric correlation between N and P in oceans and many inland lakes (figure 8.1) reveals that in most inland waters P appears to be more important in influencing productivity, probably because of the substantial input of N from agricultural land, whereas in oceanic environments, both N and P play an equal role in determining productivity.

Surveys of European inland waterways have indicated that a water course is at risk if the concentration of P exceeds $10\,\mu g\,l^{-1}$. A sequence of algal types occurs as the concentration of P increases. Diatoms including *Asterionella, Tabellaria* and *Fragilaria* spp. occur at low P concentrations, whereas Chlorophyceae of the *Scenedesmus* type, and blue-green algae, do not appear until P concentrations are high. Apart from the aesthetically unpleasant appearance of algal blooms and the eventual substantial oxygen demand, the respiration of the algae under light-limited conditions can also seriously deplete dissolved O_2. Other detrimental effects include tastes and odours, the clogging of water treatment facilities, and the

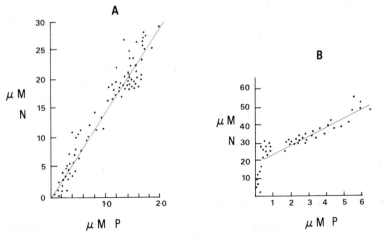

Figure 8.1 Correlations between soluble nitrate and phosphate in (A) the Western Atlantic and (B) Lake Zurich (redrawn from Stumm and Stumm-Zollinger, 1972).

production of compounds toxic to fish, livestock and man. Algicides and herbicides may provide temporary relief under certain conditions, but may be harmful in the long term because they may reduce the stability and diversity of the environment. Biological control by parasitic aquatic phycomycetes and myxobacteria has been attempted in small lakes and ponds, with varying degrees of success. There are also specific cyanophages for blue-green algae. In all cases, the procedures serve to treat the symptoms rather than the cause, and the only real cure is to limit the amount of nutrient input as far as possible.

8.5 Heat pollution

The main contributor to thermal pollution is the power industry, which returns large amounts of cooling water to source after temperature increases of 5–10°. The receiving water generally increases in temperature by less than 5°. In common with other relatively mild types of pollutant stress, this has the effect of decreasing population diversity with a concomitant increase in numbers within particular species. This is exemplified by the increased numbers of Gram-negative chromogenic rods of the genera *Pseudomonas* and *Flavobacterium* to be found in power station effluents, and the algal domination of warm waters by certain members of the Chlorophyceae and blue-green algae common to other polluted environments. Myxobacteria, *Aeromonas* spp., producing fish diseases, and aquatic phycomycetes show an increased incidence, particularly in eutrophic waters. Coliforms (and by implication a number of enteric pathogens) may survive longer in warm waters, while the pathogenic amoeba *Naegleria fowleri* is largely restricted to warm water ($\sim 40°$). However, the chief effect of raised temperatures is to promote higher metabolic rates, and since O_2 is less soluble in warmer waters, in relatively eutrophic waters a small rise in temperature may enhance the onset of the process outlined in 8.3. In general, there is little good evidence to suggest that relatively mild thermal stress produces serious deleterious effects, except under exceptional circumstances in waters already polluted in other ways.

8.6 Pollution by recalcitrant chemicals

The environment contains considerable quantities of naturally-occurring recalcitrant compounds as partially transformed plant and microbial residues in the form of humic substances and fossil fuels, but more serious

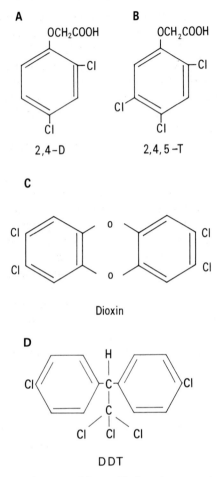

Figure 8.2 The structure of some recalcitrant chlorinated compounds: 2,4-D (2,4 dichloro-phenoxyacetate), 2,4,5-T (2,4,5-trichlorophenoxyacetate) DDT(1,1,1 trichloro-2,2-di(4-chlorophenyl) ethane), and dioxin (2,3,7,8 tetrachlorobenzo-*p*-dioxin).

concern has been focused on the persistence in the environment of some synthetic organic compounds used as pesticides, and to a lesser extent certain packaging materials, industrial chemicals, and surfactants. These compounds contain chemical structures not naturally encountered in the biosphere, and therefore sometimes called *xenobiotics*. Some of these recalcitrant materials are simply aesthetically unpleasant as they accumulate in the environment, but other recalcitrant compounds such as the insecticide DDT (figure 8.2) are toxic to man and other animals above a certain concentration, and still others such as tetrachlorodioxin, a common contaminant in the widely-used herbicides 2,4-D and 2,4,5-T (figure 8.2), are carcinogenic and teratogenic even in trace amounts. The persistence of certain of these chemicals in the environment produces a serious long-term problem with no ready solution. Considerable effort is now employed in developing appropriately active "soft" pesticides that are rapidly destroyed. Conflicts of interest may of course develop where compounds are expected to have persistent effects, and yet fail to persist in the environment.

A list of the entire spectrum of recalcitrant compounds entering the environment would be voluminous, and there are no general rules by which to predict recalcitrance. However, one factor clearly important in determining persistence is the solubility of a compound. The persistence of plastics, for instance, owes much to the insoluble nature of the material and the inaccessibility of the ends of the hydrocarbon chains. A further trend can be identified in that certain chemical groupings such as branched structures or multiple Cl atoms reduce biodegradability. An often-quoted example of this kind of effect is the relative persistence of branched alkylbenzene sulphonate surfactants which are resistant to β-oxidation, compared with the straight chain types (figure 8.3). The mechanism of microbial degradation of aromatic compounds involves an oxygenase

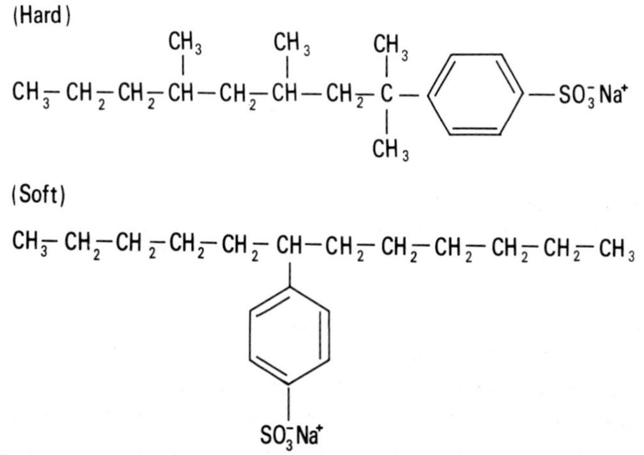

Figure 8.3 The structure of alkylbenzene sulphonates. Branched tetrapropyl side chains make the molecule persistent (hard), whereas straight-chain side chains are readily degraded (soft).

attack on the ring, leading to hydroxyl insertion and diol formation, followed by subsequent cleavage of the ring in the ortho (interdiol) or meta (adjacent) position. (In bacteria, certain of the enzymes involved in the degradation of aromatic compounds are specified by plasmids.) Substitution of the aromatic ring by a variety of groupings, including chlorine atoms, markedly inhibits enzymic attack, particularly if substitution is in the meta position. There is also increasing resistance to degradation with increased numbers of substitutions; hence 2,4,5-T is more resistant than 2,4-D, and the heavily substituted compounds DDT and tetrachlorodioxin are particularly recalcitrant (figure 8.2). In order to convert a complex aromatic to readily assimilable compounds, a considerable range of different enzymes is required, and such aromatics are therefore recalcitrant because of their inability to function as a carbon and energy source for any one microorganism. Complex compounds may, however, slowly be degraded by groups of microorganisms, or by co-metabolism. Co-metabolism is defined as occurring when an organism degrades a compound which cannot be used for growth, while growing at the expense of another compound. Co-metabolism in the natural environment is usually a slow process since the levels of suitable growth substrates are likely to be very low.

In the past it has been claimed that the effect of the more common recalcitrant pesticides on non-target microorganisms was negligible, or at worst transient, at field concentrations, and in general it is still believed that microorganisms are sufficiently resilient to cope with most perturbations of this type. However, recently, some disturbing trends have emerged, particularly with respect to rhizosphere effects, where even very low concentrations of common pesticides inhibit key organisms like *Rhizobium* spp. More work is needed to determine effects of this nature, and there is still no simple way of predicting the long-term effects of pesticide applications (1.2).

8.7 Oil pollution

Oil pollution is not exclusively a consequence of human activity, since oil seepage occurs from fissures in the earth's crust. The total contribution by natural means is probably small, and in recent times, most concern has been voiced over the increasing artificial input of oil into the environment as a consequence of accidental spills, and the accepted practice of discharging oily wastes at sea. Crude oil is an extremely complex mixture of aliphatic and aromatic hydrocarbons, including volatile components of the gasoline or petrol fractions, the higher boiling point kerosine and lubricant fraction, and the largely solid asphaltene residue. The water-insoluble kerosine fraction poses the greatest pollution problem, since the petrol fraction evaporates rapidly, and the insoluble "tar balls" of the asphaltene residue either sink in mid-ocean or can be removed from beaches without great difficulty. About 0.02 % of crude oil partitions into the aqueous phase, and although this is a small fraction quantitatively, its importance should be emphasized since it contains phenols and anilines and most of the toxic properties of crude oil therefore reside in this fraction.

Many marine isolates of fungi and bacteria have the ability to degrade certain fractions of crude oil. Gram-negative isolates of the genera *Nocardia*, *Pseudomonas* and *Flavobacterium* are probably the most significant types, but up to 20 % of all marine isolates of fungi and bacteria have some degree of degradation capacity. Normally these organisms are present in small numbers ($10^1 \, ml^{-1}$) in oceanic waters, but oil-polluted sediments in estuaries may harbour up to 10^6 oil-decomposing bacteria per g. Degradation occurs only under oxic conditions, and less complex compounds are degraded preferentially. The biochemical mechanisms are discussed elsewhere (5.7, 8.5) and include β-oxidation and aromatic ring cleavage. Some degree of alteration and degradation of the more compli-cated compounds occurs by co-metabolism. Estimates of the rate of oil decomposition range from $0.1–1.0 \, g \, m^{-2} \, day^{-1}$ on contaminated beaches, depending on temperature and the type of oil. The marine environment is normally N and P limited, and to achieve maximum rates of degradation it is necessary to add sources of these elements. Preparations of oil-degrading bacteria, containing absorbants, surfactants and nutrients are available commercially as aids to pollution control, but it is difficult to prove conclusively that any beneficial effect is primarily due to the bacterial component. The most widely-used procedure in treating oil spills is to spray with surfactant emulsifier to disperse and sink the oil, and this changes the surface properties of the oil droplets and generally increases the rate of microbial degradation. This has proved successful in the past, although the surfactants have to be carefully chosen for minimum toxic effects.

REFERENCES

Books

Higgins, I. J. and Burns, R. G. (1975) *The Chemistry and Microbiology of Pollution*, Academic Press.

Mitchell, R. (editor) (1971) *Water Pollution Microbiology*, Vol. 1, John Wiley & Sons.

Mitchell, R. (editor) (1978) *Water Pollution Microbiology*, Vol. 2, John Wiley & Sons.
Sykes, G. and Skinner, F. A. (editors) (1971) *Microbial Aspects of Pollution*, Academic Press.

Articles

Anderson, J. R. (1978) Pesticide effects on non-target soil microorganisms, in *Pesticide Microbiology*, editors I. R. Hill and S. J. Wright, Academic Press, 313–534.

Gerhold, R. M. (editor) (1978) *Microbiology of Power Plant Thermal Effluents* (Proceedings of the Symposium). University of Iowa Press.

Gutnick, D. L. and Rosenberg, E. (1977) Oil tankers and pollution, a microbiological approach. *Ann. Rev. Microbiol.*, **31**, 379–396.

Higgins, I. J. and Gilbert, P. D. (1978) The biodegradation of hydrocarbons, in *The Oil Industry and Microbial Ecosystems*, editors K. W. A. Chater and H. J. Somerville, Heyden & Sons, 80–117.

Jernelov, A. and Martin, A. L. (1975) Ecological implications of metal metabolism by microorganisms. *Ann. Rev. Microbiol.*, **29**, 61–78.

Patrick, R. (1973) Use of algae, especially diatoms, in an assessment of water quality, in *Biological Methods for the Assessment of Water Quality*, editors J. Cairns and K. L. Dickinson, American Society for Testing and Materials, **528**, 76–95.

Perry, J. J. (1979) Microbial co-oxidations involving hydrocarbons. *Microbiol. Rev.*, **43**, 59–72.

Rudd, J. W. M. and Taylor, C. D. (1980) Methane cycling in aquatic environments, in *Advances in Aquatic Microbiology*, Vol. 2, editors M. R. Droop and H. W. Jannasch, Academic Press, 77–150.

Stiff, M. J. (1978) Biodegradation of surfactants, in *The Oil Industry and Microbial Ecosystems*, editors K. W. A. Chater and H. J. Somerville, Heyden & Sons, 118–128.

Zajic, J. E. (1971) Stream surveillance, in *Water Pollution: Disposal and Re-use*, Vol. 1, Marcel Dekker, 89–198.

CHAPTER NINE

THE BIOLOGICAL TREATMENT OF WASTE

9.1 General aspects of waste treatment

At the present time we are dependent on biological processes for treating many types of waste, and more expensive chemical treatments are largely confined to particularly recalcitrant or toxic industrial wastes. In microbiological terms, biological waste-treatment processes are effectively large man-made microbial culture systems designed to transform large amounts of carbonaceous material into inoffensive products (including relatively innocuous microbial biomass). Processes range from thermophilic composting of materials with relatively low water content (3.1) to the transformation of matter dissolved or suspended in relatively large volumes of water. The transformation of dilute aqueous wastes brought about by microorganisms encompasses specific treatments for certain industrial chemicals and the treatment of domestic sewage. In quantitative terms the treatment of dilute aqueous waste greatly exceeds all other waste treatment processes, and this chapter concentrates on this aspect of the biological treatment of waste.

A consideration of the treatment of domestic sewage serves to illustrate some of the features of waste processing in general. Most commonly, sewage is transported by gravity through concrete or iron sewers to a central processing facility (figure 9.1). Microbial decomposition starts during transit and a considerable reduction in BOD (8.3) has occurred before arrival at the sewage works, where large objects are first removed by a scraping device, and grit is sedimented in channels where the flow is slowed. Most large sewage works have storm overflow tanks which come into operation during flood conditions, but during periods of prolonged flooding, sewage may have to be discharged untreated directly into water courses. This procedure is not so hazardous as it seems since the water course will generally be in spate at the time. From the sedimentation

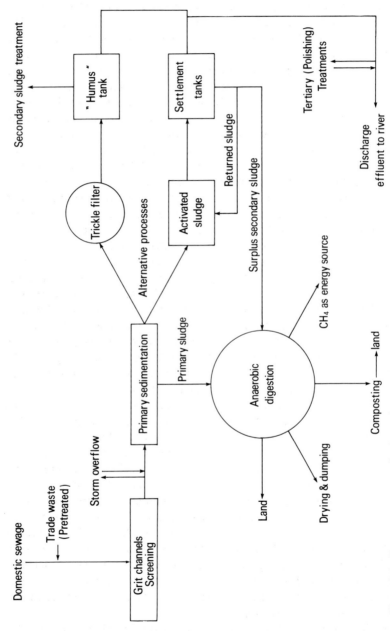

Figure 9.1 Treatment processes for domestic sewage.

channels, the flow enters a primary sedimentation tank which serves to remove "gross" solids and floating materials such as fats and oils. The organic material which settles (*primary sludge*) accounts for some 50 % of the total BOD of raw sewage. The supernatant (*settled sewage*) is usually then trickled through beds of small stones or other material (the trickle filter or bacteria bed process), or else aerated in tanks (the activated sludge process). Both processes reduce the BOD of the settled sewage by $\sim 90\%$ by aerobically transforming large amounts of carbonaceous material, mainly into CO_2 and H_2O. Both processes generate a certain amount of microbial biomass (humus or *secondary sludge*) that is removed by sedimentation before the final effluent is discharged to water courses (occasionally after tertiary "polishing" treatments). Primary and secondary sludges have to be removed, and sometimes de-watered material is dumped directly at sea or in appropriate landfill sites, but often costly chemical treatments such as liming are necessary to render the material safe and less offensive. At large sewage works some of the energy available from such material is recovered by anaerobically digesting primary and secondary sludges (figure 9.1). This produces a different microbial biomass (*digested sludge*), which is easier to de-water, is reduced by 60 % in volume compared with the original material, and is microbiologically less hazardous and suitable for direct application to agricultural land as a fertilizer and soil conditioner. A further useful feature of the process is the generation of large amounts of CH_4 which can be used to power the sewage works. The obvious returns from anaerobic digestion have made this process increasingly popular throughout the world.

Each sewage plant usually has a set of operating standards determined by local conditions, and these take account of inevitable periods of less good performance when environmental conditions fluctuate. The BOD standard for sewage works effluent depends on the dilution factor produced by the receiving water course and on the cleanliness of the water course (table 9.1). Standards for suspended solids (SS) must also be met (table 9.1), as well as a number of other standards, depending on local circumstances. Most British rivers produce a dilution factor of between 8 and 150, which permits the operation of the so-called 20/30 standard for BOD and SS respectively (table 9.1). Systems treating domestic sewage are designed to process sewage which has a BOD between 200 and 400, and wastes having a BOD higher than this have to be pretreated before discharge into the municipal sewerage system, usually by modifications of the basic biological processes.

Biological treatment processes are designed primarily to reduce BOD,

Table 9.1 Royal Commission Standards for sewage discharged into British rivers*

Dilution factor	BOD (mg l^{-1})	SS (mg l^{-1})
500	no standard	no standard
300–500	no standard	150
150–300	no standard	60
8–150	20	30
< 8	standard depends on local circumstances	standard depends on local circumstances

* Standards may also depend on how clean the receiving water is.

but fortunately are also effective to some extent in removing pathogens. Substantial numbers of pathogens do, however, survive the processes (table 9.2). Microbiological standards such as the Presumptive Coliform Test (8.2) are not generally applied to sewage effluents, but come into force at the other end of the water cycle where the potability of drinking water is in question.

9.2 Trickle filters

Trickle filters (also called bacteria beds or percolating filters) are essentially columns, commonly 1–4 m high, filled with graded media (stones, clinker, slag, etc.). Synthetic plastic media are also coming into use. Because of their lightness, these can be stacked to a great height and are thus particularly suitable for the on-site biological treatment of strong industrial wastes. Settled sewage is evenly distributed over the top surface, and percolates down the filter to a collection drain. A film of microbial growth develops on the packing medium at the expense of the carbonaceous matter in the continuous flow of sewage. A film in equilibrium is anything from

Table 9.2 Percentage reductions in various microorganisms* brought about by different stages of sewage treatment (modified from Carrington, 1978).

	Salmonella spp.	Viruses	Protozoa and metazoa
Activated sludge	70–99	80–99	0–99
Trickle filters	84–99	40–80	60–99
Anaerobic digestion	84–93	90–99	45–97

* Very much depends on the particular species monitored, particularly with regard to metazoa and protozoa.

0.2 to 2 mm thick and constantly sheds biomass that requires settlement from the effluent in secondary sedimentation tanks or humus tanks (figure 9.1). The attached population is not readily washed out even if subjected to a toxic waste, and trickle filters are therefore relatively resistant to shock. For settled sewage of BOD 200–400, the normal rate of dosage producing a 20/30 effluent is about $400 \, \mathrm{l \, m^{-3} \, day^{-1}}$. Stronger wastes requires lower loadings, and the capacity of the system can be increased by running two filters in series (alternating double filtration), or by effectively recycling the sewage by mixing some of the effluent with incoming settled sewage.

Trickle filters contain a much greater diversity of organisms than do activated sludge plants (9.3) and the trophic levels range from bacteria to worms and insect larvae. Bacteria dominate the film and make up 70–80 % of the film biomass, and protozoa, fungi and metazoa account for roughly equal portions of the remainder. Many of the bacteria in the film produce exopolysaccharides that are assumed to form the adhesive matrix of the

Table 9.3 Organisms recorded in trickle filter slime (compiled from Curds and Hawkes, 1975).

Prokaryotes	Bacteria > 20 genera	e.g. *Pseudomonas* *Zoogloea* *Flavobacterium*
	Blue-green algae > 10 genera	e.g. *Oscillatoria* *Phormidium*
Eukaryotes	Fungi > 20 genera, mainly imperfect fungi and ascomycetes	e.g. *Geotrichum* *Fusarium* *Arthrobotrys*
	Algae > 10 genera, mainly Chlorophyta and Bacillariophyta	e.g. *Chlorella* *Nitzschia* *Ulothrix*
	Protozoa > 120 genera ciliates numerically dominant	e.g. *Paramecium* *Opercularia* *Vorticella*
	Nematodes > 25 genera, mainly Rhabditinae	e.g. *Diplogasteritus* *Rhabditoides*
	Rotifers > 25 genera, mainly Bdelloidea	e.g. *Habrotrocha* *Epiphanes*
	Worms > 10 genera, mainly Enchytraedae	e.g. *Enchytraeus* *Lumbricillus*
	Insects > 15 genera, mainly Collembola and Diptera	e.g. *Metriocnemus* *Psychoda*

film. The bacteria found in trickle filter slime are essentially similar to those found in activated sludge flocs and are mainly Gram-negative aerobic chemoorganotrophs. Table 9.3 lists some of the more commonly described organisms, although it should be remembered that the operating conditions determine the population. Bacteria of the genera *Achromobacter*, *Alcaligenes*, *Flavobacterium*, *Pseudomonas*, *Zoogloea* and *Bacillus* often make up 90% of the bacterial flora isolated; viable counts of bacteria in the film (10^9–10^{10} bacteria per g) compared with total counts (10^{11}–10^{12} bacteria per g), indicate that a substantial proportion of the population may be moribund.

Microbial successions and activities are induced throughout the body of the filter in response to the changes in concentrations of substrates in the percolating liquor. Some types of activities at various levels can be modelled mathematically (for example, nitrification occurs as predicted in the lower levels of the filter). However, modelling of more than a few features is difficult in view of the heterogeneity of the system, and little is really known about the successive location and activity of different groups of microorganisms in filters. Fungi create operating problems in trickle filters due to the filamentous mode of growth predisposing towards blockage (ponding). It is reasonable to suppose that protozoa play as important a role as they do in the activated sludge process in grazing the film, although their significance is not so easily demonstrated as it is in the activated sludge process (9.3). The effect of higher organisms is probably primarily in assisting the sloughing of the film and preventing blockage by excessive film build-up. During winter months the higher organisms are suppressed, and it is during this time that most problems with blockage occur.

9.3 Activated sludge

The simplest form of this kind of treatment is the mechanically mixed oxidation ditch (e.g. the Pasveer ditch where sewage is aerated by being propelled round and round an oval or circular track), but the activated sludge process proper is comparable to a large open continuous culture system with feedback. Settled sewage is fed into aeration tanks at one end, and excess microbial biomass is removed by settlement in sedimentation tanks at the other end of the process, generating a low BOD supernatant. An important feature is that a certain amount of the sedimented biomass is fed back to the aeration tanks ("sludge return") to maintain a high reaction rate.

Table 9.4 Organisms recorded in activated sludge (compiled from Curds and Hawkes, 1975).

Bacteria	*Pseudomonas*	Protozoa	11 genera of phytoflagellates
	Nitrosomonas		7 genera of zooflagellates
	Nitrobacter		13 genera of amoebae
	Zoogloea		4 genera of actinopods
	Sphaerotilus		59 genera of ciliates
	Beggiatoa		(35 % of species Peritrichida)
	Azotobacter	Fungi	*Arthrobotrys*
	Achromobacter		*Zoophagus*
	Chromobacterium		*Cephalosporium*
	Flavobacterium		*Geotrichum*
	Arthrobacter		*Pullularia*
	Mycobacterium		*Penicillium*
	Bdellovibrio		*Cladosporium*
	Escherichia		*Alternaria*
	Leucothrix		*Candida*
	Nocardia		*Trichosporium*
	Bacillus	Rotifers	5 genera, mainly Bdelloidea

Because of the continual feedback of gravity-settled biomass, there is a strong selective pressure for organisms that produce easily sedimented flocs. Gram-negative bacteria dominate the activated sludge process, making up more than 90% of the biomass in the aeration tanks, protozoa comprising most of the remainder. Viable and total counts of bacteria are comparable to those of bacteria in filter slime, although the activated sludge floc is much less dense. Fungi are commonly present in aeration tanks, but are seldom significant in the process. The microbial population of activated sludge flocs differs from that of trickle filter slime in that metazoa are seldom present in numbers which suggest a significant role in the process. Table 9.4 lists some of the microorganisms most commonly seen in, or cultured from, aeration tank liquor (mixed liquor). Enumeration and culture of bacteria from such an environment presents similar problems to those encountered in the examination of filter slime, so that the bacteria listed in table 9.4 reflect ease of isolation as much as anything else.

Filamentous growth can also be a problem in aeration tanks, since the loose flocculent masses produced do not settle well, and are liable to exit with the supernatant. *Sphaerotilus* spp., *Beggiatoa* spp., and occasionally fungi are known to be associated with this phenomenon, which is known as "bulking", and actinomycete-like organisms such as *Nocardia* spp. may also contribute towards the production of massive amounts of foam in aeration tanks. It is not however entirely clear why these organisms should proliferate under certain conditions. Although flocs contain significant amounts of polysaccharides (2–3 % w/w), floc formation is clearly not simply an entrapment process, since flocs disaggregated by ultrasonic treatments reform rapidly within a few minutes. Charge effects are probably important, but the precise nature of floc formation is still a mystery. There is no dispute, however, that operating conditions designed to promote slow floc growth produce compact readily settleable flocs, and one of the functions of sludge return is to reduce the growth rate of the flocs. The requirement for ready floc settleability and very low BOD effluent may not be so pressing in the treatment of trade wastes, and nutrient supplementation and chemically or physically assisted settlement may then be necessary. Quite specific and very restricted populations, unlike the normal sludge floc population, may build up in plants designed to cope with particular trade wastes.

Conventional activated sludge plants treat about 3 l of sewage per l mixed liquor per day, with an aeration time of 8–10 h. Under these conditions the mixed liquor suspended solids concentration (MLSS) is about $2-5 \mathrm{g} \mathrm{l}^{-1}$ and the sludge floc has a generation time exceeding 3 days. Since the process is essentially a carbon-limited continuous culture system, increasing the carbon concentration by decreasing the rate of sludge return ("wasting" more sludge), or increasing the strength or flow rate of the sewage, will promote faster floc growth, and treat more carbonaceous material at the expense of the effluent, which is less satisfactory because of poor settleability. Certain "high rate" plants operate under these conditions where the normal 20/30 standards do not have to be met.

In theory, if a higher O_2-transfer rate can be achieved, a denser suspension of flocs can be maintained, and larger amounts of carbonaceous material can be transferred per volume of mixed liquor without significantly increasing the floc growth rate. Recent systems such as the Unox process and the ICI Deep Shaft process have sought to achieve this aim. The Unox process is essentially a closed aeration vessel pressurized with air or O_2, whereas the Deep Shaft process is a deep (or tall) aeration tube, 100 m long, injected with air or O_2 near the base, to exploit the increased solution of O_2 induced by hydrostatic pressure. In both cases, O_2 transfer rates are more than ten times the rates achieved with conventional systems, and the success of these treatments in the transformation of strong trade wastes will presumably encourage their adoption in the domestic sphere, and lead to an analysis of their microbiology.

Protozoa are known to be important in the conventional activated sludge process, commonly reaching numbers of $50\,000 \mathrm{ml}^{-1}$ mixed liquor.

Diversity at class level is somewhat less than is found in the trickle filter, and about 60% of the 200 or so species described are ciliates, many of these belonging to the sessile Peritrichida. Laboratory-scale activated sludge systems deliberately kept free of protozoa produce inferior effluents (table 9.5), and the main function of protozoa is probably in lowering numbers of bacteria by grazing, although some contribution to floc structure may be made.

Table 9.5 Effect of ciliated protozoa on the effluent quality of bench-scale activated sludge plants (from Pike and Curds, 1971).

Effluent analysis	Without ciliates	With ciliates
BOD (mg/l)	53–70	7–24
COD (mg/l)	198–250	124–142
Permanganate value (mg/l)	83–106	52–70
Organic nitrogen (mg/l)	14–21	7–10
Suspended solids (mg/l)	86–118	26–34
Optical density at 620 nm	0.95–1.42	0.23–0.34
Viable bacteria count (millions/ml)	106–160	1–9

It would be extremely useful if predictions as to the performance of a plant could be made by monitoring a few simple microbial parameters and mathematically modelling the system. Nitrifiers have been singled out and studied as a group since their substrates and products are readily determined. Normally, nitrification does not occur significantly in activated sludge plants, since nitrifiers tend to be O_2-limited and incapable of growing fast enough under most operating conditions to be retained in the aeration tanks. Mathematical modelling has provided some useful practical information on how to run plants to achieve nitrification when local conditions demand low NH_4^+ levels. Other useful information on protozoan behaviour has come from modelling studies. The prediction of all aspects of plant performance is still some way off in the absence of enough data on how the complex floc ecosystem behaves under dynamic conditions, but an approach to this kind of analysis has been started by restricting the microbiological determinations to the enumeration of a few physiological groups by MPN techniques (1.3). Principal component analyses of such data have indicated that the system can be described quite well by the behaviour of a few groups of bacteria, and eventually monitoring of this kind may be carried out automatically, and operating conditions adjusted to achieve a particular result.

9.4 Anaerobic digestion

In most anoxic environments CO_2 is ultimately used as an electron acceptor when other acceptors such as O_2, NO_3^- and SO_4^{2-} have been exhausted. The anaerobic digestion process in sewage works is merely a technological intensification of the process occurring naturally in swamps, anoxic sediments, and the gastrointestinal tracts of ruminants and other animals. Sewage digesters differ from other systems in that the substrate is largely derived from microbial cells instead of plant material, and this is reflected to some extent in the microbial population of the sewage digester. Bacteria are considered to be exclusively responsible for the trans-formations leading to methanogenesis, although a variety of different anaerobic protozoa are seen in digesters from time to time (in the rumen, protozoa make up some 50 % of the total biomass). However, it is thought that eukaryotes are not significant in the sewage digestion process; similarly, protozoa can be dispensed with in the re-populated rumens of germ-free animals. The absence of typical fungi is to be expected under the highly anoxic conditions that pertain in digesters (redox potentials < -150 mV), although it is now thought that certain of the flagellates often seen are probably the zoospores of certain aquatic fungi.

Sewage digesters have their empirical origins in the septic tanks which have been in use for more than a hundred years, and "conventional" digesters are little more than unmixed septic tanks with facilities for gas collection and removal of sedimented solids. "High rate" digesters where the contents are stirred and heated to 35–40° require 10–40 days for complete treatment of wastes, compared with several months for the unmixed "conventional" types. The process of digestion reduces solids by up to 60 % in weight, producing a material which is easy to sediment and de-water, innocuous in appearance, and considerably reduced in pathogens compared with secondary sludge (table 9.2). The material can be directly applied to land, and may also be composted at 60–65° with biodegradable municipal garbage to produce a fertilizer which is appropriate for domestic use. Digester gas contains 70 % CH_4 and 30 % CO_2, with traces of H_2S and NH_3, and this gas can be burnt to produce energy to heat the digesters and power the entire sewage plant.

Anaerobic digestion is considered to have two separate and distinct phases brought about by different populations of bacteria: (a) the non-methanogenic phase, where a variety of anaerobic bacteria transform complicated substrates to a variety of soluble and gaseous fermentation products including acetate, CO_2 and H_2; and (b) the methanogenic phase, where methanogenic bacteria utilize acetate, CO_2 and H_2 as substrates in methanogenesis. The process is thus dependent on a complicated succession of bacteria, and one of the practical problems encountered in running a sewage digester is that the non-methanogenic process may result in the production of excessive quantities of steam volatile fatty acids (VFAs) such as butyrate and propionate, with subsequent acid-inhibition of methanogenesis. The key organisms in the process are extremely strict anaerobes that require redox potentials of $-150\,mV$ for growth. The conventional experimental anaerobic systems, such as the Fildes and McIntosh jar, are incapable of achieving or maintaining such redox potentials, and the study of the anaerobic digestion process has necessitated the development of a new series of manipulative skills and techniques. Originally the techniques were developed by R. E. Hungate to study the rumen (the most economically significant digester!), but they have now been applied with great success to a variety of anoxic environments including the sewage digester. In essence, an O_2-free environment is achieved by adding appropriate reducing agents to media, and maintaining O_2-free conditions during all manipulations by constantly sparging cultures with O_2-free gas (CO_2 or N_2 rendered O_2-free by passing over heated copper filings). These procedures are collectively known as the "Hungate technique".

Table 9.6 lists some of the methanogenic and non-methanogenic

Table 9.6 Bacteria isolated from digester sludge (compiled from Toerien and Hattingh, 1969, Curds and Hawkes, 1975, and Balch et al. 1979).

Non-Methanogens		
Facultative anaerobes	*Lactobacillus*	*Bacillus*
	Spirillum	*Micrococcus*
	Klebsiella	*Pseudomonas*
	Actinomyces	*Alcaligenes*
	Vibrio	*Sarcina*
	Corynebacterium	*Aerobacter*
Anaerobes	*Bacteroides*	*Fusobacterium*
	Clostridium	*Veillonella*
	Bifidobacterium	*Peptococcus*
	Sphaerophorus	*Desulfovibrio*
Methanogens	*Methanobacterium*	
	Methanosarcina	
	Methanococcus	
	Methanospirillum	
	Methanobrevibacter	
	Methanomicrobium	

isolates from digesters. Viable counts of non-methanogens range from 10^8–10^{10} ml^{-1}, and strict anaerobes greatly outnumber facultative anaerobes. The strict anaerobes are not unique to digesters, and are found in other anoxic environments such as sediments and marshes. (The rumen however differs from other digester systems in that there are bacteria which appear to be specific to the rumen, including *Ruminococcus* spp., *Selenomonas* spp. and *Megasphaera* spp.) The facultative anaerobes in sewage digesters may be derived from primary and secondary sludges, and may be in transit rather than essential components of the process. Non-methanogens, which include cellulose, protein, and lipid digesters, break down insoluble polymers to a mixture of alcohols, VFAs, CO_2, and H_2. Many anaerobes can reoxidize NADH and NADPH by proton reduction mediated through hydrogenase, instead of the normal formation of reduced products derived from pyruvate (4.8). In the digester the partial pressure of H_2 is low (3×10^{-4} atm) because H_2 is constantly removed as a substrate for methanogenesis, and therefore (as in the rumen) a "mass action" effect occurs, where reducing equivalents are directed away from the formation of electron sink products derived from pyruvate, towards the formation of H_2 (table 4.4). Some insight into this remarkable process was originally obtained by the discovery that a supposedly pure culture of an ethanol-utilizing methanogen known as "*Methanobacillus omelianskii*" was in fact a mixed culture consortium between an H_2-producing ethanol utilizer (the "S" organism), and an H_2-utilizing methanogen. A number of similar consortia have now been described, particularly from the rumen (4.8), and it is clear that interspecies H_2 transfer is vital in carbonaceous transformations in anoxic environments.

Viable counts of methanogens in digesters usually vary from 10^5–10^8 ml^{-1}, and unlike the rumen which appears to harbour only *Methanobrevibacter* and *Methanomicrobium* spp., digesters contain representatives of all the known genera of methanogens (table 5.3), with the exception of the recently described marine genus *Methanogenium*. All methanogens oxidize H_2 (sometimes derived from the cleavage of formate) with the concomitant reduction of CO_2 to CH_4, and several species are capable of producing CH_4 from the methyl groups of acetate and methanol. The methanogenic bacteria are the most fastidious anaerobes known, and because of the difficulty of culturing them, they are still relatively obscure. Considerable interest in the group has been stimulated by the discovery that these organisms are archaebacteria, and related to certain of the thermophiles and halophiles (3.5). As well as possessing the usual archaebacterial traits, they contain unique compounds thought to be involved in methanogenesis. One of these compounds, coenzyme F_{420}, a flavin nucleotide analogue, may have a similar function to ferredoxin in other anaerobic bacteria, and another coenzyme, coenzyme M (2-mer-captoethanesulphonic acid), appears to be involved in methyl transfer reactions in methanogenesis. However, many aspects of the intermediary metabolism of this group remain to be elucidated, not least the question of how such odd chemolithotrophs obtain their cell carbon.

9.5 Tertiary treatments (polishing treatments)

In the past, the rationale of aqueous waste treatment was largely restricted to the attainment of an effluent of acceptable BOD. It has, however, been increasingly realized that sewage effluents pose problems other than that of endangering the O_2 balance in the receiving waters. In particular, N and P are not removed by conventional sewage treatment systems (apart from a certain amount of incorporation into microbial biomass). The majority (70%) of N and P exits with the effluent, P as PO_4^{3-}, and N as NH_4^+ or NO_3^-.

High NH_4^+ levels are toxic to fish and, most commonly, the solution to the NH_4^+ problem has been to nitrify NH_4^+ to NO_3^-. Trickle filters nitrify quite well (9.2), but unusual operating conditions are required to achieve nitrification in activated sludge plants (9.3), and a secondary nitrifying filter may have to be used to treat activated sludge plant effluent. Such nitrifying filters consist of a bed of stones similar to a conventional trickle filter, and a presumed population of nitrifying bacteria converts NH_4^+ to NO_3^-. However, high NO_3^- levels in water courses are increasingly regarded as unsatisfactory, partly because they encourage eutrophication, and partly because of their potential toxicity (6.4). Denitrification may be induced in closed tanks and towers where anoxic conditions develop, and bacteria (presumably mainly of the genera *Pseudomonas* and *Bacillus*) denitrify. Denitrification can also be induced in the activated sludge process by allowing a proportion of the sedimented sludge normally fed back to aeration tanks (return sludge) to sit unaerated for 3–4 hours.

P is more difficult to remove biologically, and is usually precipitated chemically by substances such as lime. N and P can be removed together by incorporation into other biomass, such as grass or algae, by percolation through cultivated plots, or by retention in aerobic lagoons. Such tertiary "polishing" procedures have the advantage that potentially valuable biomass is generated.

The trend is more and more towards the conservation of energy and minerals, and sewage plants of the future, by judicious combinations of aerobic, anaerobic and tertiary treatments will surely seek to achieve this as an objective of comparable importance to the generation of satisfactory effluent.

REFERENCES

Books

Curds, C. R. and Hawkes, H. A. (eds.) (1975) *Ecological Aspects of Used Water Treatment*. Vol. 1 — *The Organisms and their Ecology*, Academic Press.

Articles

Balch, E., Fox, G. E., Magrum, L., Woese, C. R. and Wolfe, R. S. (1979) Methanogens. Re-evaluation of a unique biological group. *Microbiol. Rev.* **43**, 260–296.

Carrington, E. G. (1978) The contribution of sewage sludges to the dissemination of pathogenic microorganisms in the environment. *Water Research Centre Technical Report* TR 71.

Christensen, M. H. and Harremoës, P. (1978) Nitrification and denitrification in waste water treatment. In *Water Pollution Microbiology*, Vol. 2, ed. R. Mitchell, Academic Press, pp. 391–414.

Hobson, P. N., Bousfield, S. and Summers, R. (1974) The anaerobic digestion of organic matter. *Critical Reviews in Environmental Control*, **4**, 131–191.

Mah, R. A., Ward, D. M., Baresi, L. and Glass, T. L. (1977) Biogenesis of methane. *Ann. Rev. Microbiol.* **31**, 309–342.

La Riviere, J. W. M. (1977) Microbial ecology of liquid waste treatment. *Adv. Microbial Ecol.* **1**, 215–260.

Pike, E. B. and Carrington, E. G. (1972) Recent developments in the study of bacteria in the activated sludge process. *J. Water Pollution Control*, **6**, 1–21.

Pike, E. B. and Curds, C. R. (1971) The microbial ecology of the activated sludge process. In *Microbial Aspects of Pollution*, eds. G. Sykes and F. A. Skinner, Academic Press, pp. 123–148.

Pirt, S. J. (1975) A quantitative theory of the activity of microbes attached to a packed column: relevant to trickle filter effluent purification and to microbial activity in soils. *J. Appl. Chem. Biotechnol.* **23**, 389–400.

Taber, W. A. (1976) Wastewater microbiology. *Ann. Rev. Microbiol.* **30**, 263–278.

Toerien, D. I. and Hattingh, W. H. J. (1969) Anaerobic digestion. *Water Research* **3**, 385–416.

Wolin, M. J. (1978) The rumen fermentation: A model for microbial interactions in anaerobic systems. *Adv. Microbial Ecol.* **2**, 49–77.

INDEX

207